2nd edition
STARTING
F O R T H

AN INTRODUCTION
TO THE **FORTH** LANGUAGE
AND OPERATING SYSTEM
FOR BEGINNERS
AND PROFESSIONALS

LEO BRODIE
and
FORTH, INC.

With a foreword by
Charles H. Moore

PRENTICE-HALL, INC.
Englewood Cliffs, New Jersey 07632

Library of Congress Cataloging-in-Publication Data

Brodie, Leo. (date)
  Starting Forth.

  Includes index.
  1. Forth (Computer program language) I. Title.
QA76.73.F24B76 1987   005.13'3   86-5032
ISBN 0-13-843087-X
ISBN 0-13-843079-9 (pbk.)

Editorial/production supervision: **Lisa Schulz**
Interior design: **Lorraine Mullaney**
Cover design: **Lundgren Graphics, Ltd.**
Manufacturing buyer: **Ed O'Dougherty**

Prentice-Hall Software Series
Brian W. Kernighan, *Advisor*

© 1987 by Prentice-Hall, Inc.
A division of Simon & Schuster
Englewood Cliffs, New Jersey 07632

Printed in the United States of America

10 9 8 7 6

ISBN 0-13-843087-X
ISBN 0-13-843079-9 025 {PBK.}

Prentice-Hall International (UK) Limited, *London*
Prentice-Hall of Australia Pty. Limited, *Sydney*
Editora Prentice-Hall do Brasil, Ltda., *Rio de Janeiro*
Prentice-Hall Canada Inc., *Toronto*
Prentice-Hall Hispanoamericana, S.A., *Mexico*
Prentice-Hall of India Private Limited, *New Delhi*
Prentice-Hall of Japan, Inc., *Tokyo*
Prentice-Hall of Southeast Asia Pte. Ltd., *Singapore*

CONTENTS

FOREWORD

by
Charles H. Moore
The Creator of Forth

The Forth community can celebrate a significant event with the publication of *Starting Forth*. A greater effort, talent, and commitment have gone into this book than into any previous introductory manual. I, particularly, am pleased at this evidence of the growing popularity of Forth, the language.

I developed Forth over a period of some years as an interface between me and the computers I programmed. The traditional languages were not providing the power, ease, or flexibility that I wanted. I disregarded much conventional wisdom in order to include exactly the capabilities needed by a productive programmer. The most important of these is the ability to add whatever capabilities later become necessary.

The first time I combined the ideas I had been developing into a single entity, I was working on an IBM 1130, a "third-generation" computer. The result seemed so powerful that I considered it a "fourth-generation computer language." I would have called it FOURTH, except that the 1130 permitted only five-character identifiers. So FOURTH became Forth, a nicer play on words anyway.

One principle that guided the evolution of Forth, and continues to guide its application, is bluntly: Keep It Simple. A simple solution has elegance. It is the result of exacting effort to understand the *real* problem and is recognized by its compelling sense of rightness. I stress this point because it contradicts the conventional view that power increases with complexity. Simplicity provides confidence, reliability, compactness, and speed.

Starting Forth was written and illustrated by Leo Brodie, a remarkably capable person whose insight and imagination will become apparent. This book is an original and detailed prescription for learning. It deftly guides the novice over the thresholds of understanding that all Forth programmers must cross.

Although I am the only person who has never had to learn Forth, I do know that its study is a formidable one. As with a human language, the usage of many words must be memorized. For beginners, Leo's droll comments and superbly cast characters appear to make this study easy and enjoyable. For those like myself who already know Forth, a quick reading provides a delightful trip and fresh views of familiar terrain. But I hope this book is not so easy and enjoyable that it seems trivial. Be warned that there is heavy content here and that you can learn much about computers and compilers as well as about programming.

Forth provides a natural means of communication between man and the smart machines he is surrounding himself with. This requires that it share characteristics of human languages, including compactness, versatility, and extensibility. I cannot imagine a better language for writing programs, expressing algorithms, or understanding computers. As you read this book, I hope that you may come to agree.

ABOUT THIS BOOK

Welcome to *Starting Forth*, your introduction to an exciting and powerful computer language called Forth.

If you're a beginner who wants to learn more about computers, Forth is a great way to learn. Forth is more fun to write programs with than any language that I know of. (See the "Introduction for Beginners.")

If you are a seasoned professional who wants to learn Forth, this book is just what you need. Forth is a very different approach to computers, so different that everyone from newcomers to old hands, learns Forth best from the ground up. If you're adept at other computer languages, put them out of your mind, and remember only what you know about *computers*. (See the "Introduction for Professionals.")

Since many people with different backgrounds are interested in Forth, I've arranged this book so that you'll only have to read what you need to know, with footnotes addressed to different kinds of readers. The first half of Chapter 7 provides a background in computer arithmetic for beginners only.

This book explains how to write simple applications in Forth. It includes all standard Forth words that you need to write a high-level, single-task application. This word set is an extremely powerful one, including everything from simple math operators to compiler-controlling words.

Excluded from this book are all commands that are related to the multi-programmer, printing and disking utilities, and target compiler. These commands are available on some versions of Forth such as polyFORTH.

I've chosen examples that will actually work at a Forth system with a terminal and disk. Don't infer from this that Forth is limited to string-handling tasks, since there is really no limit to Forth's usefulness.

Here are some features of this book that will make it easy to use:

All commands are listed twice: first, in the section in which the word is introduced, and second, in the summary at the end of that chapter. Appendix B indexes all Forth words alphabetically, while Appendix C lists them by category.

Each chapter also has a review of terms and a set of exercise problems. Appendix A lists the answers.

Several "Handy Hints" have been included to reveal procedural tips or optional routines that are useful for learners but that don't merit an explanation as to how or why they work.

A personal note: Forth is a very unusual language. It violates many cardinal rules of programming. My first reaction to Forth was skeptical, but as I tried to develop complicated applications I began to see its beauty and power. You owe it to yourself to keep an open mind while reading about some of its peculiarities. I'll warn you now: Many programmers who learn Forth never go back to other languages.

Good luck, and enjoy learning!

Leo Brodie
March 1981

PREFACE
TO THE
SECOND EDITION

When I wrote the first edition of this book in 1980, Forth was relatively little known. Things have changed considerably in the meantime. Forth has seen a steady rise in interest over the years, even as other languages have waxed and waned in popularity (Pascal was "in" back then; at the moment C reigns, with Modula 2 now appealing to the *avant-garde*). While enthusiasm for Forth grows at its own pace, it appears that the release of Charles Moore's Forth microprocessor this year will trigger an explosion of interest among engineers and programmers.

Meanwhile, *Starting Forth* has been lucky enough to ride the tail of Forth's popularity. The first edition has been translated into German, French, Japanese, Dutch and Chinese. For this, and for your encouragement and support, I thank all of you.

Of course, nothing stands still (least of all Forth). Since the first edition was published, the FORTH-83 Standard has been ratified and widely adopted. Upgrading the syntax of this book to that of the 83 Standard was the primary reason for undertaking this revision. However, I took the opportunity to make extensive improvements in other ways as well.

For one, there are still a lot of fig-Forth (Forth Interest Group) systems out there. In this edition, I've added footnotes that flag the major differences for those users.

For another, this edition follows the more rigorous coding style and conventions described in my second book, *Thinking Forth*. Also, this revision documents the nicer screen-oriented version of the editor described in the first edition. The user commands are the same, but the display is more friendly (see Chapter 3).

I've corrected the sore lack of an alphabetical general index, while retaining the index to Forth words by category.

I've rewritten the explanations of many topics including input-stream parsing, defining words, and compiling words, which upon re-reading I found somewhat obtuse. Also I've added a new example—code for a Forth assembler—to the last chapter, and a new section on fixed-point (fractional) arithmetic (see Chapter 5). Finally, at the request of many readers, I've added more self-study problems.

Two other differences that reflect the changing times should be noted here. First, the word *screen*, as it applies to a "block," has been stricken. Whatever differences there may have been between the two terms (a "screen" is usually regarded as a "block" that contains source code), this appears to be a rationalization that belongs to the distant past. Today, many newcomers are confused by the two terms.

Second, I have succumbed to fashion and converted the spelling of FORTH to Forth. Exceptions include polyFORTH, which is a trade name, and FORTH-83, which the standard spells that way.

In making all these additions and changes with the second edition, I hope I have not interfered with the original spirit of clarity and fun. I sincerely wish you the best of experiences learning and working with Forth.

Leo Brodie

ACKNOWLEDGMENTS

I'd like to thank the following people who helped to make the first edition possible:

For consultation on Forth technique and style: Dean Sanderson, Michael LaManna, James Dewey, Edward K. Conklin, and Elizabeth D. Rather; for providing insights into the art of teaching Forth and for writing several of the problems in this book: Kim Harris; for proofreading, editorial suggestions, and enormous amounts of work formatting the pages: Carolyn A. Rosenberg; for help with typing and other necessities: Sue Linstrot, Carolyn Lubisich, Kevin Weaver, Kris Cramer, and Stephanie Brown Brodie; for help with the graphics: Carolyn Lubisich, Jim Roberts, Janine Ritscher, Dana Rather, Winnie Shows, Natasha Elbert, Barbara Roberts, and John Dotson of Sunrise Printery (Redondo Beach, CA); for technical assistance, Bill Patterson and Gary Friedlander; for constructive criticism, much patience and love: Stephanie Brown Brodie; and for inventing Forth, Charles H. Moore.

For their contributions to the second edition, I thank the following people: all the kind readers who wrote to offer comments and suggestions; for the original version of the 8080 assembler, John J. Cassady; for reviewing the revised manuscript, Kurt Hambacker; and for his voluminous letters and considered critiques, a special thanks to Michael Ham.

ABOUT THE AUTHOR

Leo Brodie's inability to express even the most complex technical concepts without adding a twist of humor comes from an early love of comedy. He has had several comedies produced at UCLA, his alma mater, and later honed his skills as a copywriter for an ad agency.

When his fancy turned to programming, a career as a technical writer seemed the natural choice. He stayed at Forth, Inc. for two years, during which time he penned this book and wrote his first word processor. Since 1982 Leo has worked as a freelance consultant, documentor, programmer and lecturer. In 1985 he formed Brodie Educational Services to provide writing, classes, and tutorial media on Forth and other computer-related topics.

Leo enjoys songwriting and puppetry. He has two sons: Brandon and Ryan.

0
INTRODUCTIONS

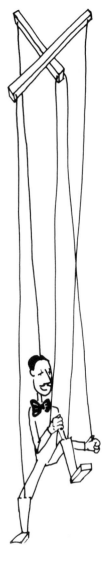

INTRODUCTION FOR BEGINNERS:
WHAT IS A COMPUTER LANGUAGE?

At first, when beginners hear the term *computer language*, they wonder, "What kind of language could a computer possibly speak? It must be awfully hard for people to understand. It probably looks like:

976#!ƏNX714&+

if it looks like anything at all."

Actually, a computer language should not be difficult to understand. Its purpose is simply to serve as a convenient compromise for communication between person and computer.

Consider the marionette. You can make a marionette "walk" simply by working the wooden control, without even touching the strings. You could say that rocking the control means "walking" in the language of the marionette. The puppeteer guides the marionette in a way that the marionette can understand and that the puppeteer can easily master.

Computers are machines, just like the marionette. They must be told exactly what to do, in specific language. And so we need a language that possesses two seemingly opposite traits:

On the one hand, it must be precise in its meaning to the computer, conveying all the information that the computer needs to know to perform the operation. On the other hand, it must be simple and easy-to-use by the programmer.

Many languages have been developed since the birth of computers: FORTRAN is the elder statesman of the field; COBOL is the standard language for business data processing; BASIC was designed as a beginner's language along the road toward languages like FORTRAN and COBOL. This book is about a very different kind of language: Forth. Forth's popularity has been gaining steadily for more than a decade, and its popularity is shared among programmers in all fields.

All of these languages, including Forth, are called "high-level" languages. It's important for beginners to recognize the difference between a high-level language and the computer it runs on. A high-level language looks the same to a programmer regardless of which make or model of computer it's running on. But each make or model has its own internal language, or "machine language." To explain what a machine language is, let's return to the marionette.

Imagine that there is no wooden control and that the puppeteer has to deal directly with the strings. Each string corresponds to exactly one part of the marionette's body. The harmonious combinations of movements of the individual strings could be called the marionette's "machine language."

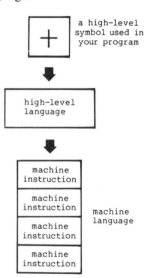

Now tie the strings to a control. The control is like a high-level language. With a simple turn of the wrist, the puppeteer can move many strings simultaneously.

So it is with a high-level computer language, where the simple and familiar symbol "+" causes many internal functions to be performed in the process of addition.

Here's a very clever thing about a computer: it can be programmed to translate high-level symbols (such as "+") into the computer's own machine language. Then it can proceed to carry out the machine instructions. A high-level language is a computer program that translates humanly understandable words and symbols into the machine language of the particular make and model of computer.

What's the difference between Forth and other high-level languages? It has to do with the compromise between man and computer. A language should be designed for the convenience of its human users, but at the same time for compatibility with the operation of the computer.

Forth is unique among languages because its solution to this problem is unique. This book will explain how.

INTRODUCTION FOR PROFESSIONALS: FORTH IN THE REAL WORLD

Forth has enjoyed a rising tide of popularity since 1978, although it has been used since the early '70s in critical scientific and industrial applications. Whatever your application, chances are that Forth can run it more efficiently than the language you're presently using.

To get a clear understanding of Forth, you should read this book and, if possible, find a Forth system and try it for yourself. For those of you who are still at the bookstore browsing, however, this section will answer two questions: "What is Forth?" and "What is it *good* for?"

Forth is many things:

—a high-level language
—an assembly language
—an operating system
—a set of development tools
—a software design philosophy

As a language, Forth begins with a powerful set of standard commands, then provides the mechanism by which you can define your own commands. The process of building definitions upon previous definitions in modular fashion is Forth's equivalent of high-level coding. Alternatively, words may be defined directly in assembler mnemonics, using Forth's assembler. All commands are interpreted by the same interpreter and compiled by the same compiler, giving the language tremendous flexibility.

The highest level of your code will resemble an English-language description of your application. Forth has been called a "meta-application language"—a language that you can use to create application-oriented languages.

Forth lets you break a problem into small pieces, write small words that handle those pieces, and then group them a few at a time into other words. This fits ideally with the way the human mind works. At any step, the programmer has to deal with only a few concepts, which fits the capacity of our short-term memory. And those concepts are named and called by name, which fits the way we think.

Forth is truly interactive. New words can be compiled on the spot, so that the programmer can immediately test each new command and learn about the problem at hand with instant feedback. (Many languages require loading an editor, editing, leaving the editor, loading a compiler, compiling, leaving the compiler, loading a linker, etc.) This *iterative* approach, in which optimal solutions are found by testing prototypes, works best in an integrated and responsive environment such as Forth provides.

Forth's structured control operators force a nested program design that reduces program complexity. And because it is optimized for the calling of words, Forth encourages the use of even smaller subroutines (words) than the most traditional "modular" languages. At virtually no cost in efficiency, Forth encourages information hiding, which in turn simplifies program enhancement.

For these reasons, Forth has been known to cut program development time by a factor of ten for equivalent assembly-language programming and by a factor of two for equivalent high-level programming.

Forth not only lets you program more productively, it lets your computer run more efficiently. Forth is fast. High-level Forth executes faster than most other high-level languages and roughly half as fast as equivalent assembly-language programs. Time-critical code may be written in assembler to run at full processor speed.

Also, Forth code is compact. Applications require less memory than their equivalent *assembly-language* programs! Written in Forth, the entire operating system and its standard word set resides in less than 8K bytes; a full development environment comfortably fits in 16–32K. Support for a target application may require less than 1K bytes.

Forth is transportable. The Forth virtual machine has been implemented on just about every mini- and microcomputer known to the industry. In fact, the Forth architecture has even been implemented in silicon.

Here is a small selection of Forth applications in the real world:

The Arts—Forth controls the equipment that has produced several rock videos and the title sequence for the Bill Cosby Show. At San Jose State University's electronic music studio, a Forth extension language called MASC allows composers to write music for analog synthesizers.

Business and Personal Computer Software—Forth was used to develop Peachtree's "Back to Basics" accounting software, the Savvy database package, Quest Research's Simplex (an integrated database system with word processing, communications, MacIntosh-like windows, and graphics), Data Ace, and Master Type. Bell Canada chose Forth for its telephone-switching network troubleshooting and analysis database network on which a single 68000 processor supports thirty-two terminals and a 200MB database. Cycledata Corp. uses Forth to create and maintain a large financial database of stocks for their investors with real-time modeling reports.

Data Acquisition and Analysis—Forth is used in many of the world's major observatories. For instance, a single PDP-11/34 running under Forth controls an observatory telescope, dome, several CRTs, printer and disk drive while recording data on infrared emissions from space, analyzing the data, and displaying the results on a graphics monitor. The U.S. Forestry Service uses a Forth-based image processing system for analyzing and reformatting contour maps. Dysan uses a Forth-based integrated test instrument built around an IBM-PC which analyzes bit patterns on floppy disks to assess various parameters of manufacturing quality. Towboats on the Mississippi River use Forth-based depth-sounding devices. NASA, the Naval Oceans Systems Center, and Naval Weapons Center use Forth for sophisticated data analysis of various kinds. Applications of this type often make use of Fast Fourier and Walsh Transforms, numerical integration, and other math routines written in Forth.

Expert Systems—A diesel electric locomotive troubleshooting and expert system was developed in Forth for General Electric Corporate Research and Development. Forth is also used by Applied Intelligence Systems and IRI, Inc., in industrial vision applications. The Stanford University Sleep Research Center uses a Forth-based real-time expert system for identifying sleep patterns.

Graphics—The Easel program, and its successor Lumena, by Time Arts Inc., are paint programs sold in connection with a variety of popular graphics/CAD systems; both were written in Forth.

Medical—On a single PDP-11 at a major hospital, Forth maintains a large patient database, manages thirty-two terminals and an optical reader, analyzes blood samples, monitors heartbeats in real time, and performs statistical analysis to correlate physical types, diseases, treatments, and results. NCR's Medical Systems Division also uses Forth on its 9300 system in hospital applications. The Palo Alto Veterans Administration Rehabilitation Research and Development Center uses Forth to build devices that serve disabled individuals, including an ultrasonic detector that translates the position of the user's head into signals that control devices such as electric wheelchairs.

Portable Intelligent Devices—The variety of applications that run Forth internally include a heart monitor for outpatients, two companies' automotive ignition analyzers, a hand-held instrument to measure relative moisture in different types of grain, and the Craig Language Translator.

Process Control—Both Jet Propulsion Lab and The McDonnell Douglas Astronautics Company have separately chosen Forth to design custom devices related to materials manufacturing under weightless conditions. Lockheed California and TRW each use Forth in different ways as aids to designing radar antennas. Northrup has made Forth their standard test language. Johnson Filaments uses Forth to control a laser micrometer robot to monitor the diameter of plastic fibers. At Union Carbide, Forth is used to develop laboratory automation and process control automation systems.

Robotics—A voice-controlled servomotion control system used by TRW was written in Forth. A suspended robot video camera called Skycam shoots football games, while Elicon's motion-picture cameras create space-chase scenes. Other applications range from a baggage handler for a major U.S. airline to a peach sorter for a California cannery.

Forth in Silicon—The R65F11 and R65F12 from Rockwell International Corp. are eight-bit processors that carry 133 Forth words in on-chip ROM, and mate with separate ROM chips that contain additional Forth words for program development. The MA2000 family from National Semiconductor Corp. consists of a stackable set of modules that form a full self-contained Forth computer when assembled. The Novix NC4000 family of high-speed engines implements the Forth architecture directly in silicon, executing high-level Forth instructions in a single clock cycle.

There's a catch, we must admit. It is that Forth makes *you* responsible for your computer's efficiency. To draw an analogy, a manual transmission is tougher to master than an automatic, yet for many drivers it offers improved control over the vehicle.

Similarly, Forth is tougher to master than traditional high-level languages, which essentially resemble one another (i.e., after learning one, it is not difficult to learn another). Once mastered, however, Forth gives you the capability to minimize CPU time and memory space, as well as an organizing philosophy by which you can dramatically reduce project development time.

And remember, all of Forth's elements enjoy the same protocol, including operating system, compiler, interpreters, text editor, virtual memory, assembler, and multiprogrammer. The learning curve for Forth is much shorter than that for all these separate elements added together.

If this sounds exciting to you, read on and start Forth.

1
FUNDAMENTAL FORTH

In this chapter, we'll acquaint you with some of the unique properties of the Forth language. After a few introductory pages, we'll have you sitting at a Forth computer. If you don't have a Forth computer, don't worry. We'll show you the result of each step along the way.

A LIVING LANGUAGE

Imagine that you're an office manager and you've just hired a new, eager assistant. On the first day, you teach the assistant the proper format for typing correspondence. (The assistant already knows how to type.) By the end of the day, all you have to say is "Please type this."

On the second day, you explain the filing system. It takes all morning to explain where everything goes, but by the afternoon all you have to say is "Please file this."

By the end of the week, you can communicate in a kind of shorthand, where "Please send this letter" means "Type it, get me to sign it, photocopy it, file the copy, and mail the original." Both you and your assistant are free to carry out your business more pleasantly and efficiently.

Good organization and effective communication require that you

1. define useful tasks and give each task a name, then

2. group related tasks together into larger tasks and give each of these a name, and so on.

Forth lets you organize your own procedures and communicate them to a computer in just this way (except you don't have to say "Please").

As an example, imagine a microprocessor-controlled washing machine programmed in Forth. The ultimate command in your example is named WASHER. Here is the definition of WASHER, as written in Forth:

`: WASHER    WASH SPIN RINSE SPIN ;`

In Forth, the colon indicates the beginning of a new definition. The first word after the colon, WASHER, is the name of the new procedure. The remaining words, WASH, SPIN, RINSE, and SPIN, comprise the "definition" of the new procedure. Finally, the semicolon indicates the end of the definition.

Each of the words comprising the definition of WASHER has already been defined in our washing-machine application. For example, let's look at our definition of RINSE:

`: RINSE    FILL AGITATE DRAIN ;`

As you can see, the definition of RINSE consists of a group of words: FILL, AGITATE, and DRAIN. Once again, each of these words has already been defined elsewhere in our washing-machine application. The definition of FILL might be

`: FILL    FAUCETS OPEN  TILL-FULL  FAUCETS CLOSE ;`

In this definition, we are referring to *things* (faucets) as well as to *actions* (open and close). The word TILL-FULL has been defined to create a "delay loop" that does nothing but mark time until the water-level switch has been activated, indicating that the tub is full.

If we were to trace these definitions back, we would eventually find that they are all defined in terms of a group of commands that form the basis of all Forth systems. For example, polyFORTH includes about 300 such commands. Many of these commands are themselves "colon definitions," just like our example words; others are defined directly in the machine language of the particular computer. In Forth, a defined command is called a *word*.†

---

† **For Old Hands:** This meaning of *word* is not to be associated with a 16-bit value, which in the Forth community is referred to as a "cell."

The ability to define a word in terms of other words is called "extensibility." Extensibility leads to a style of programming that is extremely simple, naturally well-organized, and as powerful as you want it to be.

Whether your application runs an assembly line, acquires data for a scientific environment, maintains a business application, or plays a game, you can create your own "living language" of words that relate to your particular need.

In this book we'll cover the most useful of the standard Forth commands.

ALL THIS AND ... INTERACTIVE!

One of Forth's many unique features is that it lets you "execute"† a word by simply naming the word. This can be as simple as typing in the word and pressing the RETURN key.

Of course, you can also use the same word in the definition of any other word, simply by putting its name in the definition.

Forth is called an "interactive" language because it carries out your commands the instant you enter them.

We're going to give an example that you can try yourself, showing the process of combining simple commands into more powerful commands. We'll use some simple Forth words that control your video screen or printer. But first, let's get acquainted with the mechanics of "talking" to Forth through your keyboard.

Take a seat at your real or imaginary Forth computer. We'll assume that someone has been kind enough to set everything up for you, or that you have followed all the instructions given for loading your particular computer.

Now press the key labeled

RETURN‡

The computer will respond by saying

_ok

The RETURN key is your way of telling Forth to acknowledge your request.

---

† **For Beginners:** To "execute" a word is to order the computer to carry out a command.

‡ **For People at Computers:** RETURN may have a different name on your keyboard. Other possible names are NEW LINE and ENTER.

Backspace also may have a different name on your terminal, such as DEL or RUBOUT.

The ok is Forth's way of saying that it's done everything you asked it to do without any hangups. In this case, you didn't ask it to do anything, so Forth obediently did nothing and said ok.

Now enter this:

```
15 SPACES
```

Many Forth systems do care whether you're typing in upper- or lowercase, so when you type "SPACES", be sure it's in uppercase, just as we show it here.

If you make a typing mistake, you can correct it by pressing the "backspace" key. Back up to the mistake, enter the correct letter, then continue. When you have typed the line correctly, press the RETURN key. (Once you press RETURN, it's too late to correct the line.)

In this book, we use the symbol `RETURN` to mark the point at which you must press the RETURN key. We also underline the computer's output (even though the computer does not) to indicate who is typing what.

Here's what has happened:

```
15 SPACES RETURN _____ok
```

As soon as you pressed the RETURN key, Forth printed fifteen blank spaces and then, having processed your request, it responded ok (at the end of the fifteen spaces).

Now enter this:

```
42 EMIT RETURN _*ok
```

The phrase "42 EMIT" tells Forth to print an asterisk (we'll discuss this command later in the book.) Here Forth printed the asterisk, then responded ok.

We can put more than one command on the same line. For example,

```
15 SPACES   42 EMIT   42 EMIT RETURN _____**ok
```

This time, Forth printed fifteen spaces and two asterisks. A note about entering words and/or numbers: We can separate them from one another by as many spaces as we want for clarity. But they must be separated by *at least one space* for Forth to be able to recognize them as words and/or numbers.

Instead of entering the phrase

```
42 EMIT
```

over and over, let's define it as a word called "STAR."

Enter this:

```
: STAR   42 EMIT ; RETURN _ok
```

Here "STAR" is the name; "42 EMIT" is the definition. Notice that we set off the colon and semicolon from adjacent words with a space. Also, to make

Forth definitions easy for human beings to read, we conventionally separate the name of a definition from its contents with three spaces.

After you have entered the above definition and pressed RETURN, Forth responds <u>ok</u>, signifying that it has recognized your definition and will remember it. Now enter

STAR `RETURN` _*<u>ok</u>

Voila! Forth executes your definition of "STAR" and prints an asterisk.

There is no difference between a word such as STAR that you define yourself and a word such as EMIT that is already defined. In this book, however, we will put boxes around those words that are already defined, so that you can more easily tell the difference.

Another system-defined word is CR , which performs a carriage return and line feed at your terminal.† For example, enter this:

CR `RETURN` _
<u>ok</u>

As you can see, Forth executed a carriage return, then printed an <u>ok</u> (on the next line).

Now try this:

CR STAR CR STAR CR STAR`RETURN`
*
*
*<u>ok</u>

Let's put a CR in a definition, like this:

: MARGIN   CR   30 SPACES ;`RETURN` _<u>ok</u>

Now we can enter

MARGIN STAR MARGIN STAR MARGIN STAR `RETURN`

and get three stars lined up vertically, thirty spaces in from the left.

Our MARGIN STAR combination will be useful for what we intend to do, so let's define

: BLIP   MARGIN STAR ;`RETURN` _<u>ok</u>

We will also need to print a horizontal row of stars. So let's enter the following definition (we'll explain how it works in a later chapter):

: STARS   0 DO STAR LOOP ;`RETURN` _<u>ok</u>

---

† **For Beginners:** Be sure to distinguish between the key labeled RETURN and the Forth word CR .

Now we can say

5 STARS `RETURN`_*****ok

or

35 STARS `RETURN`_***********************************ok

But don't say "0 STARS", especially not on a Forth-83 system. Wait until Chapter 6.

We will need a word that performs MARGIN and then prints five stars. Let's define it like this:

: BAR   MARGIN 5 STARS ; `RETURN`_ok

Now we can enter

BAR BLIP BAR BLIP BLIP   CR

and get a letter "F" (for Forth) made up of stars. It should look like this:

```
                              *****
                              *
                              *****
                              *
                              *
```

The final step is to make this new procedure a word. Let's call the word "F":

: F   BAR BLIP BAR BLIP BLIP   CR ; `RETURN`_ok

You've just seen an example of the way simple Forth commands can become the foundation for more complex commands. A Forth application, when listed,† consists of a series of increasingly powerful definitions rather than a sequence of instructions to be executed in order.

To give you a sample of what a Forth application really looks like, here's a listing of our experimental application:

```
0 ( LARGE LETTER-F )
1 : STAR    42 EMIT ;
2 : STARS    0 DO STAR LOOP ;
3 : MARGIN   CR 30 SPACES ;
4 : BLIP    MARGIN STAR ;
5 : BAR    MARGIN 5 STARS ;
6 : F    BAR BLIP BAR BLIP BLIP   CR ;
7
8
```

---

† **For Beginners:** We'll explain more about listing, as it applies to Forth, in Chapter 3.

THE DICTIONARY

Each word and its definition are entered into Forth's "dictionary." The dictionary already contained many words when you started, but your own words are now in the dictionary as well.

When you define a new word, Forth translates your definition into dictionary form and writes the entry in the dictionary. This process is called *compiling*.†

For example, when you enter the line

    : STAR   42 EMIT ;

the compiler compiles the new definition into the dictionary. The compiler does *not* print the asterisk.

(Want to see a list of the words in the dictionary right now? On most systems, you can type WORDS and see the names along with their "addresses" [locations in memory]. The words are listed in the order they were defined, with the most recent on top. Some older systems call this word VLIST.)

Once STAR is in the dictionary, how is it executed? Let's say you enter the following line directly (not inside a definition):

    STAR   30 SPACES RETURN

This will activate a word called INTERPRET, also known as the *text interpreter*.

---

† **For Beginners:** Compilation is a general computer term that normally means the translation of a high-level program into machine code that the computer can understand. In Forth, it means the same thing, but specifically it means writing in the dictionary.

The text interpreter scans the input stream, looking for strings of characters separated by spaces.

When he finds such a string, he looks it up in the dictionary.

If he finds the word in the dictionary, he points out the definition to a word called EXECUTE—

—who then executes the definition (in this case, he prints an asterisk). The interpreter says everything's "ok."

If the interpreter cannot find the string in the dictionary, he calls the numbers-runner (called NUMBER).

NUMBER knows a number when he sees one. If NUMBER finds a number, he runs it off to a temporary storage location for numbers.

What happens when you try to execute a word that is not in the dictionary? Enter this and see what happens:

XLERB ⌈RETURN⌉ _XLERB_?

When the text interpreter cannot find XLERB in the dictionary, it tries to pass it off on ⌈NUMBER⌉. ⌈NUMBER⌉ shines it on. Then the interpreter returns the string to you with an error message.

Many versions of Forth save the entire name of each definition in the dictionary, along with the number of characters in the name. The problem with this scheme is that in large applications, too much memory is consumed not by the program or by data, but by names.

In some versions of Forth, the compiler can be told *not* to keep the entire name, but simply the count of characters in the whole name and a specified number of characters, usually three. This technique allows the program to reside in less memory, but can result in naming conflicts. For instance, if the compiler only saves the count and the first three characters, the text interpreter cannot distinguish between STAR and STAG, while it can distinguish between STAR and START.

It's nice if the Forth system lets you switch back and forth between using shortened name fields and, for words that cause "collisions," keeping "natural-length" names. (Check your system documentation to see whether—and how—you can do this.)

To summarize: When you type a predefined word at the terminal, it gets interpreted and then executed.

Now, remember we said that ⌈:⌉ is a word? When you type the word ⌈:⌉, as in

: STAR   42 EMIT ; ⌈RETURN⌉

the following occurs:

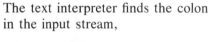

The text interpreter finds the colon in the input stream,

and points it out to EXECUTE .

: STAR   42 EMIT ;

EXECUTE says, "Please start compiling."

The compiler translates the definition into dictionary form and writes it in the dictionary.

When the compiler gets to the semi-colon, he stops,

and execution returns to the text interpreter, who gives the message <u>ok</u>.

SAY WHAT?

In Forth, a word is a character or group of characters that have a definition. Almost any characters can be used in naming a word. The only characters that cannot be used are:

return	because the computer thinks you've finished entering.†
backspace	because the computer thinks you're trying to correct a typing error, and
space	because the computer thinks it's the end of the word.

Here is a Forth word whose name consists of two punctuation marks. The word is ." and is pronounced *dot-quote*. You can use ." inside a definition to type a "string" of text at your terminal. Here's an example:

```
: GREET   ." Hello, I speak Forth " ; RETURN_ok
```

We've just defined a word called GREET. Its definition consists of just one Forth word, ." , followed by the text we want typed. The quotation mark at the *end* of the text will not be typed; it marks the end of the text. It's called a *delimiter*.

When entering the definition of GREET, don't forget the closing ; to end the definition.

Let's execute GREET:

```
GREET RETURN _Hello, I speak Forth ok
```

RUN-TIME VERSUS COMPILE-TIME: A SUMMARY

You'll be hearing two terms in your study of Forth: *compile-time* and *run-time*. Their meanings are actually quite simple. When we compile a definition, that is compile-time for that word. When we execute a word, that is its run-time.

For example, in the definition of GREET just given, at compile-time, Forth simply responds "ok"; at the definition's run-time, the word prints "Hello, I speak Forth." In the case of a predefined word such as CR, compile-time was when the person who created your Forth system compiled it; run-time is whenever you invoke it (or invoke a word that invokes it).

To take another example, when we compile GREET, the Forth compiler—or the set of "compiling words" that do the compiling—is actually running. It's compile-time for GREET, but run-time for the Forth compiling words.

The terms *compile-time* and *run-time* will be especially helpful in talking about the behavior of more complicated words later on.

---

† **For Philosophers:**   No, the computer doesn't "think." Unfortunately, there's no better word for what it really does. We say "think" on the grounds that it's all right to say, "the lamp needs a new light bulb." Whether the lamp really *needs* a bulb depends on whether it *needs* to provide light (that is, incandescence is its karma). So let's just say the computer thinks.

THE STACK: FORTH'S WORKSITE
FOR ARITHMETIC

A computer would not be much good if it couldn't do arithmetic. If you've never studied computers before, it may seem pretty amazing that a computer (or even a pocket calculator) can do arithmetic at all. We can't cite all the mechanics in this book, but believe us, it's not a miracle.

In general, computers perform their operations by breaking everything they do into ridiculously tiny pieces of information and ridiculously easy things to do. To you and me, "3 + 4" is just "7," without even thinking. To a computer, "3 + 4" is actually a very long list of things to do and remember.

Let's say you have a pocket calculator which expects its buttons to be pushed in this order:

Here's a generalized picture of what might occur:
When you press

—the number 3 goes into one place (we'll call it Box A);

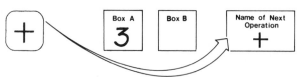

—the intended operation (addition) is remembered somehow;

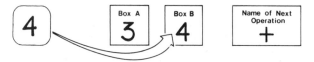

—the number 4 is stored into a second place (Box B); and

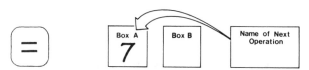

—the calculator performs the operation that is stored in the "Next Operation" Box on the contents of the number boxes and leaves the result in Box A.

Many calculators and computers approach arithmetic problems in a way similar to what we've just described. You may not be aware of it, but these machines are actually storing numbers in various locations and then performing operations on them.

In Forth, there is *one* central location where numbers are temporarily stored before being operated on. That location is called the *stack*. Numbers are "pushed onto the stack," and *then* operations work on the numbers on the stack.†

The best way to explain the stack is to illustrate it. If you enter the following line at your terminal:

3 4 + . RETURN 7 ok

here's what happens, key by key.

Recall that when you enter a number at your keyboard, the text interpreter hands it over to NUMBER , who runs it to some location. That location, it can now be told, is the stack. In short, when you enter the number three from the keyboard, you push it onto the stack.

Now the four goes onto the "top" of the stack and pushes the three downward.

---

† **For Pocket-Calculator Experts:** Hewlett-Packard calculators feature a stack and postfix arithmetic.

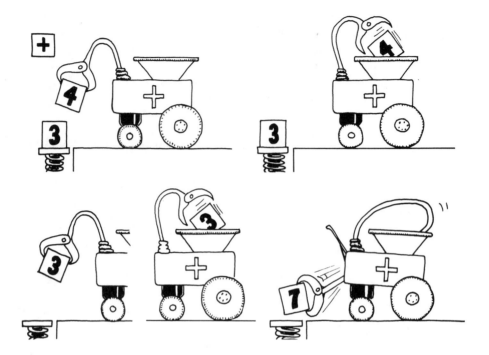

The next word in the input stream *can* be found in the dictionary. ☐+ has been previously defined to "take the top two numbers off the stack, add them, and push the result back onto the stack."

The next word, ☐., is also found in the dictionary. It has been previously defined to take the number off the stack and display it.

POSTFIX POWER

Now wait, you say. Why does Forth want you to type

3 4 +

instead of

    3 + 4

which is more familiar to most people?

Forth uses *postfix* notation (so called because the operator is affixed *after* the numbers) rather than *infix* notation (so-called because the operator is affixed *in-between* the numbers) so that all words that "need" numbers can get them from the stack. For example:

> the word $\boxed{+}$ gets two numbers from the stack and adds them;
>
> the word $\boxed{.}$ gets one number from the stack and prints it;
>
> the word $\boxed{\text{SPACES}}$ gets one number from the stack and prints that many spaces;
>
> the word $\boxed{\text{EMIT}}$ gets a number that represents a character and prints that character;
>
> even the word STARS, which we defined ourselves, gets a number from the stack and prints that many stars.

When *all* operators are defined to work on the values that are already on the stack, interaction between many operations remains simple even when the program gets complex.

We pointed out earlier that Forth lets you execute a word in either of two ways: by simply naming it, or by putting it in the definition of another word and naming *that* word. Postfix is part of what makes this possible.

Just as an example, let's suppose we wanted a word that will always add the number 4 to whatever number is on the stack (for no other purpose than to illustrate our point). Let's call the word

    FOUR-MORE

We could define it this way:

    : FOUR-MORE   4 + ; `RETURN`

and test it this way:

    3 FOUR-MORE . `RETURN` _7_ok

and again:

    -10 FOUR-MORE . `RETURN` _-6_ok

The "4" *inside* the definition goes onto the stack, just as it would if it were outside a definition. Then the $\boxed{+}$ adds the two numbers on the stack. Since $\boxed{+}$ always works on the stack, it doesn't care that the "4" came from inside the definition and the "3" from outside.

As we begin to give some more complicated examples, the value of the stack and of postfix arithmetic will become increasingly apparent to you. The more operators that are involved, the more important it is that they all be able to "communicate" with each other. Using a stack makes that communication simple.

KEEP TRACK OF YOUR STACK

We've just begun to demonstrate the philosophy behind the stack and postfix notation. Before we continue, however, let's look more closely at the stack in action and get accustomed to its peculiarities.

Forth's stack is described as "last-in, first-out" (LIFO). You can see from the earlier illustration why this is so. The three was pushed onto the stack first, then the four was pushed on top of it. Later, the adding machine took the four off first because it was on top. Hence, "last-in, first-out."

Let's use [.] to further demonstrate. Remember that each [.] removes one number from the stack and prints it. Four dots, therefore, remove four numbers and print them.

2 4 6 8 . . . . RETURN 8 6 4 2 ok

The system reads input from left to right and executes each word in turn.

For input, the rightmost value on the screen will end up on *top* of the stack.

For output, the rightmost value on the screen came from the *bottom* of the stack.

Let's see what kind of trouble we can get ourselves into. Type

10 20 30 . . . .

(that's *four* dots) then RETURN. What you get is:

10 20 30 . . . . [RETURN] _30_20_10_0_._Stack_empty†

Each dot removes one value. The fourth dot found no value left on the stack to send to the display, and it told you so.

This error is called "stack underflow." (Notice that a stack underflow is *not* "ok.")

The opposite condition, when the stack completely fills up, is called "stack overflow." The stack is usually so deep, however, that this condition will never occur except when you've done something terribly wrong.

Ordinarily you needn't worry about everything that's on the stack at any given moment—just the numbers you're working with now. Other numbers that may have been pushed on the stack previously will safely stay there—below your awareness—until they are needed.

For example, suppose we want to draw a box, using the same techniques we developed to display the letter "F." For the sides, we could write the word

    : SIDES   STAR 5 SPACES   STAR ;

This would produce:

    *   *

However, suppose we want to draw *any* size box. We don't want to put the "5" *inside* the definition, we want to pass it to SIDES from the *outside*. Thus we write

    : SIDES   STAR   SPACES   STAR ;

and then say, for instance,

    5 SIDES

---

† **For the Curious:** Actually, dot always prints whatever is on the top, so if there is nothing on the stack, it prints whatever is just below the stack, which is usually zero. Only then is the error detected; the offending word (in this case, *dot*) is returned to the screen, followed by the "error message."

The point is this: Even as the first STAR was executed (which involves pushing a "42" on the stack, then consuming it with $\boxed{\text{EMIT}}$, the number "5" stayed on the stack, patiently waiting to be consumed by $\boxed{\text{SPACES}}$.

STACK EFFECT COMMENTS

The stack provides an easy, consistent way to pass arguments to a definition.† In using the stack, however, we bear the responsibility for keeping track of "stack effects." This means that when we define a word, we must decide on what arguments the word will consume and what arguments it will leave behind, or "return," and then make sure the word behaves accordingly.

To use our previous simplistic example, FOUR-MORE, we know that it requires one argument on the stack (before we execute it) and leaves, or "returns," one result on the stack (after we execute it). If we put a "dot" inside the definition, to print the result, that would change the stack effect: the word would no longer return the result to the stack.

To communicate stack effects in a visual way, Forth programmers use a special notation called the *stack effect comment*. These should appear in program listings and "glossaries" (a kind of documentation that lists the words written for your application). Before we can show you what a stack effect comment looks like, we must pause and talk about "comments" in Forth.

A comment is anything written for human readers only; text that is neither executed nor compiled. In Forth, the word $\boxed{(}$, "*left parenthesis*," begins a comment by telling the text interpreter to skip all the following text up to the terminating right parenthesis. Because $\boxed{(}$ is a word, we must follow it with a space, just as we do with $\boxed{."}$.‡

---

† **For Semantics Freaks:** In mathematics, the word *argument* refers to an independent variable of a function. Computer linguists have borrowed this term to refer to numbers being operated on by functions or subroutines. They also have borrowed the word *parameters* to describe pretty much the same thing.

‡ **For Beginners:** The closing parenthesis is not a word, it is simply a character called a delimiter that is looked for by $\boxed{(}$. (Recall that the delimiter for $\boxed{."}$ is the closing quotation mark.)

Here's how we might use an ordinary comment inside a definition:

```
: NOTHING  ( do nothing )  ;
```

The words *do nothing* are the comment.

Now, back to stack effect comments. Here's the basic form of a stack effect comment:

```
( -- )
```

This particular comment shows that the definition has no apparent effect on the stack. An example of such a word is CR, or our own word STAR. (Internally, STAR puts a 42 on the stack, but consumes it before it's through—hence, no stack effect worth commenting.) The conventional place to put a stack effect comment is two spaces after the name, like this:

```
: STAR  ( -- )  42 EMIT ;
```

Remember that the stack effect comment means nothing to Forth, but plenty to any programmer trying to understand the code!

If a word *consumes* any arguments, list the arguments to the *left* of the double-hyphens. For example, the stack notation for the word . ("dot") is

```
( n -- )
```

(The "n" stands for "number.") If a word *returns* any arguments, list them to the *right* of the double-hyphens. The stack notation for the word + is

```
( n1 n2 -- sum)
```

When there is more than one argument, we may use names to describe what the arguments are, or abbreviations, or simply number them n1, n2, n3, and so on, as we've done here.

When you have more than one argument on either side of the dashes, obviously it's important to express the correct order. Here's the rule to remember: the *right-most* item in the comment is the *top-most* on the stack.

```
( n1 n2 -- sum)
```

You're the top

This is easy to remember if you think of the stack effect comment as a picture of what you entered. If you type the numbers 1 2 3 as input to a word, the stack effect comment would be:

```
( 1 2 3 -- )
```

that is, "1" on the bottom and "3" on the top.

Since you probably have the hang of it by now, we'll be leaving out the RETURN symbol except where we feel it's needed for clarity. You can usually tell where to press RETURN because the computer's response is always underlined.

Here's a list of the Forth words you've learned so far, including their stack notations ("n" stands for number; "c" stands for character):

: xxx yyy ;	(--)	Creates a new definition with the name *xxx*, consisting of word or words *yyy*.
CR	(--)	Performs a carriage return and line feed at the current output device.
SPACES	(n --)	Displays the given number of blank spaces.
SPACE	(--)	Displays one blank space.
EMIT	(c --)	Transmits a character to the output device.
." xxx"	(--)	Displays the character string *xxx*. The " character terminates the string.
+	(n1 n2 -- sum)	Adds.
.	(n --)	Displays a number, followed by one space.
(xxx)	(--)	Begins a comment that will be ignored by the text interpreter. The character) is the delimiter.

In the next chapter, we'll discuss how to get the computer to perform some fancier arithmetic.

REVIEW OF TERMS

Compile   to generate a dictionary entry in computer memory from source text (the written-out form of a definition). Distinct from "execute."

Dictionary   in Forth, a list of words and definitions including both "system" definitions (predefined) and "user" definitions (which you invent). A dictionary resides in computer memory in compiled form.

Execute   to perform. Specifically, to execute a word is to perform the operations specified in the compiled definition of the word.

Extensibility	a characteristic of a computer language that allows a programmer to add new features or modify existing ones.
Glossary	a list of words defined in Forth, showing their stack effects and an explanation of what they do, which serves as a reference for programmers.
Infix notation	the method of writing operators between the operands they affect, as in "2 + 5."
Input stream	the text to be read by the text interpreter. This may be text that you have just typed in or it may be text that is stored on disk.
Interpret	(when referring to Forth's text interpreter) to read the input stream, then to find each word in the dictionary or, failing that, to convert it to a number.
LIFO	(last-in, first-out) the type of stack which Forth uses. A can of tennis balls is a LIFO structure; the last ball you drop in is the one you must remove first.
Postfix notation	the method of writing operators after the operands they affect, as in "2 5 +" for "2 + 5." Also known as Reverse Polish Notation.
Stack	a region of memory that is controlled in such a way that data can be stored or removed in a last-in, first-out (LIFO) fashion.
Stack overflow	the error condition that occurs when the entire area of memory allowed for the stack is completely filled with data.
Stack underflow	the error condition that occurs when an operation expects a value on the stack, but there is no valid data on the stack.
Word	in Forth, the name of a definition.

PROBLEMS

Before you work on these problems, remember these simple rules:
Every `:` needs a `;`.
Every `."` needs a `"`.
and
Every `(` needs a `)`.

1-1. Define a word called GIFT that, when executed, will type out the name of some gift. For example, you might try:

```
: GIFT   ." bookends" ;
```

Now define a word called GIVER that will print out a person's first name.

Finally, define a word called THANKS that includes the new words GIFT and GIVER, and prints out a message something like this:

```
Dear_Stephanie,
      Thanks_for_the_bookends._ok
```

1-2. Define a word called TEN-LESS that takes a number on the stack, subtracts ten, and returns the answer on the stack. (Hint: You can use $\boxed{+}$.) Be sure to include a stack effect comment.

1-3. After entering the words in Problem 1-1, enter a new definition for GIVER to print someone else's name, then without redefining THANKS, execute THANKS again. Can you explain why THANKS still prints out the first giver's name?

HOW TO GET RESULTS

In this chapter, we'll dive right into some specifics that you need to know before we go on. Specifically, we'll introduce some of the arithmetic instructions besides ⊞ and some special operators for rearranging the order of numbers on the stack, so that you'll be able to write mathematical equations in Forth.

FORTH ARITHMETIC—CALCULATOR STYLE

Here are the four simplest integer-arithmetic operators in Forth:†

pronounced:

+	(n1 n2 -- sum)	Adds.	plus
−	(n1 n2 -- diff)	Subtracts ($n1 - n2$).	minus
∗	(n1 n2 -- prod)	Multiplies.	star
/	(n1 n2 -- quot)	Divides ($n1/n2$).	slash

† **If Math Is Not Your Thing:** Don't worry if this chapter looks a little like an algebra textbook. Solving math problems is only one of the things you can do with Forth. Later we'll explore some of the other things Forth can do.

Unlike calculators, computer keyboards don't have special keys for multiplication and division. Instead, we use ⟨*⟩ and ⟨/⟩.

In the first chapter, we learned that we can add two numbers by putting them both on the stack, executing the word ⟨+⟩, and finally executing the word ⟨.⟩ (dot) to display the result.

    17 5 + ._22_ok

We can use this method with all of Forth's arithmetic operators. In other words, we can use Forth like a calculator to get answers, even without writing a "program." Try a multiplication problem:

    7 8 * ._56_ok

By now we've seen that the operator comes after the numbers. In the case of subtraction and division, however, we must also consider the *order of numbers* ("7 − 4" is not the same as "4 − 7").

Just remember this rule:

To convert to postfix, simply move the operator to the end of the expression:

INFIX	POSTFIX
3 + 4	3 4 +
500 − 300	500 300 −
6 × 5	6 5 *
20 / 4	20 4 /

So to do this subtraction problem:

    7 − 4 =

simply type in

    7 4 − ._3_ok

Meanwhile, we'd like to remind you that integers are whole numbers, such as

... −3, −2, −1, 0, 1, 2, 3, ...

Integer arithmetic (logically enough) is arithmetic that concerns itself only with integers, not with decimal-point numbers, such as 2.71.

FOR ADVENTURESOME NEWCOMERS SITTING AT A COMPUTER

If you're one of those people who likes to fool around and figure out things for themselves without reading the book, then you're bound to discover a couple of weird things. First off, as we told you, these operators are *integer operators*. That not only means that you can't do calculations with decimal values, like

10.00 2.25 +

it also means that you can only get integer results, as in

21 4 / ._5_ok instead of **5.25_ok**

Another thing is that if you try to multiply:

10000 10 *

or some such large numbers, you'll get a crazy answer. So we're telling you up front that with the operators introduced so far and with ▯.▯ to print the results, you can't have any numbers that are higher than 32767 or lower than −32768. Numbers within this range are called "single-length signed numbers."

> +32767 ┼ ⎫
> 0 ┼ ⎬ Allowable range of single-length signed numbers.
> −32768 ┼ ⎭

Notice, in the list of Forth words a few pages back, the letter "n," which stands for "number." Since Forth uses single-length numbers more often than other types of numbers, the "n" signifies that the number must be single-length. And yes, there are other operators that extend this range ("double-length" operators, which are indicated by "d").

All of these mysteries will be explained in time, so stay tuned.

The order of numbers stays the same. Let's try a division problem:

20 4 / ._5_ok

The word ⟨/⟩ is defined to divide the second number on the stack by **the** top number:

SAMURAI DIVIDER

What do you do if you have more than one operator in an expression like:

`4 + (17 * 12)`

Let's take it step by step: the parentheses tell you to first multiply seventeen by twelve, *then* add four. So in Forth you would write:

`17 12 * 4 + . 208 ok`

and here's why:

17 and 12 go onto the stack. ⟦*⟧ multiplies them and returns the result.

Then the four goes onto the stack, on top of the 204. ⟦+⟧ rolls out the adding machine and adds them together, returning only the result.

Or suppose you want to add five numbers. You can do it in Forth like this:

```
17 20 +  132 + 3 + 9 +  . _181_ok
```

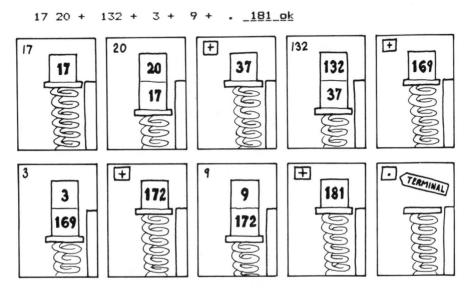

Now here's an interesting problem:

(3+9) * (4+6)

To solve it, we have to add three to nine first, then add four to six, then finally multiply the two sums. In Forth, we can write

3 9 +   4 6 +   *   . _120 ok

and here's what happens:

Notice that we very conveniently saved the sum twelve on the stack while we went on about the business of adding four to six.

Remember that we're not concerned yet with writing definitions. We are simply using Forth as a calculator.

If you're like most beginners, you probably would like to try your hand at a few practice problems until you feel more comfortable with postfix.

POSTFIX PRACTICE PROBLEMS (QUIZZIE 2-A)

First convert the algebraic equations in the left column to postfix, using pencil and paper. For example, given

ab + c   2 · 3 + 4   (10)

you would write

a b * c +

Next, test your new equation by substituting the numbers given in the middle column, and by using Forth "calculator style" to obtain the correct result (right column); that is,

2 3 * 4 + . _10 ok

1.	$c(a + b)$	$3(4 + 5)$	(27)
2.	$\dfrac{ab}{100}$	$\dfrac{80 \cdot 90}{100}$	(72)
3.	$\dfrac{3a - b}{4} + c$	$\dfrac{(3 \cdot 9) - 7}{4} + 2$	(7)

4. $$\dfrac{a + 1}{4}$$ $$\dfrac{7 + 1}{4}$$ (2)

5. $x(7x + 5)$ $10 \cdot ((7 \cdot 10) + 5)$ (750)

Convert the following postfix expressions to infix:

6. a b - b a + /

7. a b 10 * /

ANSWERS—QUIZZIE 2-A

1. a b c * + or
    c a b * +

2. a b 100 * /

3. 3 a * b - 4 / c +

4. a 1 + 4 /

5. 7 x * 5 + x *

6. $\dfrac{a - b}{b + a}$

7. $\dfrac{a}{10b}$

FORTH ARITHMETIC—DEFINITION STYLE

In Chapter 1, we saw that we could define new words in terms of numbers and other predefined words. Let's explore some further possibilities, using some of our newly learned math operators.

Let's say that we want to convert various measurements to inches. We know that

1 yard = 36 inches

and

1 foot = 12 inches

so we can define these two words:

```
: YARDS>INCHES  ( yards -- inches)  36 * ;_ok
: FEET>INCHES   ( feet -- inches )  12 * ;_ok
```

where the names symbolize "yards-to-inches" and "feet-to-inches." Here's what they do:

```
10 YARDS>INCHES . _360_ok
2 FEET>INCHES . _24_ok
```

If we *always* want our result to be in inches, we can define:

```
: YARDS  ( yards -- inches)  36 * ;_ok
: FEET   ( feet -- inches)   12 * ;_ok
: INCHES ( -- ) ;_ok
```

so that we can use the phrase

```
10 YARDS  2 FEET +  9 INCHES + . _393_ok
```

Notice that the word INCHES doesn't do anything except remind the human user what the nine is there for. If we really want to get fancy, we can add these three definitions:

```
: YARD   YARDS ;_ok
: FOOT   FEET ;_ok
: INCH ;_ok
```

so that the user can enter the singular form of any of these nouns and still get the same result:

```
1 YARD  2 FEET +  1 INCH + . _61_ok
2 YARDS  1 FOOT + . _84_ok
```

So far, we have only defined words whose definitions contain a single math operator. But it's perfectly possible to put many operators inside a definition, if that's what you need to do.

Let's say we want a word that computes the sum of five numbers on the stack. A few pages back, we summed five numbers like this:

```
17 20 +  132 +  3 +  9 +  . _181_ok
```

But we can also enter

17 20 132 3 9 + + + + . _181_ok

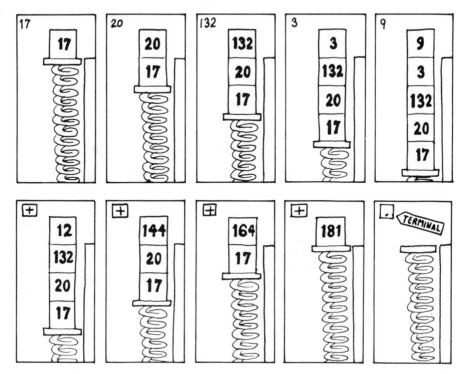

We get the same answer, even though we've clustered all the numbers into one group and all the operators into another group. We can write our definition like this:

: 5#SUM   (n1 n2 n3 n4 n5 -- sum)   + + + + ;_ok

and execute it like this:

17 20 132 3 9 5#SUM . _181_ok

Here's another equation to write a definition for:†

`(a + b) ✻ c`

As we saw in Quizzie 2-A, this expression can be written in postfix as

`c a b + ✻`

Thus, we could write our definition

`: SOLUTION   ( c a b -- n )   + ✻ ;`

DEFINITION-STYLE PRACTICE PROBLEMS (QUIZZIE 2-B)

Convert the following infix expressions into Forth definitions and show the stack order required by your definitions. The values represented in the formula by letters (a, b, and c) must come from the stack, in whatever order is most convenient. Since this is Quizzie 2-B, you can name your definitions 2B1, 2B2, and so on. For example,

1. $ab + c$ would become `: 2B1   ( c a b -- x )   ✻ + ;`

2. $\dfrac{a - 4b}{6} + c$

3. $\dfrac{a}{8b}$

4. $\dfrac{0.5\,ab}{100}$

5. $a(2a + 3)$

6. $\dfrac{a - b}{c}$

† **For Beginners Who Like Word Problems:** If a jet plane flies at an average air speed of 600 mph and if it flies with a tail wind of 25 mph, how far will it travel in five hours?

If we define

`: DISTANCE   ( hours mph tail-wind -- distance)`
`   + ✻ ;`

we could enter

`5 600 25 DISTANCE . 3125 ok`

Try it with different values, including head winds (negative values).

ANSWERS—QUIZZIE 2-B

2. : 2B2 (c a b -- x)
        4 * 6 - / + ;
3. : 2B3 (a b -- x)
        8 * / ;
4. : 2B4 (a b -- x)
        * 200 / ;
5. : 2B5 (a a -- x)
        2 * 3 + * ;
6. If you said this one's impossible,
    you're right—at least without the stack
    manipulation operators, which we'll
    introduce very shortly.

THE DIVISION OPERATORS

The word $\boxed{/}$ is Forth's simplest division operator. *Slash* supplies only the quotient; any remainder is lost. If you type

        22 4 / . _5_ok

you get only the quotient five, not the remainder two.

If you're thinking of a pocket calculator's divide operator, then five is not the full answer. And Forth doesn't even round up its integer answer!

But $\boxed{/}$ is only one of several division operators supplied by Forth to give you the flexibility to tell the computer exactly what you want it to do. In many applications, in fact, you *don't* want a floating point or rounded result.

Take this problem: "How many dollar bills can I get for 22 quarters?" The real answer, of course, is exactly 5, not 5.5. A computerized money changer, for example, would not know how to give you 5.5 dollar bills. What we need is a way to compute the integer quotient and remainder. Which leads us to two relatives of $\boxed{/}$:

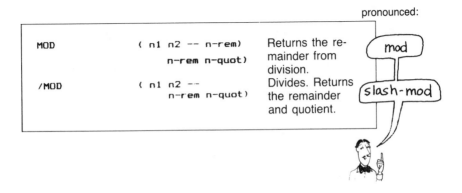

pronounced:

MOD	(n1 n2 -- n-rem)	Returns the re-	mod
	n-rem n-quot)	mainder from division.	
/MOD	(n1 n2 --	Divides. Returns	slash-mod
	n-rem n-quot)	the remainder and quotient.	

To summarize:

Use ☐/ when you want just the quotient.
Use ☐MOD when you want just the remainder.†
Use ☐/MOD when you want both the remainder and the quotient.

Let's try ☐/MOD:

22 4 /MOD . .5 2 ok

SAMURAI /MOD (slash's older brother)

With what we've learned so far, we can easily define this set of words:

```
: $>QUARTERS  ( dollars -- quarters dollars)  4 /MOD ;
: .DOLLARS  ( dollars -- )  .  ." dollar bills" ;
: .QUARTERS  ( quarters -- )  .  ." quarters " ;
: QUARTERS  ( dollars -- )
    $>QUARTERS  ." Gives " .DOLLARS  ."  and " .QUARTERS ;
```

so that we can type

22 QUARTERS

with this result:

22 QUARTERS Gives 5 dollars and 2 quarters ok

---

† For the Curious: "Mod" is short for "modulo," which basically means "remainder."

In the FORTH-83 Standard, in all of Forth's division operators, the quotient is *floored*.†

What about those applications that require rounding? Have no fear: the elementary Forth math operators can easily be combined and extended to provide this ability, as we'll see in the section called "Rounding" in Chapter 5.

STACK MANEUVERS

If you worked Problem 6 in the last set, you discovered that the infix equation

$$\frac{a - b}{c}$$

cannot be solved with a definition unless there is some way to rearrange values on the stack.

Well, there *is* a way: by using a "stack manipulation operator" called SWAP.

---

† **For the Mathematically Bent:**   Believe it or not, controversy in computer science surrounds even a simple math problem such as -31 divided by 7. The answer can be either -4 with a remainder of -3 ($-4 \times 7 = -28$; $-28 + -3 = 31$) OR -5 with a remainder of 4 ($-5 \times 7 = -35$; $-35 + 4 = 31$).

The choice made by the FORTH-83 Standards team was that division should be defined so that the quotient is *floored*; that is, if the real quotient lies between two integers, the lesser integer is chosen. In this example, -5 is less than -4, and hence is the floor. Using floored division is the same as saying that the remainder should have the same sign as the divisor. Thus, in the FORTH-83 Standard, the quotient of -31 divided by 7 is -5 and the remainder is 4.

This rule results in signed division not having awkward inconsistencies around zero.

SWAP

The word SWAP is defined to switch the order of the top two stack items:

As with the other stack manipulation operators, you can test SWAP at your keyboard in "calculator style"; that is, it doesn't have to be contained within a definition.

First, enter

    1 2 . ._2_1_ok

then again, this time with SWAP:

    1 2 SWAP . ._1_2_ok

Thus, Problem 6 can be solved with this phrase:

    - SWAP /

with (c a b --) on the stack.

Let's give a, b, and c these test values:

    a = 10   b = 4   c = 2

then put them on the stack and execute the phrase, like so:

    2 10 4 - SWAP / ._3_ok

Here is a list of several stack manipulation operators, including SWAP .

SWAP	(n1 n2 -- n2 n1)	Reverses the top two stack items.
DUP	(n -- n n)	Duplicates the top stack item.
OVER	(n1 n2 -- n1 n2 n1)	Makes a copy of the second item and pushes it on top.
ROT	(n1 n2 n3 -- n2 n3 n1)	Rotates the third item to the top.
DROP	(n --)	Discards the top stack item.

DUP

The next stack manipulation operator on the list, DUP , simply makes a second copy (duplicate) of the top stack item.

For example, if we have "a" on the stack, we can compute:

a^2

as follows:

    DUP *

in which the following steps occur:

OPERATION	CONTENTS OF STACK
	a
DUP	a a
✻	a^2

OVER

Now somebody tells you to evaluate the expression:

a ✻ (a + b)

given the following stack order:

(a b --)

But, you say, I'm going to need a new manipulation operator: I want two copies of the "a," and the "a" is *under* the "b." Here's the word you need: OVER. OVER simply makes a copy of the "a" and leapfrogs it *over* the "b":

(a b -- a b a)

Now the expression

a ✻ (a + b)

can easily be written as

OVER + ✻

Here's what happens:

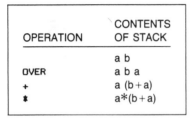

OPERATION	CONTENTS OF STACK
	a b
OVER	a b a
+	a (b + a)
✻	a*(b + a)

Always look for ways to simplify stack manipulations. For example, if somebody asks you to evaluate:

$$a^2 + ab$$

in Forth, you'll find the stack manipulations trickier than if you algebraically refactor the expression to read:

```
a * (a + b)
```

which is the expression we just evaluated so easily.

ROT

The fourth stack manipulator on the list is ROT (pronounced *rote*), which is short for "rotate." Here's what ROT does to the top three stack values:

For example, if we need to evaluate the expression:

$$ab - bc$$

we should first factor out the "b"'s:

```
b * (a - c)
```

Now if our starting-stack order is this:

```
( c b a -- )
```

we can use:

    ROT - *

in which the following steps will occur:

OPERATION	CONTENTS OF STACK
	c b a
ROT	b a c
-	b (a−c)
*	(b*(a−c))

| DROP |

The final stack manipulation operator on the list is | DROP |. All it does is discard the top stack value.

Pretty simple, huh? We'll see some good uses for | DROP | later on.

A NONDESTRUCTIVE STACK PRINT

When testing code, Forth programmers very often want to see what's on the stack. One way to do this, of course, is to type a series of dots. The problem with dots, however, is that they don't leave the numbers on the stack for future manipulations.

Most Forth systems have an invaluable tool called | .S | that prints out all the values on the stack "nondestructively"—that is, without removing them. This means that, in checking a definition, you can type a few words, do | .S | to ensure that the stack looks the way it should, type a few more words, do | .S | again, and so on.

Let's test it:

```
1 2 3 .S
1_2_3_ok

ROT .S
2_3_1_ok
```

In learning the stack manipulation words just covered, some beginners play the following trick:

```
: SWAP    SWAP .S ;
: DUP     DUP .S ;
: OVER    OVER .S ;
: ROT     ROT .S ;
: DROP    DROP .S ;
```

This gives them immediate feedback on what each of the commands has done. (It works because the interpreter uses the most recent definition found in the dictionary.)

STACK MANIPULATION AND MATH DEFINITION PROBLEMS (QUIZZIE 2-C)

1. Write a phrase that flips three items on the stack, leaving the middle number in the middle; that is,

    a b c   becomes   c b a

2. Write a phrase that does what OVER does, without using OVER.

    Write definitions for the following equations, given the stack effects shown:

3. $\dfrac{n + 1}{n}$ (n -- result)

4. $x(7x + 5)$ (x -- result)

5. $9a^2 - ba$ (a b -- result)

```
ANSWERS—QUIZZIE 2-C

1.       SWAP ROT

2.       SWAP DUP ROT SWAP

3.  : 2C3  DUP 1 + SWAP / ;    or
    : 2C3  DUP 1+ SWAP / ;

4.  : 2C4  DUP 7 * 5 + * ;

5.  : 2C5  OVER 9 * SWAP - * ;
```

PLAYING DOUBLES†

The next four stack manipulation operators should look vaguely familiar:

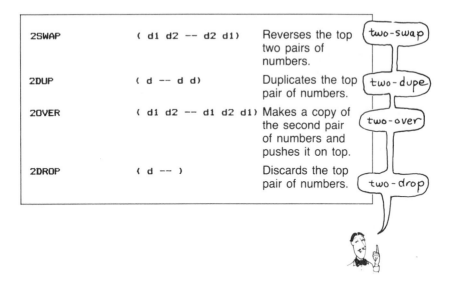

2SWAP	(d1 d2 -- d2 d1)	Reverses the top two pairs of numbers.	two-swap
2DUP	(d -- d d)	Duplicates the top pair of numbers.	two-dupe
2OVER	(d1 d2 -- d1 d2 d1)	Makes a copy of the second pair of numbers and pushes it on top.	two-over
2DROP	(d --)	Discards the top pair of numbers.	two-drop

The prefix "2" indicates that these stack manipulation operators handle numbers in pairs.‡ The letter *d* in the stack effects column stands for "double." "Double" has a special significance that we will discuss in Chapter 7.

The "2"-manipulators listed above are so straightforward, we won't even bore you with examples.

One more thing: There are still some stack manipulators that we haven't talked about yet, so don't go crazy by trying too much fancy footwork on the stack.

Guess who.

---

† **FORTH-83 Standard:** These words are part of the Standard's "Double Number Extension Word Set," which is optional in a Standard system. 2ROT is included.

‡ **For Old Hands:** They also can be used to handle double-length (32-bit) numbers.

Here are the Forth words we've covered in this chapter:

+	(n1 n2 -- sum)	Adds.
-	(n1 n2 -- diff)	Subtracts (n1 - n2).
*	(n1 n2 -- prod)	Multiplies.
/	(n1 n2 -- quot)	Divides (n1/n2).
MOD	(n1 n2 -- n-rem)	Returns the remainder from division.
/MOD	(n1 n2 -- n-rem n-quot)	Divides. Returns the remainder and quotient.
SWAP	(n1 n2 -- n2 n1)	Reverses the top two stack items.
DUP	(n -- n n)	Duplicates the top stack item.
OVER	(n1 n2 -- n1 n2 n1)	Makes a copy of the second item and pushes it on top.
ROT	(n1 n2 n3 -- n2 n3 n1)	Rotates the third item to the top.
DROP	(n --)	Discards the top stack item.
2SWAP	(d1 d2 -- d2 d1)	Reverses the top two pairs of numbers.
2DUP	(d -- d d)	Duplicates the top pairs of numbers.
2OVER	(d1 d2 -- d1 d2 d1)	Makes a copy of the second pair of numbers and pushes it on top.
2DROP	(d --)	Discards the top pair of numbers.

REVIEW OF TERMS

Double-length numbers — integers that encompass a range of over -2 billion to $+2$ billion (and that we'll introduce officially in Chapter 7).

Single-length numbers — integers that fall within the range of -32768 to $+32767$: the only numbers that are valid as the arguments or results of any of the operators we've discussed so far. (This seemingly arbitrary range comes from the way computers are designed, as we'll see later on.)

PROBLEMS

(answers in the back of the book)

2-1. What is the difference between $\boxed{\text{DUP}}$ $\boxed{\text{DUP}}$ and $\boxed{\text{2DUP}}$?

2-2. Define the word NIP to remove the stack item just under the top; that is,

(a b -- b)

2-3. Define the word TUCK to copy the top stack item under the second item; that is,

`( a b -- b a b)`

2-4. Define the word −ROT to move the top item underneath the next two items (opposite of ROT); that is,

`( a b c -- c a b)`

2-5. Write a phrase that will reverse the order of the top four items on the stack; that is,

`( 1 2 3 4 -- 4 3 2 1)`

2-6. Write a definition called 3DUP that will duplicate the top three numbers on the stack; for example,

`( 1 2 3 -- 1 2 3 1 2 3)`

Write definitions for the following infix equations, given the stack effects shown:

2-7. $a^2 + ab + c$ (c a b -- result)

2-8. $\dfrac{a - b}{a + b}$ (a b -- result)

2-9. Write a set of words to compute prison sentences for hardened criminals such that the judge can enter:

`CONVICTED-OF ARSON HOMICIDE TAX-EVASION_ok`
`WILL-SERVE_35_YEARS_ok`

or any series of crimes beginning with the word CONVICTED-OF and ending with WILL-SERVE. Use these sentences:

HOMICIDE	20 years
ARSON	10 years
BOOKMAKING	2 years
TAX-EVASION	5 years

2-10. You're the inventory programmer at Maria's Egg Ranch. Define a word called EGG.CARTONS, which expects on the stack the total number of eggs laid by the chickens today and displays the number of cartons that can be filled with a dozen each, as well as the number of left-over eggs.

WORKING WITH FORTH

Up until now, you've been compiling new definitions into the dictionary by typing them from your keyboard. This chapter introduces an alternate method, using disk storage and a Forth *editor*.

This chapter consists of two sections. The first discusses Forth's use of disk storage for writing source code, as well as certain stylistic conventions for the arrangement of code. This first section is for everyone.

The second section discusses a particular editor that has come to be known as the "Starting Forth editor." If the Forth system you're using has a different editor of its own, you'll want to skip the second part of this chapter and rely instead on your system's documentation.

ANOTHER LOOK AT THE DICTIONARY

If you've been experimenting at a real live computer, you may have discovered some things we haven't mentioned yet. In any case, it's time to mention them.

Discovery One: You can define the same word more than once in different ways—only the most recent definition will be executed.

For example, if you have entered

```
: GREET    ." Hello.   I speak Forth. " ; ok
```

you should get

```
GREET Hello.   I speak Forth. ok
```

and if you redefine

```
: GREET    ." Hi there! " ; ok
```

you get the most recent definition:

```
GREET Hi there! ok
```

Has the first GREET been erased? No, it's still there, but the text interpreter always starts at the "back of the dictionary" where the most recent entry is located. The first definition he finds is the one he shows to EXECUTE.

We can prove that the old GREET is still there. Try this:

```
FORGET GREET ok
```

and

```
GREET Hello.   I speak Forth. ok
```

(the old GREET again!).

The word FORGET looks up the given word in the dictionary and, in effect, removes it from the dictionary along with anything you may have defined since that word. FORGET, like the interpreter, searches starting from the back; he only removes the most recently defined version of the word (along with any words that follow). So now when you type GREET, the interpreter finds the original GREET.

$\boxed{\text{FORGET}}$ is a good word to know; it helps you to weed out your dictionary so it won't overflow. (The dictionary takes up memory space, so as with any other use of memory, you want to conserve it.)

> Discovery Two: When you enter definitions from the keyboard (as you have been doing), your source text[†] is not saved.

Only the compiled form of your definition is saved in the dictionary. So, what if you want to make a minor change to a word you've already defined? You must retype the entire definition with the change. This might get tedious, right? And worse:

> Discovery Three: When you turn off the computer, then turn it back on, all the definitions you typed have vanished!

Obviously, you need a way to save your source text permanently, so that you can modify it and recompile it at any time.

This is where the Forth *editor* comes in. The editor stores your source text on disk. So first, let's learn a bit about the disk and the way the Forth system uses it.

HOW FORTH USES THE DISK

Nearly all Forth systems use disk memory. To understand what disk memory does, compare it with computer memory (RAM, short for *Random Access Memory*). The difference is analogous to the difference between a filing cabinet and a rolling card-index.

---

† **For Beginners:** The *source text* is the original version of the definition, such as

```
: FOUR-MORE   ( n -- n+4)   4 + ;
```

which the compiler translates into a dictionary entry.

So far you've been using computer memory, which is like the card index. The computer can access this memory almost instantaneously, so programs that are stored in RAM can run very fast. Unfortunately, this kind of memory is limited and relatively expensive. Also, it "loses its memory" when you turn off the power.

On the other hand, the disk is called a *mass storage* device because, like a filing cabinet, it can store a lot of information at a much cheaper price per unit of information than the memory inside the computer. Also, like a tape recording, the disk retains information even when the power is off.

When you define a word, the compiler compiles it into RAM so that the definitions will be quickly accessible. The perfect place to store source text, however, is on the disk. In Forth, you can save your source text on the disk and then later read it off the disk and send it to the text interpreter.†

Forth divides disk memory into units called *blocks*. Blocks can be used for any kind of data storage onto disk. When they are used to store source text, each block of 1,024 characters is arranged, by convention, in 16 lines of 64 characters each, to fit on your computer display. (The term *screen* is sometimes used to refer to a block used in this way for source text; for simplicity, we only use the term *block*.)

† **For Beginners:** The disk is sometimes also used to save the Forth system itself. When you invoke, or *boot,* Forth, this usually means copying Forth from a portion of the disk into RAM, where it becomes the dictionary. (Other systems store Forth in Read Only Memory (ROM) where it is immediately accessible at power up.)

This is what a block of source text looks like:

```
Block#  50
   0 ( Large letter "F")
   1 : STAR    42 EMIT ;
   2 : STARS   ( #)  0 DO  STAR  LOOP ;
   3 : MARGIN   CR  30 SPACES ;
   4 : BLIP    MARGIN STAR ;
   5 : BAR     MARGIN  5 STARS ;
   6 : F    BAR BLIP BAR BLIP BLIP  CR ;
   7
   8
   9 F
  10
  11
  12
  13
  14
  15
```

The top line ("Block# 50") and the numbers shown along the left are provided for your reference by LIST; they are not actually on the disk.

To list a block for yourself, simply type the block number and the word LIST, as in:

50 LIST

How do you enter source text into a block? That's what the editor is for. Since virtually every Forth system has a different editor, refer to your system documentation for instructions. (One type of editor is documented in Section II of this chapter.)

For the sake of discussion, let's pretend that your block 50 contains the definitions shown above. Almost everything should look familiar: these are the definitions you used to print a large letter "F" on your video display.

Now, having edited your definitions into a block, how do you send block 50 to the text interpreter? With the phrase

50 LOAD

The word LOAD sends the given block to the text interpreter, causing all the definitions to be compiled.

Having "loaded" these definitions, we can now type the new word F and get the expected results. But notice that we've put our new word F on line 9. We've done this to make a point: when you load a block, you execute its contents. Loading *this* block will not only compile the definition of F, it will execute it, and display a letter "F" on your video screen.

As we've said earlier, the text interpreter scans the *input stream*. Until now, we've referred to the line that you enter from the keyboard as the input stream. Now we have learned that the source of the input stream can be *switched*.

Ordinarily, the input stream comes from the keyboard; when you $\boxed{\text{LOAD}}$ it comes from mass storage.

Note the two possible routes to the input stream: Directly from the keyboard, or from the disk.

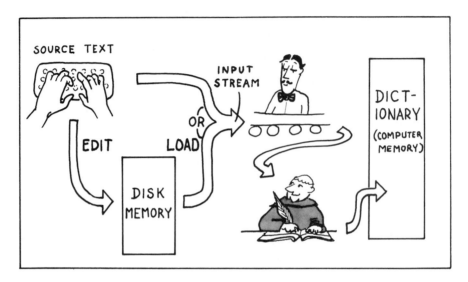

In Chapter 10, we'll discuss in greater detail the ways that Forth manages the disk. However, before you begin editing, we must introduce one more command. The word $\boxed{\text{FLUSH}}$ ensures that any change you've made to a block really gets written to the disk.

When you edit a block, each change you make is *not* immediately being recorded on the disk. Instead, you are changing an image of the block somewhere in RAM. Eventually Forth will copy this image back to the disk, complete with your corrections. But suppose you turn off the computer before Forth has recopied the block to the disk. Or suppose you change disks. You may even make a programming mistake and crash the system before Forth has copied your corrections to disk.

At least until you have read Chapter 10, play it safe and always enter $\boxed{\text{FLUSH}}$ before removing the disk, cycling power, or trying something dangerous.†

---

† **For Forths Running on Some Other Disk Operating System:** Many Forth systems run "on top of" some other operating system such as CP/M or MS-DOS. Here Forth blocks are 1K divisions of some file (or files) reserved for that purpose. How you open and close these files is explained in the documentation for your system.

Here are the commands we've learned in this section:

`FORGET name`	(--)	Forgets (removes from the dictionary) all definitions back to and including *name*.
`LIST`	(n --)	Lists a disk block.
`LOAD`	(n --)	Loads a disk block (compiles or executes). Block 0 normally cannot be loaded.
`FLUSH`	(--)	Writes all updated disk buffers to the disk, then unassigns the buffers.

RUDIMENTS OF FORTH STYLE

Look back at the example block in the last section. Good Forth style dictates that you reserve line 0 of any block as a *comment line*—a brief description of the purpose of the definitions contained in this block. The comment line often includes the date of the most recent revision and the programmer's initials.

Although we used parentheses in our example block to set off the comment, some systems include the word $\boxed{\backslash}$ (pronounced "skip-line"). And that's what it does; it tells the interpreter to skip the rest (everything to the right) of this line. It's like the word $\boxed{(}$ in that it begins a comment, yet unlike $\boxed{(}$ it doesn't need a delimiter. You can also put $\boxed{\backslash}$ in the *middle* of any line; whatever is to the left will be interpreted, whatever is to the right won't.

A similar word, $\boxed{\backslash S}$ (pronounced "skip-screen"), causes the interpreter to ignore everything else in the block. Some Forths use the word $\boxed{\text{EXIT}}$ for this purpose.

Here are a few additional ways to make your blocks easy to read:

1. Use two spaces on either side of the stack effect comment, or, if no stack comment is used, three spaces between the name and body of the definition.
2. Break up definitions into phrases, separated by double spaces.
3. If the definition takes more than one line, indent all but the first line.
4. Don't put more than one definition on a single line.
5. Keep definitions short! An average of two lines of code per definition is a good rule of thumb.

Thinking Forth [1] devotes an entire chapter to the elements of good Forth style.

Here are two commands we've learned in this section:

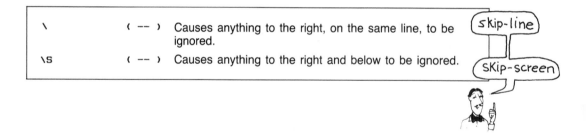

| \ | (--) | Causes anything to the right, on the same line, to be ignored. | *skip-line* |
| \s | (--) | Causes anything to the right and below to be ignored. | *skip-screen* |

THE FORTH PROGRAMMING ROUTINE

How does a Forth programmer typically develop Forth code? Here are the steps generally used:

1. Call in a block via the Forth editor.
2. Type a definition.
3. Exit the editor (if necessary).
4. Load the block.
5. Test the new word.
6. If errors are found, forget, edit, and reload the definition; if no errors, go to 1 and continue with the next definition.

The main reason that Forth programmers can work faster than users of other languages is the quick turnaround time of Forth's code-load-test cycle. Loading a block takes less than a second.

As a result, Forth programming involves a different strategy than programming in most other popular languages, such as C. Once you have an overall design and have decided what a particular word should do, you can begin coding. You can try your definitions as you write, revising them to remove bugs and to polish or refine them. Thus your later words can build on a secure foundation, and you get the advantage of being able to use hindsight from the very beginning of the program. (*Thinking Forth* describes this approach as iterative development.)

GETTING LOADED

As we've seen, the coding process may involve re LOAD ing the same block(s) over and over again. But consider: each time you load definitions, you increase the size of your dictionary.

Suppose you load a block several times, each time making an improvement on one word. Your dictionary will now contain a version of each word in the block for each time you loaded the block. The simplest way to avoid this problem is to use FORGET .

For instance, if you have changed something in the definition of the word F in block 50 and now want to reload, you would type:

```
FORGET STAR_ok
50 LOAD_ok
```

Remember, FORGET forgets everything back to, and including, the specified word.

Or you may have several variations of a program to choose from, only one of which you want compiled at any given time. Suppose you were to write a word processor. After you've finished the basic application, you want to add variations so it can use one format for correspondence, another format for magazine articles, and a third for address labels.

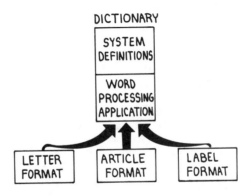

In Forth, these three variations are called *overlays*† because they are mutually exclusive and can be made to replace each other. Here's how:

The last definition at the end of the core application should be a name only, such as

```
: VARIATIONS ;
```

This is called a *null definition* because it does nothing but mark a place in your dictionary.

Then at the beginning of each variation block, include the expression

```
FORGET VARIATIONS   : VARIATIONS ;
```

Now when you load any variation, it FORGETs back to the null definition, compiles the null definition again, and then compiles the variation's definitions.

---

† **For Experts:**   More specifically, they are called *compilation overlays*. Some Forth systems offer ways to load *binary overlays,* which are precompiled sections of code that can be linked into the resident dictionary.

When you load another variation, you replace the first overlay with the second overlay.†

We've introduced $\boxed{\text{LOAD}}$ for loading a block, but how do you load a many-blocked application? The word $\boxed{\text{THRU}}$ loads a specified *range* of blocks. For example, the phrase

```
180 189 THRU
```

will load every block from 180 to 189, inclusive. On many systems, $\boxed{\text{THRU}}$ will print on the display each block number as it is loaded, to help you follow the action.

One more hint: You know that $\boxed{.\text{''}}$ used *inside* a definition will cause that definition to print a message. Another word called $\boxed{.(}$ can be used *outside* a definition. Type:

```
.( What's up, Doc?)
```

and press RETURN; you will see your text echoed back to you. This word is useful when you want a block to display a message when it is loaded. For instance,

```
Block# 10
    0 \ My application
    1
    2 CR   .( Loading my application...)
    3 20 37 THRU   \ widgets
    4 40 45 THRU   \ do-dads
    5 50 58 THRU   \ gizmos
    6
    7 CR   .( Application is loaded )
    8
    9
```

A FEW MORE BLOCK TOOLS

We've seen that $\boxed{\text{LIST}}$ will display a single block. We'll now introduce words, available in most Forth systems, for displaying groups of blocks and an index to blocks.

The word $\boxed{\text{TRIAD}}$ displays a group of three contiguous blocks, starting with a block evenly divisible by three. For instance,

```
30 TRIAD
```

will display blocks 30, 31 and 32. (The arguments "31" and "32" will produce the same triad.)

---

† **For Systems with** $\boxed{\text{EMPTY}}$**:** The word $\boxed{\text{EMPTY}}$ "forgets" all the definitions that you yourself have defined. In a multiprogrammed system, this is your own personal extension of the dictionary, not anyone else's.

The word $\boxed{\text{SHOW}}$ will display a *range* of blocks. For instance,

```
30 38 SHOW
```

will display three triads, beginning with blocks 30, 33, and 36.

These words are useful for creating application listings on the printer. How do you direct output to the printer? Unfortunately, that varies among Forth systems. You'll have to check your system's own documentation to be sure, but as a guide:

—On a multitasked system, you often will type

```
PRINT   17 TRIAD
```

The word $\boxed{\text{PRINT}}$ sends the rest of the command line to the printer *task*, while execution continues normally at the terminal task.

—On single-tasked systems, there are words which redirect output to the peripheral *devices* (not tasks). On such a system, you might type

```
PRINTER   17 LIST   CONSOLE
```

This would direct output to the printer, list the block, then direct output back to the display. You might simulate the multitasked syntax shown above by defining:

```
: PRINT    PRINTER   INTERPRET   CONSOLE ;
```

On some systems, $\boxed{\text{SHOW}}$ will automatically route the listing to the printer and return to the console upon completion.

Another important word is $\boxed{\text{INDEX}}$, which produces an index for a specified range of blocks by displaying those blocks' comment lines (0 lines) only. For example,

```
30 38 INDEX
```

will display the comment lines for blocks 30 through 38 inclusive.

Here are the commands we've learned recently:

THRU	(lo hi --)	Loads all blocks in the range *lo* through *hi*, inclusive.
.(text)	(--)	Displays the message *text* delimited by right parenthesis. Typically used outside a colon definition.
TRIAD	(n --)	Displays the three blocks that include *n*, starting with the one that is evenly divisible by three.
SHOW	(lo hi --)	Lists the range of blocks, from *lo* through *hi* inclusive, in triad form.
INDEX	(lo hi --)	Displays the comment lines only for all blocks from *lo* to *hi* inclusive.

If you haven't already done so, this is a good time to acquaint yourself with the Forth editor. If your system has a different editor from the one described in the next section (the "Starting Forth editor"), skip the rest of this chapter and read your system's editor documentation.

SECTION II
THE STARTING
FORTH EDITOR

This section describes a type of editor found on some Forth systems. It is a command-based screen editor, rather than a cursor-based screen editor more commonly seen. The difference lies in how you "move around" in the editor.

In a cursor-based editor, you "enter" the editor in some system-dependent way. To move the cursor on the screen, you must press control keys (or move a mouse, if available).

In a command-based editor, the listing of your block remains stationary in the upper part of the display, while you are free to enter Forth commands in the remaining lines at the bottom. A special set of Forth words are provided to allow editing.

Some of these commands let you position the cursor, either to a given line or, by using pattern-matching, to a given string. Letting the editor "find" a position is usually faster than holding down a cursor key while the cursor putters across the screen. Other commands let you insert or delete strings, while remembering the strings for multiple insertions/deletions. Best of all, however, you remain "in" Forth. If you want to double-check the spelling of a word, perform a hex-to-decimal conversion, or just load the block you've been editing, you can do it without having to "exit" anything. This convenience is especially important in a program development environment. Also, this type of editor is easily extensible.

Not everyone agrees, but the editor in this section appears to be more usable, flexible, and "Forth-like" than cursor-controlled editors.

(*Note:* Some older Forth systems have a "line editor." Instead of refreshing an image of the entire block, they display only the modified line. Now that all programmers use CRTs instead of teletypes, line editors are old-fashioned. Nevertheless, since such editors are command-based, they use the same type of commands described in this section. The following discussion is easily adaptable to them.)

DEAR EDITOR

First, find an empty block (using INDEX if necessary) and list it, using the form:

```
180 LIST
```

When you list an empty block, you'll see sixteen line numbers (0–15) running down the side of the screen, but nothing on any of the lines. The "ok" on the last line is the signal that the text interpreter has obeyed your command to list the block.

By listing a block, you also select that block as the one you're going to work on.

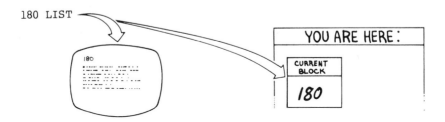

Having LISTed the block you're going to begin editing in, it's a good idea to invoke the command WIPE. Sometimes an unused block that appears empty will actually contain strange characters that might keep the block from being loaded. WIPE blanks the entire current block, ensuring it is truly empty.

Now that you've made a block "current," you can list it by simply typing the word

L

Unlike LIST , L does not want to be preceded by a block number; instead, it lists the current block.

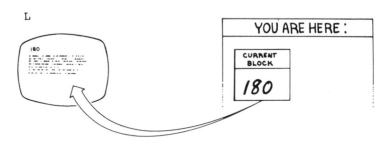

Now that you have a current block, it's time to select a current line by using the word T . Suppose we want to write something on line 3. Type:

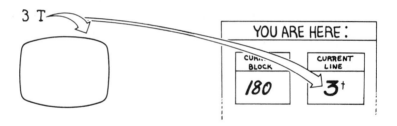

T shows the line you have selected by displaying it in reverse video.

Now that your sights are fixed, you can put some text in the current line by using P .

P HERE IT IS RETURN

---

† **For the Curious:** Actually, the cursor position, not the line number, serves as the pointer. More on this in a future footnote.

P⃞ *puts* the string that follows it (up to the carriage return) on the current line.

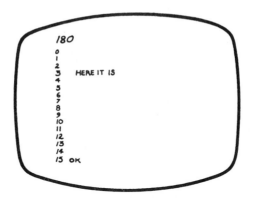

Remember that your current position remains the same, so if you were to now type

P THERE IT WENT⬛RETURN⬛

you would see that the latter string had replaced the former on line 3.

Similarly, entering P⃞ followed by at least two blank spaces (one to separate the P⃞ from the string, the other as the string itself) causes the former string to be replaced by a blank space; in other words, it blanks the line.

In this chapter, the symbol "β̸" means that you type a blank space. So to blank a line, type:

P̸β̸β̸⬛RETURN⬛

CHARACTER EDITING COMMANDS

In this section, we'll show you how to insert and delete text within a line.

F⃞

Before you can insert or delete text, you must be able to position the editor cursor (as opposed to the Forth cursor) wherever you want it. This editor indicates its cursor position by beginning the reverse-video field on the first character after the cursor. Suppose line 3 looks like this:

⃞IF MUSIC BE THE FOD OF LOVE

and you want to insert the second "O" in "FOOD." The cursor is now at the beginning of the line. To reposition it after the "FO", use the command F⃞, followed by the string, as in

F FO⬛RETURN⬛

|F| searches forward from the current position of the cursor until it *finds* the given string (in this case "FO"), then places the cursor right after it.

IF MUSIC BE THE FOD OF LOVE

IF MUSIC BE THE FOD OF LOVE

IF MUSIC BE THE FO|D OF LOVE

|I|

Now that the cursor is positioned where you want it, simply enter:

    I O RETURN

and |I| will *insert* the character "O" just behind the cursor.

    IF MUSIC BE THE FO|OD OF LOVE

|E|

To *erase* a string (using the command |E|), you must first *find* the string, using |F|. For example, if you want to erase the word "MUSIC," first reset the cursor with:

    3 T RETURN

then type

    F MUSIC RETURN

    IF MUSIC| BE THE FOOD OF LOVE

and then simply

    E RETURN

E erases the string you just found with F.

IF M*U*SIC| BE THE FOOD OF LOVE

E then redisplays the line:

IF | BE THE FOOD OF LOVE

The cursor is now is a position where you can insert another word:

I ROCK`RETURN`

IF ROCK| BE THE FOOD OF LOVE

D

The command D finds and *deletes* a string. It is a combination of F and E, giving you two commands for the price of one. For example, if your cursor is here:

IF ROCK| BE THE FOOD OF LOVE

then you can delete "FOOD" by simply typing

D FOOD`RETURN`

IF ROCK BE THE |OF LOVE

Once again, you can insert text at the new cursor position:

I CHEESEBURGERS`RETURN`

IF ROCK BE THE CHEESEBURGERS| OF LOVE

Using D is a little more dangerous than using F and then E. With the two-step method, you know exactly what you're going to erase before you erase it.

R

The command R *replaces* a string that you've already found. It is a combination of E and I. For instance, if you have

|COMPUTERS NEED A TERMINAL

and you enter

F NEED A`RETURN`

R CAN BE`RETURN`

you'll get:

> COMPUTERS CAN BE| TERMINAL

R̄ is great when you want to make an insertion *in front of* a certain string. For example, if your line 0 is missing an ''E'':

> (Sample definitions)   MPTY

then it's not easy to F̄ your way through all those spaces to get the cursor over to the space before MPTY. Better you should use the following method:

> F MPTY[RETURN]

then

> R EMPTY[RETURN]

TILL

TILL is the most powerful command for deletion. It deletes everything from the cursor position up *till* and including the given string. For example, if you have the line:

> BREVITY IS THE|SPARK, THE ESSENCE, AND THE VERY SOUL OF WIT

(note the cursor position), then the phrase:

> TILL VERY[RETURN]

or even just

> TILL Y[RETURN]

(since there's only one ''Y'') will produce

> BREVITY IS THE| SOUL OF WIT

Has a nicer ring, doesn't it?

TILL only searches to the end of the current line, not to the remainder of the block.

THE FIND BUFFER AND THE INSERT BUFFER

In order to use the editor effectively, you really have to understand the workings of its *find buffer* and its *insert buffer*.

You may not have known it, but when you typed

> F MUSIC[RETURN]

the first thing F̄ did was to move the string ''MUSIC'' into something called the find buffer. A buffer, in computer parlance, is a temporary storage place for data. The find buffer is located in computer memory (RAM).

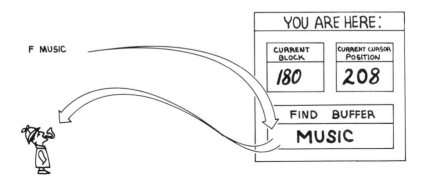

Then $\boxed{F}$ proceeded to search the line for the contents of the find buffer. Now you will be able to understand the following variation on $\boxed{F}$:

$\boxed{F}$ RETURN

that is, $\boxed{F}$ followed immediately by a return.

This variation causes $\boxed{F}$ to search for the string that is already in the find buffer, left over from the last time you used $\boxed{F}$.

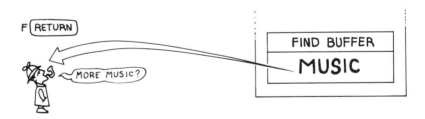

What good is this? It lets you find numerous occurrences of the same string without retyping the string. For example, suppose line 8 contains the profundity:

```
THE WISDOM OF THE FUTURE IS THE HOPE OF THE AGES          '
```

---

† **For the Curious:**   By keeping the current cursor position, the editor doesn't need to keep a separate pointer for the current line. It simply uses the word $\boxed{/MOD}$. Since there are 64 characters per line, the phrase

```
208 64 /MOD . . 3 16 ok
```

shows the cursor is located at the sixteenth character in line 3.

with the cursor at the beginning, and you want to erase the word "THE" near the end. Start by typing

```
THE │WISDOM OF THE FUTURE IS THE HOPE OF THE AGES                    │
```

Now that "THEβ" is in the find buffer, you can simply type a series of single Fs:

and so on until you find the "THE" you want, at which time you can erase it with ⎡E⎤. (⎡E⎤ counts the number of characters in the find buffer and deletes that many characters preceding the cursor.)

By the way, if you were to try entering ⎡F⎤ one more time, you'd get:

```
F_THE_none
```

This time, ⎡F⎤ cannot find a match for the find buffer, so it returns the word "THEβ" to you, with the error message "none."

Remember we said that ⎡D⎤ is a combination of ⎡F⎤ and ⎡E⎤? Well, that means that ⎡D⎤ also uses the find buffer. With "THEβ" in the find buffer, and with the cursor at the beginning of the line:

```
│THE WISDOM OF THE FUTURE IS THE HOPE OF THE AGES                    │
```

you can delete all the "THEβ"'s with single Ds:

```
D RETURN
D RETURN
D RETURN
D RETURN
```

```
WISDOM OF FUTURE IS HOPE OF │AGES                                    │
```

The other buffer is called the *insert buffer*. It is used by ⎡I⎤. Simply typing

```
I RETURN
```

will insert the contents of the insert buffer at the current cursor position. The following experiment will demonstrate how you might use both buffers at the same time. Suppose a line contains

```
THE YONDER, THE DANUBE, AND THE MAX
```

Now position the cursor:

```
F THEβ RETURN
```

```
THE │YONDER, THE DANUBE, AND THE MAX                                 │
```

and insert

I BLUEⱭ RETURN

THE BLUE ┌───┐
         │ YONDER, THE DANUBE, AND THE MAX   │
         └───┘

You have now loaded both buffers like so:

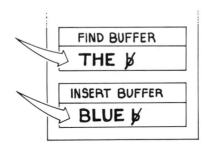

Now type

to produce

THE BLUE YONDER, THE BLUE DANUBE, AND THE BLUE ┌─────┐
                                               │ MAX │
                                               └─────┘

LINE EDITING COMMANDS

Now that we've shown you how to move letters and words around, we'll show you how to move whole lines around.

┌───┐
│ P │
└───┘

The word P, which we introduced before, uses the very same insert buffer that I uses. Assuming that you still have "BLUEⱭ" in your insert buffer from the previous example and that line 14 is still your current line, then typing:

P RETURN

will replace the old line 14 with the contents of the insert buffer, so that line 14 now contains only the single word:

BLUEⱭ

To quickly review, you have now learned three ways to use P :

1. P ALL THIS TEXT RETURN   puts the string in the insert buffer, then in the current line.

2. P░░ RETURN   blanks the insert buffer, then blanks the current line.

3. P RETURN   puts the contents of the insert buffer in the current line.

U

A very similar word is U . It places the contents of the insert buffer *under* the current line. For example, suppose your block contains:

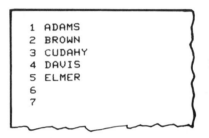

If you move your cursor to line 2 with

2 T

and then type

U CARLIN RETURN _ok
U COOPER RETURN _ok

you'll get

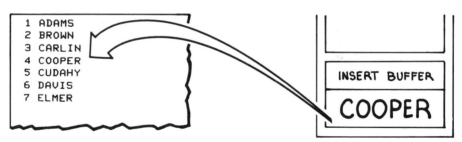

Instead of replacing the current line, U squeezes the contents of the insert buffer in below the current line, pushing all the lines below it down. If there were anything in line 15, it would roll off and disappear.

It's easier to use $\boxed{U}$ than $\boxed{P}$ when you're adding successive lines. For example,

```
1 T P ADAMS RETURN _ok
U BROWN RETURN _ok
U CUDAHY RETURN _ok
U DAVIS RETURN _ok
```

The three ways of using $\boxed{P}$ also apply to $\boxed{U}$.

$\boxed{X}$

$\boxed{X}$ is the opposite of $\boxed{U}$; it *extracts* the current line. Using the above example, if you make line 3 current (with the phrase "3 T"), then by entering

```
X RETURN
```

you extract line 3 and move the lower lines up.

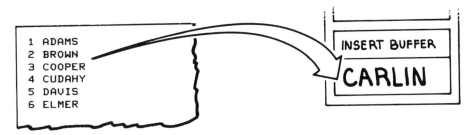

As you see, $\boxed{X}$ also moves the extracted line into the insert buffer. This makes it easy to move the extracted line anywhere you want it. For example, the combination

```
9 T RETURN
```

and

```
P RETURN
```

would now put "CARLIN" on line 9.

Here's how to insert a new line 0, thereby pushing the existing line 0 down. Begin by inserting the new line *under* line 0:

```
0 T U THIS IS MY NEW LINE ZERO. RETURN
```

Then swap the first two lines:

```
0 T X U RETURN
```

MISCELLANEOUS EDITOR COMMANDS

[N] AND [B]

When you type the word [N], you add one to the current block number. Thus, the combination:

    N L

causes the *next* block to be listed.

Similarly, the word [B] subtracts one from the current block number.

Thus, the combination:

    B L

lets you list one block *back*.

Some systems combine [N] with [L], so that [N] goes to the next block *and* lists it; the same with [B]. You can redefine your [N] and [B] to do this if you wish—Forth lets you tailor the commands to *your* needs.

[COPY]

The word [COPY] lets you *copy* one block to another, displacing whatever was in the destination block. You use it in this form:

    from to COPY

For example, entering

    153 200 COPY

will copy whatever is in block 153 into block 200.
Make it a habit to [FLUSH] after every [COPY].

[S]

[S] is an expanded version of [F]. It lets you *search* for a given string in and beyond your current block into the following blocks, up to the block that you specify.

For example, if your current block is 180, and you type

    185 S TREASURE

[S] will search for "TREASURE" in blocks 180 through 184. If it finds the string, it will display that block with the cursor at the found string.

S leaves the ending block number on the stack, letting you continue the search for the same text by simply typing S.

G AND BRING

The word B gets a single line from another block, and inserts it in front of the current line (pushing the current line and subsequent lines down).

Suppose that our cursor is on line 3 of this block:

```
1
2   Oh where, oh where has my
3   gone?  Oh where, oh where can it be?
```

The missing line appears in block 38, on line 10. So we type

38 10 G[RETURN]

This produces:

```
1
2   Oh where, oh where has my
3   missing line
4   gone?  Oh where, oh where can it be?
```

The word BRING gets a group of lines at once. The phrase

38 10 14 BRING

gets lines 10–14 from block 38.

M

Some Forth developers use M instead of G and BRING. M is the reverse of G; you move the current line to the specified screen and line number:

190 2 M[RETURN]

K

The word K swaps the contents of the find buffer with that of the insert buffer. It comes in handy when you've accidentally deleted something with D that you really want. Since the deleted string is in the find buffer, just enter K to move it to the insert buffer, then enter I.

The reverse is also true. If you've inserted a string in the wrong place, you can move the string into the find buffer with K and then erase it with a simple E.

On your own, try swapping two words on the same line, using K.

On some systems, you can type the caret character instead of RETURN to indicate the end of a character string, so that you can get more than one command on a line.

For example, you could type

    D FRUIT^ I NUTS`RETURN`

all on the same line, and get the same result as if you had typed

    D FRUIT`RETURN`

and

    I NUTS`RETURN`

That's it for the editor commands. Because Forth is naturally flexible, and because users can define their own editor commands if they want to, the set of editor commands in your system may vary from the set presented here. This chapter closes with a review of all the commands we've talked about.

One final observation about the editor: it is not a program, as it might be in another language. It is rather a collection of words. The editor, in fact, is called a *vocabulary*. We'll discuss the significance of vocabularies in a later chapter.

A HANDY HINT
HOW TO LOCATE A SOURCE DEFINITION

    Some Forth systems feature a very useful word called LOCATE (some call it VIEW). If you enter

LOCATE EGGSIZE

Forth will list the block that contains the definition of EGGSIZE. The requirement is that the word must be resident (currently in the dictionary). (On some systems you can "locate" system electives and words in your application, but you can't locate words in the precompiled portion.)

Here's a list of Forth words we've covered in this chapter:

FORGET name	(--)	Forgets (removes from the dictionary) all definitions back to and including *name*.
LIST	(n --)	Lists a disk block.
LOAD	(n --)	Loads a disk block (compiles or executes). Block 0 normally cannot be loaded.
THRU	(lo hi --)	Loads all blocks in the range *lo* through *hi*, inclusive.
FLUSH	(--)	Writes all updated disk buffers to the disk, then unassigns the buffers.
.(text)	(--)	Displays the message *text* delimited by right parenthesis. Typically used outside a colon definition.
TRIAD	(n --)	Displays the three blocks which include *n*, starting with the one that is evenly divisible by three.
SHOW	(lo hi --)	Lists the range of blocks, from *lo* through *hi* inclusive, in triad form.
INDEX	(lo hi --)	Displays the comment lines only for all blocks from *lo* to *hi* inclusive.
LOCATE xxx or VIEW	(--)	Lists the block from which *xxx* (a defined word) has been loaded.

Editing Commands — Line Operators

T	(n --)	*Types* the line.
P Pbb or P xxx	(--)	Copies the given string, if any, into the insert buffer, then *puts* a copy of the insert buffer in the current line.
U Ubb or U xxx	(--)	Copies the given string, if any, into the insert buffer, then puts a copy of the insert buffer in the line *under* the current line.
G	(block line --)	Gets a copy of the specified line and inserts on the line above the current line, pushing the current and subsequent lines down.
BRING	(block lo hi --)	Gets specified range of lines.
X	(--)	Copies the current line into the insert buffer and *extracts* the line from the block.

Editing Commands—String Operators

F or **F xxx**	(--)	Copies the given string, if any, into the find buffer, then *finds* the string in the current block.
S or **S xxx**	(n --) or (n -- n)	Copies the given string, if any, into the find buffer, then *searches* the range of blocks, starting from the current block and ending with *n*, for the string. If found, the ending block is left on the stack.
E	(--)	To be used after F. *Erases* as many characters as are currently in the find buffer, going backwards from the cursor.
D or **D xxx**	(--)	Copies the given string, if any, into the find buffer, finds the next occurrence of the string within the current line, and *deletes* it.
TILL or **TILL xxx**	(--)	Copies the given string, if any, into the find buffer, then deletes all characters starting from the current cursor position up *till* and including the string.
I or **I xxx**	(--)	Copies the given string, if any, into the insert buffer, then *inserts* the contents of the insert buffer at the point just behind the cursor.
R or **R xxx**	(--)	Combines the commands E and I to *replace* a found string with a given string or the contents of the insert buffer.
↑ or **^**	(--)	Indicates the end of the string to be placed in a buffer.

Editing Commands—Miscellaneous

WIPE	(--)	Blanks the contents of the current block.
L	(--)	Lists the current block.
N	(--)	Makes the next block current.
B	(--)	Makes the previous block current.
COPY	(source dest --)	Copies the contents of the source block to the destination block.
K	(--)	Swaps the contents of the find buffer and insert buffer.

REVIEW OF TERMS

Block	in Forth, a division of disk memory containing up to 1024 characters of source text.
Buffer	a temporary storage area for data.
Input stream	the string of characters to be processed by the text interpreter. The input stream may originate either from the current input device such as the keyboard (via the text input buffer) or from mass storage such as the disk (via a block buffer).
Load block	one block that, when loaded, itself loads the rest of the blocks for an application.
Null definition	a definition that does nothing, written in the form:

> : NAME ;

that is, a name only will be compiled into the dictionary. A null definition serves as a "bookmark" in the dictionary for FORGET to find.

Overlay	a portion of an application that, when loaded, replaces another portion in the dictionary.
Pointer	a location in memory at which a number can be stored (or changed) as a reference to something else.
Source text	in Forth, the written-out form of a definition or definitions in English-like words and punctuation, as opposed to the compiled form that is entered into the dictionary.

REFERENCES

[1] Brodie, Leo, *Thinking Forth* (Englewood Cliffs, N.J.: Prentice-Hall, 1984).

PROBLEMS

3-1. (a) Enter your definitions of GIFT, GIVER, and THANKS from Problems 1-1 and 1-3 into a block, then load and execute THANKS.

(b) Using the editor, change the person's name in the definition of GIVER, then load and execute THANKS again. What happens this time?

3-2. Try loading some of your mathematical definitions from Chapter 2 into an available block, then load it. Fool around.

4

DECISIONS, DECISIONS, . . .

In this chapter, we'll learn how to program the computer to make "decisions." This is the moment when you turn your computer into something more than an ordinary calculator.

THE CONDITIONAL PHRASE

Let's see how to write a simple decision-making statement in Forth. Imagine that we are programming a mechanical egg-carton packer. Some sort of mechanical device has counted the eggs on the conveyor belt, and now we have the number of eggs on the stack. The Forth phrase

```
12 =  IF  FILL-CARTON  THEN
```

tests whether the number on the stack is *equal* to *12*, and *if* it is, the word FILL-CARTON is executed. If it's not, execution moves right along to the words that follow THEN .

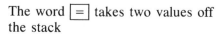
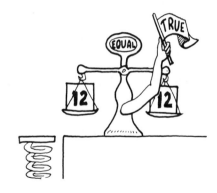

The word $=$ takes two values off the stack

and compares them to see whether they are equal.

If the condition is true, IF allows the flow of execution to continue with the next word in the definition.

But if the condition is false, IF causes the flow of execution to skip to THEN, from which point execution will proceed.

Let's try it. Define this example word:

```
: ?FULL   ( #eggs)   12 = IF   ." It's full. " THEN ;_ok
11 ?FULL_ok
12 ?FULL_It's_full._ok
```

Notice that an IF THEN statement must be contained within a colon definition. You can't just enter these words in "calculator style."

Don't be misled by the traditional English meanings of the Forth words IF and THEN. The words that follow IF are executed *if* the condition is true. The words that follow THEN are *always* executed, as though you were telling the computer, "After you make the choice, *then* continue with the rest of the definition." (In this example, the only word after THEN is ;, which ends the definition.)

If it helps, think of the Forth syntax as *postfix notation*. Instead of the usual

```
   IF   ( condition)   THEN   ( do-something)   ENDIF
```

we have

```
( condition)  IF  ( do-something)  THEN
```

Remember that every IF needs a THEN to come home to. Both words must be in the same definition.

A CLOSER LOOK AT IF

The comparison operator doesn't really wave the flag† in the air as our earlier cartoon suggests. Instead, it *puts the flag on the stack*, like any other argument. "True" is represented by −1 (negative one); "false" is represented by 0 (zero).‡ The word IF knows to find the flag on the stack, and eats (consumes) it.

Try entering the following phrases at the terminal, letting $\lfloor . \rfloor$ show you what's on the stack as a flag.

```
12 12 = . -1 ok        Yes, 12 is equal to 12.

11 12 = . 0 ok         No, 11 is not equal to 12.
```

(It's okay to use comparison operators directly at your keyboard like this, but remember that an IF THEN statement must be wholly contained within a definition because it involves branching.)

---

† **For Beginners:** In computer jargon, when one piece of program leaves a value as a signal for another piece of program, that value is called a *flag*.

‡ **For Pre-83 Standard Systems:** In older Forth systems, "true" was represented by "1."

IF will take a "−1" as a flag that means true and a "0" as a flag that means false. However, IF may be preceded by another word, NOT†, which reverses the flag on the stack.

```
0 NOT . -1 ok
```

```
-1 NOT . 0 ok
```

NOT is used to reverse the sense of IF. Thus, we could write

```
: ?TWELVE  ( n)   12 = NOT IF ." Not a twelve. " THEN ;
```

which will print "Not a twelve" only when "n" is *not* twelve.

Forth's use of the stack for flags is one of its many delightful simplicities. It's possible, for instance, to pass a flag as an argument to another word ("across colon," as it were). By way of example,

```
: .TRUE?  ( ? -- )  IF  ." True "  THEN ;
12 12 = .TRUE? True ok
```

(The question mark, used inside a stack comment, signifies a flag.) Does any other language let you put a comparison test in one routine and the IF in another?

OTHER COMPARISON OPERATORS

Here is a partial list of comparison operators that you can use before an IF THEN statement:

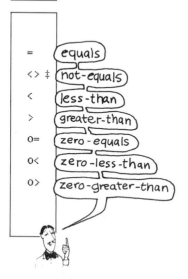

=	equals
<> ‡	not-equals
<	less-than
>	greater-than
0=	zero-equals
0<	zero-less-than
0>	zero-greater-than

† **For fig-Forth Systems:** Use 0= instead.

‡ **For Those Who Don't Have** <> : Use − (minus); see "The Secret of IF" later in this chapter.

The words $<$ and $>$ expect the same stack order as the arithmetic operators, that is:

INFIX	POSTFIX
2 < 10 is equivalent to	2 10 <
17 > −39 is equivalent to	17 −39 >

Let's look at another example. This definition checks whether the temperature of a laboratory boiler is too hot. It expects to find the temperature on the stack:

```
: ?TOO-HOT   ( temp -- )
    220 > IF   ." DANGER!   Reduce heat " THEN ;
```

If the temperature on the stack is *greater than* 220, the danger message will be displayed. You can execute this one yourself, by entering the definition, and then typing in a value just before the word.

```
290 ?TOO-HOT DANGER!  Reduce heat ok
130 ?TOO-HOT ok
```

The three words $0=$, $0<$, and $0>$ are used to test whether a number is equal to zero, negative, or positive. They are equivalent to writing out "0 =", "0 <", and "0 >", respectively. The only difference is that these one-word operators are more efficient.

THE ALTERNATIVE PHRASE

Forth allows you to provide an alternative phrase in an IF statement, with the word $ELSE$.

The following example is a definition that tests whether a given number is a valid day of the month:

```
: ?DAY  ( day)
    32 < IF ." Looks good " ELSE   ." No way " THEN ;
```

If the number on the stack is less than thirty-two, the message "Looks good" will be printed. Otherwise, "No way" will be printed.

Imagine that IF pulls a railroad-track switch, depending on the outcome of the test. Execution then takes one of two routes, but either way, the tracks rejoin at the word THEN.

In computer terminology, this whole business of rerouting the path of execution is called *branching*.†

Here's another example. You know that dividing any number by zero is impossible, so if you try it on a computer, you'll get an incorrect answer. We might define a word that only performs division if the denominator is not zero:

```
: /CHECK   ( numerator denominator -- result )
    DUP 0= IF ." Invalid " DROP  ELSE  /  THEN ;‡
```

Notice that we first have to DUP the denominator because the phrase

```
0= IF
```

will destroy it in the process.

Also notice that the word DROP removes the denominator if division won't be performed, so that whether or not we divide, the stack effect will be the same; that is, one argument will be left on the stack whether we do the IF part or the ELSE part. (A subtle source of program bugs occurs when these two parts leave a different number of arguments on the stack—sometimes the program will work, sometimes it won't. Very mysterious.)

NESTED IF THEN STATEMENTS

It's possible to put an IF THEN (or IF ELSE THEN) statement inside another IF THEN statement. In fact, you can get as complicated as you like, as long as every IF has one THEN.

Consider the following definition, which determines the size of commercial eggs (extra large, large, etc.), given their weight in ounces per dozen:§

```
: EGGSIZE   ( ounces-per-dozen -- )
    DUP  18  < IF ." Reject "         ELSE
    DUP  21  < IF ." Small "          ELSE
    DUP  24  < IF ." Medium "         ELSE
    DUP  27  < IF ." Large "          ELSE
    DUP  30  < IF ." Extra Large "    ELSE
                 ." Error "
       THEN  THEN  THEN  THEN  THEN   DROP ;‖
```

† **For Old Hands:**   Forth has no GOTO statement. If you think you can't live without GOTO, just wait. By the end of this book, you'll be telling your GOTO where to GOTO.

‡ **For Experts:**   There are better ways to do this, as we'll see.

§ **For People at Keyboards:**   Because this definition is fairly long, we suggest that you load it from a disk block.

‖ **For Trivia Buffs:**   Here is the official table on which this definition is based:

Extra Large	27–30
Large	24–27
Medium	21–24
Small	18–21

Once EGGSIZE has been loaded, some results you'd get are:

```
23 EGGSIZE Medium ok
29 EGGSIZE Extra Large ok
40 EGGSIZE Error ok
```

We'd like to point out a few things about EGGSIZE:

The entire definition is a series of "nested" IF THEN statements. The word *nested* does not refer to the fact that we're dealing with eggs, but to the fact that the statements nest inside one another, like a set of mixing bowls.

The five THEN s at the bottom close off the five IF s in reverse order; that is,

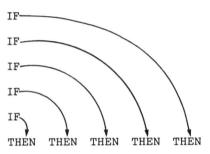

Also notice that a DROP is necessary at the end of the definition to get rid of the original value. Could you have eliminated the final DUP so that the number would be removed by the last comparison, and also eliminate the DROP ? No. Why not?

Finally, notice that the definition is visually organized to be read easily by human beings. Most Forth programmers would rather waste a little space in a block (there are plenty of blocks) than let things get any more confused than they have to be.

THE SECRET OF IF

We've seen that IF considers −1 to represent "true." Actually, Forth programmers often capitalize on the fact that IF will recognize *any nonzero value* as "true"; only zero is "false."† Ordinarily you don't have to think about it, but there are times when it's handy to know.

---

† **For the Doubting Few:** Just to prove it, try entering this test:

```
: TEST  ( ? )  IF ." Non-zero " ELSE  ." Zero " THEN ;
```

Even though there is no comparison operator in this definition, you'll still get

```
0 TEST Zero ok
-1 TEST Non-zero ok
8000 TEST Non-zero ok
```

For instance, if you're only testing whether a number is zero, you don't need a comparison operator at all. A slightly simpler version of /CHECK, which we saw earlier, could be

```
: /CHECK   ( numerator denominator -- result)
   DUP IF  /  ELSE ." Invalid " DROP  THEN ;
```

Or say you want to test whether a number is an even multiple of ten, such as 10, 20, 30, and so on. You know that the phrase

```
10 MOD
```

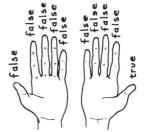

divides by ten and returns the remainder only. An even multiple of ten would produce a zero remainder, so the phrase

```
10 MOD 0=
```

gives the appropriate "true" or "false" flag.

Another interesting result is that you can often use $\boxed{-}$ (minus) as a comparison operator that tests whether two values are "not equal." When you subtract two equal numbers, you get zero (false); when you subtract two unequal numbers, you get a nonzero value (true). Some Forth systems omit the word $\boxed{<>}$ for this reason. Still, $\boxed{<>}$ not only reads better as "not equal," it also returns an actual minus-one as a flag meaning "true." This is sometimes more useful than a simple, arithmetic difference, as we'll see in Chapter 7.

A LITTLE LOGIC

Forth (like most languages) lets you combine flags. An example is the "either/or" decision. Given two flags, if either or both are true, then Forth will execute something. If neither is true, it won't.

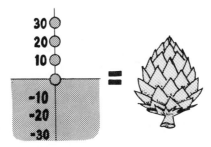

Here's a rather simple-minded example, just to show you what we mean. Say you want to print the name "artichoke" if an input number is *either* negative *or* a multiple of ten.

How do you do this in Forth? Consider the phrase:

```
DUP O<   SWAP   10 MOD   0=   OR
```

Here's what happens when the input number is, say, 30:

OPERATOR	CONTENTS OF STACK		OPERATION
		30	
DUP	30	30	Duplicate it so we can test it twice.
O<	30	0	Is it negative? No (zero).
SWAP	0	30	Swaps the flag with the number.
10 MOD 0=	0	–1	Is it evenly divisible by 10? Yes (negative-one).
OR		–1	"Or"s the flags.

"Or"s the flags? What happens when you "or" two flags? You get a "true" if either (or both) of the two flags are true. Here are the four possible combinations of two flags, and the corresponding results of the "or" operation:

1st flag

2nd flag

result

Our simple-minded definition, then, would be:

```
: VEGETABLE   ( n)   DUP O<   SWAP   10 MOD 0=   OR
     IF ." Artichoke "   THEN ;
```

The following is an improved version of a previous example called ?DAY. The old ?DAY only caught entries over thirty-one. But zero or negative numbers shouldn't be allowed either. How about this:

```
: ?DAY   ( day)   DUP 1 <   SWAP 31 >   OR
   IF   ." Try again "   ELSE   ." Thank you "   THEN ;
```

(Many Forth systems provide the word WITHIN for situations like this. See the questions at the end of this chapter.)

Another kind of decision is called an "and" decision. In an "and" decision, *both* conditions must be true for the result to be true.

For example, the front door *and* the back door must both be open for a breeze to come through. Contrast this with an "or" decision: if either the front door *or* the back door is open (or both), flies may get in.†

Forth includes the word AND. Here's what AND would do with the four possible combinations of flags that we saw earlier:

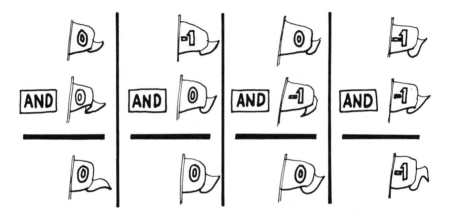

In other words, only a pair of "true"'s will produce a true result.

Let's say we're looking for a cardboard box that's big enough to fit a disk drive that measures:

height 6″
width 19″
length 22″

---

† **For the Curious Newcomer:** The use of words like *or* and *and* to structure an application is called *logic*. A form of notation for logical statements was developed in the nineteenth century by George Boole; it is now called Boolean algebra. Thus, the term *Boolean flag* (or even just *boolean*) simply refers to a flag that will be used in a logical statement.

The height, width, *and* length requirements all must be satisfied for the box to be big enough. If we have the dimensions of a box on the stack, we can define:

```
: BOXTEST  ( length width height -- )
   6 >  ROT 22 >  ROT 19 >  AND AND
   IF ." Big enough "  THEN ;
```

You can test BOXTEST with the phrase:

```
23 20 7 BOXTEST Big enough ok
```

A third kind of decision is called "exclusive or." This operation, performed by the Forth word $\boxed{XOR}$, yields "true" if *either* of two flags is true, *but not both.*

As an example, here's a word that will take two numbers from the stack. If they are both the same sign (both positive or both negative), the word prints "Same sign"; otherwise, it prints "Different signs."

```
: ?SIGNS   ( n1 n2 -- )
   0<  SWAP 0<  XOR IF ." Different signs "
   ELSE  ." Same sign " THEN  ;
```

As your applications become more sophisticated, you will be able to write statements in Forth that look like postfix English and are very easy to read. Just define the individual words within the definition to check some condition somewhere, then leave a flag on the stack.

An example is

```
: SNAPSHOT   LIGHT? FILM? AND  IF PHOTOGRAPH THEN ;
```

which checks that there is available light *and* that there is film in the camera before taking the picture. Another example, which might be used in a computer-dating application, is

```
: MATCH   HUMOROUS SENSITIVE AND
   ART-LOVING MUSIC-LOVING OR  AND  SMOKING NOT  AND
   IF ." I have someone you should meet "  THEN ;
```

where words like HUMOROUS and SENSITIVE have been defined to check a record in a disk file that contains information on applicants of the appropriate sex.

Special Note: Until we've had a chance to explain certain ramifications (in Chapter 7), use the words $\boxed{NOT}$, $\boxed{OR}$, $\boxed{AND}$, and $\boxed{XOR}$ *only* with values that you know to be logical flags; that is, either zero or minus-one. All the comparison operators we've discussed so far (except $\boxed{-}$ for "not-equal") return logical flags. (Experiment to see what $\boxed{NOT}$, $\boxed{OR}$, $\boxed{AND}$, and $\boxed{XOR}$ do to numbers other than 0 and -1.)

TWO WORDS WITH BUILT-IN IFS

| ?DUP |

question-dupe

abort-quote

The word | ?DUP | duplicates the top stack value only if it is nonzero. This can sometimes eliminate a few surplus words. For example, the definition

```
: ?EMIT   ( c -- )   DUP IF EMIT ELSE DROP THEN ;
```

will emit any character-code except 0 (null). With | ?DUP |, we can shorten the definition to:

```
: ?EMIT   ( c -- )   ?DUP IF EMIT THEN ;
```

| ABORT" |

It may happen that somewhere in a complex application an error might occur way down in one of the low-level words. When this happens you don't just want the computer to keep on going, and you also don't want it to leave anything on the stack.

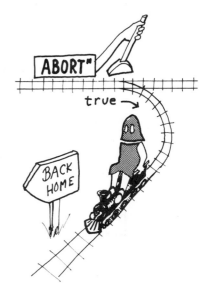

   If you think such an error might occur, you can use the word | ABORT" |. | ABORT" | expects a flag on the stack: a "true" flag tells it to "abort," which in turn clears the stack and returns execution to the terminal, waiting for someone to type something. | ABORT" | also prints the name of the last interpreted word, as well as whatever message you want.†

Let's illustrate. Here is yet another version of /CHECK:

```
: /CHECK   ( numerator denominator -- result)
   DUP 0=   ABORT" Zero denominator "   / ;
```

In this version, if the denominator is zero, any numbers that happen to be on the stack will be dropped and Forth will respond:

```
8 0 /CHECK /CHECK Zero denominator
```

---

† **For Experts:**   Forth also provides the word | QUIT |, which stops the program but does not clear the stack, and | ABORT |, which does a | QUIT | and also clears the stack, but doesn't print a message. We'll discuss these words in Chapter 9.

Just as an experiment, try putting /CHECK inside another definition:

```
: ENVELOPE    /CHECK   ." The answer is "   . ;
```

and try

```
8 4 ENVELOPE The answer is 2 ok
8 0 ENVELOPE ENVELOPE Zero denominator
```

The point is that when /CHECK aborts, the rest of ENVELOPE is skipped. Also notice that the name ENVELOPE, not /CHECK, is displayed.

Here's a list of the Forth words we've covered in this chapter.

IF xxx
  ELSE yyy
  THEN zzz
	IF: (? --)	If ? is true (nonzero) executes xxx; otherwise, executes yyy; continues with zzz regardless. The phrase ELSE yyy is optional.

=	(n1 n2 -- ?)	Returns true if n1 and n2 are equal.
<>	(n1 n2 -- ?)	Returns true if n1 and n2 are not equal.
<	(n1 n2 -- ?)	Returns true if n1 is less than n2.
>	(n1 n2 -- ?)	Returns true if n1 is greater than n2.
0=	(n -- ?)	Returns true if n is zero (i.e., reverses the truth value).
0<	(n -- ?)	Returns true if n is negative.
0>	(n -- ?)	Returns true if n is positive.
NOT	(? -- -?)	Reverses the sense of a flag.
AND	(n1 n2 -- and)	Returns the logical "and."
OR	(n1 n2 -- or)	Returns the logical "or."
XOR	(n1 n2 -- xor)	Returns the logical "exclusive-or."
?DUP	(n -- n n) or (0 -- 0)	Duplicates only if n is nonzero.
ABORT" xxx"	(? --)	If the flag is true, types out the last word interpreted, followed by the text. Also clears the user's stacks and returns control to the terminal. If false, takes no action.
	Key	
n, n1 ... 16-bit signed numbers	? boolean flag	

REVIEW OF TERMS

Abort	as a general computer term, to cease execution abruptly if a condition occurs that the program is not designed to handle, in order to avoid producing nonsense or possibly doing damage.
"And" decision	two conditions that are combined such that if *both* of them are true, the result is true.
Branching	breaking the normally straightforward flow of execution, depending on conditions in effect at the time of execution. Branching allows the computer to respond differently to different conditions.
Comparison operator	in general, a command that compares one value with another (for example, determines whether one is greater than the other) and sets a flag accordingly, which normally will be checked by a conditional operator. In Forth, a comparison operator leaves the flag on the stack.
Conditional operator	a word, such as $\boxed{\text{IF}}$, that routes the flow of execution differently depending on some condition (true or false).
"Exclusive-or" decision	two conditions that are combined such that if either of them is true, *but not both,* the result is true.
Flag	as a general computer term, a value stored in memory that serves as a signal as to whether some known condition is true or false.
Logic	in computer terminology, the system of representing conditions in the form of "logical variables," which can be either true or false, and combining these variables using such "logical operators" as "and," "or," and "not," to form statements that may be true or false.
Nesting	placing a branching structure within an outer branching structure.
"Or" decision	two conditions that are combined such that if *either* of them is true, the result is true.

PROBLEMS

(answers in the back of the book)

4-1. What will the phrase

```
0= NOT
```

leave on the stack when the argument is

−1?
0?
200?

4-2. Explain what an artichoke has to do with any of this.

4-3. Define a word called CARD which, given a person's age on the stack, prints out either of these two messages (depending on the relevant laws in your area):

```
Alcoholic beverages permitted        or
Under age
```

4-4. Define a word called ?SIGN that will test a number on the stack and display one of three messages:

```
Positive
Zero
Negative
```

4-5. Write a definition of $\boxed{<>}$ (not-equal) so that, unlike $\boxed{-}$ (minus), it always returns either true or false.

4-6. Write a definition for $\boxed{\text{XOR}}$ in terms of other logical operators such as $\boxed{\text{AND}}$, $\boxed{\text{OR}}$, and $\boxed{\text{NOT}}$.

4-7. In Chapter 1, we defined a word called STARS, but it won't work right with an argument of zero. (In Forth-83 systems, it will print 65,535 stars; in earlier systems it will print one star.) Using the word STARS, as we defined it, define a new version of STARS that corrects this problem.

4-8. Write the definition for a word called $\boxed{\text{NEGATE}}$ (which, by the way, already exists in your Forth system) that changes the sign of the number on the stack (4 becomes −4 and vice-versa). Next, using $\boxed{\text{NEGATE}}$, define a word called $\boxed{\text{ABS}}$ that, given "n," produces its absolute value. (The word $\boxed{\text{ABS}}$ also exists in your system.)

4-9. Write the definition of a word called /UP that rounds up if the remainder of division is not zero. (For instance, "How many boxes are needed for n items?" The remainder will require a complete additional box.)

4-10. Write the definition for a word called WITHIN which expects three arguments:

`( n low-limit hi-limit -- )`

and leaves a "true" flag only if *n* is within the range

`low-limit ≤ n < hi-limit`

4-11. Here's a number-guessing game that you may enjoy writing more than anyone will enjoy playing. First, you secretly enter a number onto the stack (you can hide your number after entering it by executing the word PAGE, which clears the video screen). Then you ask another player to enter a guess followed by the word GUESS, as in

`100 GUESS`

The computer will either respond "Too high," "Too low," or "Correct!" Write the definition of GUESS, making sure that the answer-number will stay on the stack through repeated guessing until the correct answer is guessed, after which the stack should be clear.

4-12. Using nested tests and $\boxed{\text{IF}}$ $\boxed{\text{ELSE}}$ $\boxed{\text{THEN}}$ statements, write a definition called SPELLER that will spell out a number that it finds on the stack, from −4 to 4. If the number is outside this range, it will print the message "Out of range." For example:

```
2 SPELLER Two ok
-4 SPELLER Negative four ok
7 SPELLER Out of range ok
```

Make it as short as possible. (Hint: The Forth word $\boxed{\text{ABS}}$ gives the absolute value of a number on the stack.)

4-13. Using your definition of WITHIN from Problem 4-10, write another number-guessing game, called TRAP, in which you first enter a secret value, then a second player tries to home in on it by trapping it between two numbers, as in this dialogue:

```
0 1000 TRAP Between ok
330 660 TRAP Between ok
440 550 TRAP Not between ok
330 440 TRAP Between ok
```

and so on, until the player guesses the answer:

```
391 391 TRAP You got it!
```

Hint: You may have to modify the arguments to WITHIN so that TRAP does not say "BETWEEN" when only one argument is equal to the hidden value.

5

THE PHILOSOPHY
OF INTEGER ARITHMETIC

In this chapter, we'll introduce a new batch of arithmetic operators. Along the way, we'll tackle the problem of handling decimal points using only whole-number arithmetic.

QUICKIE OPERATORS

Let's start with the real easy stuff. You should have no trouble figuring out what the words in the following table do.†

1+	(n -- n+1)	Adds one.
1-	(n -- n-1)	Subtracts one.
2+	(n -- n+2)	Adds two.
2-	(n -- n-2)	Subtracts two.
2*	(n -- n*2)	Multiplies by two (arithmetic left shift).
2/	(n -- n/2)	Divides by two (arithmetic right shift).

one-plus
one-minus
two-plus
two-minus
two-star
two-slash

† **For Beginners:** We'll explain what "arithmetic left shift" is later on.

96

There are three reasons to use a word such as ⌐1+⌐ , instead of one and ⌐+⌐ , in your definitions. First, you save a little dictionary space each time. Second, since such words have been specially defined in the "machine language" of each individual type of computer to take advantage of the computer's architecture, they execute faster than one and ⌐+⌐ . Finally, you save a little time during compilation.

MISCELLANEOUS MATH OPERATORS

Here's a table of four miscellaneous math operators. Like the quickie operators, these functions should be obvious from their names.

Aunt Min and Uncle Max

ABS	(n -- ¦n¦)	Returns the absolute value.
NEGATE	(n -- -n)	Changes the sign.
MIN	(n1 n2 -- min)	Returns the minimum.
MAX	(n1 n2 -- max)	Returns the maximum.

Here are two simple word problems, using ⌐ABS⌐ and ⌐MIN⌐ :

⌐ABS⌐

Write a definition that computes the difference between two numbers, regardless of the order in which the numbers are entered.

```
: DIFFERENCE   ( n1 n2 -- difference)   - ABS ;
```

This gives the same result whether we enter

```
52 37 DIFFERENCE . 15 ok        or
37 52 DIFFERENCE . 15 ok
```

MIN

Write a definition that computes the commission that furniture salespeople will receive if they've been promised $50 or 1/10 of the sale price, whichever is less, on each sale they make.

```
: COMMISSION  ( price -- commission)  10 /  50 MIN ;
```

Three different values would produce these results:

```
600 COMMISSION . _50_ok
450 COMMISSION . _45_ok
50 COMMISSION . _5_ok
```

THE RETURN STACK

We mentioned before that there were still some stack manipulation operators we hadn't discussed yet. Now it's time.

Up until now we've been talking about "the stack" as if there were only one. But in fact there are two: the *data stack* and the *return stack*. The data stack is used more often by Forth programmers, so it's simply called "the stack" unless there is cause for doubt.

As you've seen, the data stack holds arguments that are being passed from word to word. The return stack, however, holds any number of *pointers* that Forth uses to make its merry way through the maze of words that are executing *other* words. We'll elaborate later on.

You can employ the return stack as a kind of "extra hand" to hold values temporarily while you perform operations on the data stack.

The return stack is a last-in, first-out structure, just like the data stack, so it can hold many values. But here's the catch: Whatever you put on the return stack you must remove again before you get to the end of the definition (the semicolon), because at that point the Forth system will expect to find a pointer there. You cannot use the return stack to pass arguments from one word to another.†

The following table lists the words associated with the return stack. Remember, the stack notation refers to the data stack.

>R	(n --) Takes a value off the data stack and pushes it onto the return stack.	*to-r*
R>	(-- n) Takes a value off the return stack and pushes it onto the data stack.	*r-from*
R@	(-- n) Copies the *top* of the return stack without affecting it.	*r-fetch*

The words >R and R> transfer a value to and from the return stack, respectively. In the foregoing cartoon, where the stack effect was:

    (2 3 1 -- 3 2 1)

this is the phrase that did it:

    >R SWAP R>

Each >R and its corresponding R> must be used together in the same

---

† **FORTH-83 Standard:** Other restrictions include (1) There must be symmetry around DO LOOPs (see "Loop Limitations" in Chapter 6); and (2) You cannot invoke an EXIT while any values are still saved on the return stack.

definition or, if executed interactively, in the same line of input (before you hit the RETURN key).

The word $\boxed{\text{R@}}$ only copies a value from the return stack without removing it. Thus, the phrase

```
>R SWAP R@
```

would produce the same result as far as it goes, but unless you clean up your trash† before the next semicolon (or return key), you will crash the system.

To see how $\boxed{\text{>R}}$, $\boxed{\text{R>}}$, and $\boxed{\text{R@}}$ might be used, imagine you are so unlucky as to need to solve the equation:

$$ax^2 + bx + c$$

with *all four* values on the stack in the following order

```
( a b c x -- )
```

(remember to factor out first).

OPERATOR	DATA STACK	RETURN STACK
	a b c x	
>R	a b c	x
SWAP ROT	c b a	x
R@	c b a x	x
*	c b ax	x
+	c (ax+b)	x
R> *	c x (ax+b)	
+	x (ax+b)+c	

Go ahead and try it. Load the following definition:

```
: QUADRATIC   ( a b c x -- n)
    >R SWAP ROT R@ *  +  R> *  + ;
```

Now test it:

```
2 7 9 3 QUADRATIC 48 ok
```

---

† You might call such an error in your program a "litter bug."

AN INTRODUCTION TO FLOATING-POINT ARITHMETIC

There are many controversies surrounding Forth. Certain principles that Forth programmers adhere to are considered foolhardy by the proponents of more traditional languages. One such controversy is the question of *scaled-integer arithmetic* versus floating-point arithmetic.

If you already understand these terms, skip ahead to the next section, where we'll express our views on the controversy. If you're a beginner, you may appreciate the following explanation.

First, what does floating point mean? Take a pocket calculator, for example. After each entry, the display looks like this:

YOU ENTER	DISPLAY READS
1 . 5 0 ×	1.5
2 . 2 3	2.23
=	3.345

The decimal point "floats" across the display as necessary. This is called a *floating-point display*.

Floating-point representation is a way to store numbers in computer memory using a form of scientific notation. In scientific notation, twelve million is written:

$$12 \times 10^6$$

since ten to the sixth power equals one million. In many computers, twelve million could be stored as two numbers: 12 and 6, where it is understood that 6 is the power of ten to be multiplied by 12, while 3.345 could be stored as 3345 and -3.

The idea of floating-point representation is that the computer can represent an enormous range of numbers, from atomic to astronomic, with two relatively small numbers.

What is scaled-integer arithmetic? It is simply the method of storing numbers in memory without storing the positions of each number's decimal point. For example, in working with dollars and cents, all values can be stored in cents. The *program*, rather than each individual *number*, can remember the location of the decimal point.

For example, let's compare scaled-integer and floating-point representations of dollars-and-cents values.

REAL-WORLD VALUE	SCALED-INTEGER REPRESENTATION	FLOATING-POINT REPRESENTATION
1.23	123	$123(-2)$
10.98	1098	$1098(-2)$
100.00	10000	$1(2)$
58.60	5860	$586(-1)$

As you can see, with scaled integer all the values must conform to the same "scale," and the computer treats all the numbers as integers. If the program needs to display an answer, however, it simply inserts the decimal point two places in from the right before it sends the number to the terminal or to the printer.

WHY FORTH PROGRAMMERS ADVOCATE SCALED INTEGER

Many respectable languages and many distinguished programmers use floating-point arithmetic as a matter of course. Their opinion might be expressed like this: "Why should I have to worry about moving decimal points around? That's what computers are for."

That's a valid question—in fact it expresses the most significant advantage to floating-point implementations. For translating a mathematical equation into program code, having a floating-point language makes the programmer's life easier.

Many Forth applications are real-time, however. They use the computer to control some device or manage displays and keyboards. These programs need to be as fast as possible to get the most out of the devices. Therefore, a Forth programmer is often interested in maximizing the efficiency of *the machine* rather than the efficiency of the *programmer*. In many cases (such as hand-held computers), it is also desirable to use as little memory as possible.

If your application must repeat the same calculations millions of times, scaled-integer arithmetic will give you the speed you need. Is the extra speed that noticeable? Yes, it is. A floating-point multiplication or division can take many times as long as its equivalent scaled-integer counterpart. And to perform addition or subtraction, the realignment of the values prior to the operation is at least as time-consuming as the addition itself. Most mini- and microcomputers don't "think" in floating point; you pay a heavy penalty for making them act as though they do.

For over a decade, Forth programmers have been writing complex applications with scaled-integer arithmetic involving solutions of fancy things such as differential equations, Fast Fourier Transforms, nonlinear least squares fitting, linear regression, and so on. What other programmers do on mainframe computers, Forth programmers do on mini- and microcomputers, sometimes with an overall *increase* in computation rate.

It's not that Forth *can't* support floating point. Several people have written floating-point functions in Forth ([1]–[7]), and some Forth systems support a floating-point coprocessor (a separate "chip" whose only job is to perform floating-point arithmetic at high speeds) ([8], [9]).

It's just that floating point is not the necessity most programmers think it is. Most problems with physical inputs and outputs have a dynamic range of no more than a few thousand to one, and thus fit comfortably in a 16-bit integer word. (Some calculations may require 32-bit intermediate values, which Forth accommodates.) Such problems include weather modeling, image reconstruction, automated electrical measurements, and the like.

The "trick" to eliminating wasteful floating-point operations from your code is to ensure that values are always scaled according to the range of possible values that you're interested in.

Forth does not just make outrageous claims and then leave you high and dry; it supplies a unique set of high-level commands called *scaling operators* to support techniques such as *rational approximations* and *fractional arithmetic*. The following sections are meant to serve as mere introductions to the world of possibilities for integer arithmetic.

STAR-SLASH THE SCALAR

The following operator is as useful as it is unusual: $\boxed{*/}$

`*/`	`( n1 n2 n3 --` `result)`	Multiplies, then divides (*n1* × *n2/n3*). Uses a 32-bit intermediate result.

star-slash

As its name implies, $\boxed{*/}$ performs multiplication, then division. For example, let's say that the stack contains these three numbers:

`( 225 32 100 -- )`

$\boxed{*/}$ will first multiply 225 by 32, then divide the result by 100.

This operator is particularly useful as an integer-arithmetic solution to problems such as percentage calculations.

For example, you could define the word % like this:

`: % ( n % -- n') 100 */ ;`

$*/$

so that by entering the number 225 and then the phrase

    32 %

you'd end up with 32% of 225 (that is, 72) on the stack.†

    $\boxed{*/}$ is not just a $\boxed{*}$ and a $\boxed{/}$ thrown together, though. It uses a *double-length intermediate result*. What does that mean, you ask?

    Suppose you want to compute 34% of 2000. Remember that single-length operators, $\boxed{*}$ and $\boxed{/}$, only work with arguments and results within the range of -32768 to $+32767$. If you were to enter the phrase

    2000 34 * 100 /

you'd get an incorrect result, because the "intermediate result" (in this case, the result of multiplication) exceeds 32767, as shown in the left column in this pictorial simulation.

    2000 34 * 100 /   2000 34 100 */

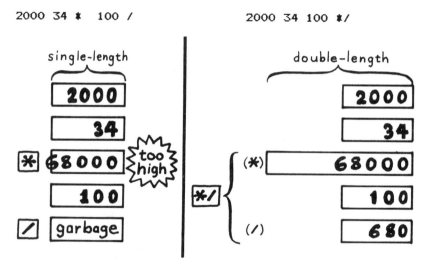

    However, $\boxed{*/}$ uses a double-length intermediate result, so that its range will be large enough to hold the result of any two single-length numbers multiplied together. The phrase

    2000 34 100 */

returns the correct answer because the end result falls within the range of single-length numbers.

---

    † **For the Curious:** The method of first multiplying two integers, then dividing by 100 is identical to the approach most people take in solving such problems on paper.

ROUNDING

The previous example brings up another question: How do you round off?
Let's assume that this is the problem:

If 32% of the students eating at the school cafeteria usually buy bananas,
how many bananas should be on hand for a crowd of 225? Naturally, we
are only interested in whole bananas, so we'd like to round off any decimal
remainder.

As our definition now stands, any value to the right of the decimal is simply
dropped. In other words, the result is "truncated."

32% OF:	RESULT:
225 = 72.00	72—exactly correct
226 = 72.32	72—correct, rounded down
	(truncated)
227 = 72.64	72—truncated, not rounded.

There is a way, however, with any decimal value of 0.5 or higher, to round
upwards to the next whole banana. We could define the word R%, for "rounded
percent," like this:

```
: R%  ( n % -- result )   10 */   5 +   10 / ; †
```

so that the phrase

```
227 32 R% .
```

will give you 73, which is correctly rounded up.
Notice that we first divide by 10 rather than 100. This gives us an extra
decimal place to work with, to which we can add five:

OPERATION	STACK CONTENTS		
	227	32	10
*/			726
5 +			731
10 /			73

† **For Experts:** An even faster definition with greater range is

```
: R%  ( n % -- result )   50 */   1+   2/ ;
```

The final division by ten sets the value to its rightful decimal position. Try it and see.

A disadvantage to this method of rounding is that you lose one decimal place of range in the final result; that is, it can only go as high as 3,276 rather than 32,767. However, if that's a problem, you can always use double-length numbers, which we'll introduce later, and still be able to round.

SOME PERSPECTIVE ON SCALING

Take the simple problem of computing two-thirds of 171. Basically, there are two ways to go about it.

1. We could compute the value of the fraction 2/3 by dividing 2 by 3 to obtain the repeating decimal 0.666666, etc. Then we could multiply this value by 171. The result would be 113.9999999, etc., which is not quite right but which could be rounded up to 114.

2. We could multiply 171 by 2 to get 342. Then we could divide this by 3 to get 114.

Notice that the second way is simpler and more accurate.

Most computer languages support the first way. "You can't have a fraction like two-thirds hanging around inside a computer," it is believed. "You must express it as 0.666666, etc."

Forth supports the second way. $\boxed{*/}$ lets you have a fraction like two-thirds, as in:

`171 2 3 */`

Now that we have a little perspective, let's take a slightly more complicated example:

We want to distribute $150 in proportion to two values:†

7,105	?
5,145	?
12,250	150

Again, we could solve the problem this way:

$(7{,}105 / 12{,}250) \times 150$

and

$(5{,}145 / 12{,}250) \times 150$

---

† **For People Who Like Word Problems:**   Here's a word problem for the above example.
The boss says he'll divide a $150 bonus between the two top-selling marketing representatives according to their monthly commissions. When the receipts are counted, the top two commissions are $7,105 and $5,145. How much of the bonus does each marketing rep get?

but for greater accuracy, we should say:

(7,105 × 150) / 12,250

and

(5,145 × 150) / 12,250

which in Forth is written:

7105 150 12250 */ . _87_ok

then

5145 150 12250 */ . _63_ok

It can be said that the values 87 and 63 are "scaled" to 7105 and 5145. Calculating percentages, as we did earlier, is also a form of scaling. For this reason, ⏍*/⏍ is called a *scaling operator.*

Another scaling operator in Forth is ⏍*/MOD⏍:

*/MOD	(n1 n2 n3 -- n-rem n-result)	Multiplies, then divides (n1 × n2/n3). Returns the remainder and the quotient. Uses a double-length intermediate result.	star-slash-mod

We'll let you dream up a good example for ⏍*/MOD⏍ yourself.

USING RATIONAL APPROXIMATIONS†

So far, we've only used scaling operations to work on rational numbers. They also can be used on rational approximations of irrational constants, such as *pi*

† **For Math-block Victims:** You can skip this section and the next one, if it starts making your brain itch. However, if you're feeling particularly smart today, try this:

A rational number is one that can be made equal to a fraction in which the numerator and denominator are both whole numbers. Seventeen is a rational number, as is 2/3. Even 1.02 is rational, because it's the same as 102/100. $\sqrt{2}$, on the other hand, is irrational.

or the square root of two. For example, the real value of *pi* is

3.14159265358, etc.

But to multiply a number by *pi*, yet stay within the bounds of single-length arithmetic, we could write

    31416 10000 */

and get a pretty good approximation.

Now we can write a definition to compute the area of a circle, given its radius. We'll translate the formula:

$$\pi r^2$$

into Forth. The value of the radius will be on the stack, so we DUP it and multiply it by itself, then multiply by the ratio *pi*.

    : PI   (n -- n')   31416 10000 */ ;
    : AREA   (radius -- area)   DUP * PI ;

Try it with a circle whose radius is ten inches:

    10 AREA . 314 ok

But for even more accuracy, we might wonder if there is a pair of integers besides 31416 and 10000 that is a closer approximation to *pi*. Surprisingly, there is. The fraction

    355 113 */

is accurate to more than six places beyond the decimal, as opposed to less than four places with 31416.

Our new and improved definition, then, uses:

    : PI   (n -- n')   355 113 */ ;

It turns out that you can approximate nearly any constant by many different pairs of integers, all numbers less than 32768, with an error of less than 10^{-8}.†

FRACTIONAL ARITHMETIC

We've just seen how to express fractions as a pair of integers, for scaling. Some applications require noninteger values in situations other than scaling. For instance, how might you add these two fractions

$$\frac{7}{34} + \frac{23}{99} =$$

without using floating-point? We can do it in Forth with a simple technique called *fractional arithmetic* (sometimes called *fixed-point arithmetic*).

Fixed-point arithmetic involves scaling and an implied decimal point. However, instead of scaling by multiples of ten (which we humans are used to), we scale by multiples of two (which computers are fond of). Thus, the implied decimal point might be more aptly called a "binary point."‡

Suppose we define

```
: +1  ( -- scaled-"one" )  16384 ;
```

(constants are introduced in Chapter 8) to establish a scale wherein 16384 represents the positive integer one. In binary, 16384 looks like this:

0100000000000000

The "1" is scaled up in binary, along with the implied binary point.

---

† **For Really Dedicated Mathephiles:** Here's a handy table of rational approximations to various constants. Thanks to Ned Conklin and Robert T. Corry.

NUMBER	APPROXIMATION	ERROR
$\pi = 3.141\ldots$	355/ 113	8.5×10^{-8}
$\sqrt{2} = 1.414\ldots$	19601/13860	1.5×10^{-9}
$\sqrt{3} = 1.732\ldots$	18817/10864	1.1×10^{-9}
$e = 2.718\ldots$	25946/ 9545	2.0×10^{-9}
$\sqrt{10} = 3.162\ldots$	27379/ 8658	6.7×10^{-10}
$\sqrt[12]{2} = 1.059\ldots$	26797/25293	1.0×10^{-9}
$\log_{10} 2/1.6384 = 0.183\ldots$	2040/11103	1.1×10^{-8}
$\ln 2/16.384 = 0.042\ldots$	846/19997	1.2×10^{-8}
$.001°/22$-bit rev $= 0.858\ldots$	18118/21109	1.4×10^{-9}
arc-sec/22-bit rev $= 0.309\ldots$	9118/29509	1.0×10^{-9}
$c = 2.9979248$	24559/ 8192	1.6×10^{-9}

---

‡ **For Beginners:** Binary arithmetic is introduced in Chapter 7.

Now let's extend Forth to define two new math operators—fractional multiply and fractional divide—based on our new scale:

```
: *.  ( n n -- n)  +1  */ ;
: /.  ( n n -- n)  +1  SWAP */ ;
```

To show what we have here, let's start simply. If we divide 1 by 1, we should get 1:

```
1 1 /. . 16384 ok
```

(Remember that 16384 represents positive 1.) If we divide 1 by 2, we get:

```
1 2 /. . 8192
```

Here, 8192 represents the value "one-half" (it's half of 16384).

Thus, we can solve our opening problem like this:

```
7 34 /.  23 99 /.  +
```

Look at the final operation; we simply used good old [+] to add the two fractions!

Of course, this doesn't look too useful so far, since we have no way of recognizing the answer in its present form. To scale the result back to decimal form, we merely type

```
10000 *. . 4381 ok
```

Our answer, then, is 4381/10000, better known as

0.4381

With fractional arithmetic we can add, subtract, multiply and divide using fast integer operations, even though we are dealing with non-integer values. In *number-crunching* applications (those that do a lot of arithmetic computation), the speed of these internal calculations is crucial.

By contrast, the problem of converting numbers to human-readable (decimal) form is relatively unimportant, because only the final result needs to be displayed. In fact, with applications such as graphics and robotics the result *never* needs to be converted to decimal form, but rather to a form suitable to the graphics buffer, plotter, robot arm, or whatever.

Much as we'd like to think otherwise, it really makes sense to let the computer do things its own way, rather than impose a system we were taught in school.

Be that as it may, we might still want to input and output these fractions using customary notation. Would you like Forth to print the result with the decimal in the correct place? All we need is a customized number-formatting word. We'll have to borrow some techniques from Chapter 7, but here goes:†

```
: #.#### 	DUP ABS  0 <#  # # # #  46 HOLD  # ROT SIGN  #>
	TYPE SPACE ;
: .F 	( fraction -- )	10000 *.  #.#### ;
```

Now, the complete statement:

```
7 34 /.  23 99 /.  + .F_0.4381_ok
```

It's not floating point, but it's the same result and a lot faster.

Say we want to express *input* arguments as floating-point numbers as well; for example,

.1250 + .3750 = ?

To do this in Forth, we first need a word to convert a number with a decimal point into a scaled fraction. We'll explain the details in Chapter 7, but for now we can define such a word as:

```
: D>F 	( d -- fraction)  DROP  10000 /. ;
```

("D>F" stands for double-number to fraction.) Now we can enter

```
.1250 D>F .3750 D>F + .F_0.5000_ok
```

Notice that we must express the inputs complete to four decimal places.
We can multiply two fractions with [*.].

```
.7500 D>F  .5000 D>F  *.  .F _.3750_ok
```

Interestingly, if we [*.] a fraction times an integer, the result is an integer. For example,

```
28  .5000 D>F  *.  ._14_ok
```

With [/.], we can divide, say, −0.3 by 0.95 like this:

```
-.3000 D>F  .9500 D>F /.  .F_-0.3160
```

We can also get a fraction result by using [/.] on two integers. Thus,

```
22 44 /. .F_.5000_ok
```

And we get an integer result if we [/.] an integer by a fraction. To summarize, using the letter "f" for fraction and "i" for integer, the following input/output

† **For fig-Forth, Pre-83 polyFORTHs, or Old Starting Forth Systems:** Omit the [ROT] before [SIGN].

combinations of fractional numbers or combinations of fractions and integers are possible:

f f $\boxed{+}$ gives f
f f $\boxed{-}$ gives f
f i $\boxed{*}$ gives f
i f $\boxed{*}$ gives f
f i $\boxed{/}$ gives f
f f $\boxed{*.}$ gives f
f i $\boxed{*.}$ gives i
i f $\boxed{*.}$ gives i
f f $\boxed{/.}$ gives f
i i $\boxed{/.}$ gives f
i f $\boxed{/.}$ gives i

Using a binary-oriented scalar such as 16384 instead of a decimal number such as 10000 allows greater accuracy within 16 bits (by a ratio of 16 to 10). Also, $\boxed{*.}$ and $\boxed{/.}$ can be coded in assembler extremely efficiently.

But the choice of 16384 as the value of "one" is arbitrary. Had we chosen 256, we would get 8 bits (including sign) to the left and eight bits to the right of the binary point.

This same technique can be extended, of course, into 32-bit numbers if the precision is truly needed.

A great use for $\boxed{*.}$ and $\boxed{/.}$ is with trig functions, since an angle can be represented internally as a fraction of a circle (well-behaved, between 0 and 1). Conversions to and from degrees become easy as well.

CONCLUSION

We've covered scaling operators, rounding, rational approximations, and fixed-point techniques. To get a feel for solving a complex mathematical problem keeping intermediate values properly scaled at all times, see the second example in Chapter 12.

As we said before, there's nothing in Forth to prevent you from adding floating-point operations. But Forth does not easily come by its virtues of compactness, high performance, simplicity, and elegance. It requires a rigorous and continual rejection of anything that is not absolutely necessary. By the judicious use of scaling and double-length integers where required, you can eliminate the expense of floating-point operations from your code.

You might prefer to add floating-point if:

1. You want to use your computer like a calculator, for one-shot computations.

2. You value the initial programming time more highly than the execution time spent whenever the calculation is performed.

3. You need a number to be able to describe a very large dynamic range (greater than −2 billion to +2 billion).

All of these are valid reasons. In many environments, however, you don't need to pay for floating point, certainly not in software.

The following list of Forth words were covered in this chapter:

1+	(n -- n+1)	Adds one.
1-	(n -- n-1)	Subtracts one.
2+	(n -- n+2)	Adds two.
2-	(n -- n-2)	Subtracts two.
2*	(n -- n*2)	Multiplies by two (arithmetic left shift)
2/	(n -- n/2)	Divides by two (arithmetic right shift)
ABS	(n -- |n|)	Returns the absolute value.
NEGATE	(n -- -n)	Changes the sign.
MIN	(n1 n2 -- min)	Returns the minimum.
MAX	(n1 n2 -- max)	Returns the maximum.
>R	(n --)	Takes a value off the data stack and pushes it onto the return stack.
R>	(-- n)	Takes a value off the return stack and pushes it onto the data stack.
R@	(-- n)	Copies the *top* of the return stack without affecting it.
*/	(n1 n2 n3 -- result)	Multiplies, then divides ($n1 \times n2/n3$). Uses a 32-bit intermediate result.
*/MOD	(n1 n2 n3 -- n-rem n-result)	Multiplies, then divides ($n1 \times n2/n3$). Returns the remainder and the quotient. Uses a double-length intermediate result.

REVIEW OF TERMS

Data stack   in Forth, the region of memory which serves as common ground between various operations to pass arguments (numbers, flags, or whatever) from one operation to another.

Double-length intermediate result
: a double-length value that is created temporarily by a two-part operator, such as $\boxed{*/}$, so that the "intermediate result" (the result of the first operation) is allowed to exceed the range of a single-length number, even though the initial arguments and the final result are not.

Floating-point arithmetic
: arithmetic that deals with numbers which themselves indicate the location of their decimal points. The program must be able to interpret the true value of each individual number before any arithmetic can be performed.

Fractional arithmetic
: (also called "fixed-point arithmetic") Arithmetic that allows fractions to be expressed as integers with an implied binary point at a particular bit position.

Return stack
: in Forth, a region of memory distinct from the data stack which the Forth system uses to hold "return addresses" (to be discussed in Chapter 9), among other things. The user may keep values on the return stack temporarily, under certain conditions.

Scaled-integer arithmetic
: arithmetic that deals with numbers that do not themselves indicate the location of their decimal points. Instead, for any group of numbers, the program assumes the location of the decimal point or keeps the decimal location for all such numbers as a separate number.

Scaling
: the process of multiplying (or dividing) a number by a ratio. Also refers to the process of multiplying (or dividing) a number by a power of ten so that all values in a set of data may be represented as integers with the decimal point assumed to be in the same place for all values, or by a power of two for fractional arithmetic.

REFERENCES

1. Bowhill, Sidney A., "A Variable-Precision Floating-Point System for Forth," *1983 FORML Conference Proceedings*, Asilomar, California.

2. Bumgarner, John O., and Jonathan R. Sand, "Dysan IEEE P-754 Binary Floating Point Architecture," *1983 Rochester Forth Conference Proceedings*, pp. 185–94.

3. Jesch, Michael, "Floating Point in FORTH?" *1981 FORML Conference Proceedings*, pp. 61–78; reprinted as "Floating Point FORTH?", *Forth Dimensions*, 4/1, May–June 1982, pp. 23–25.

4. Harwood, James V., "FORTH Floating Point," *1981 Rochester Forth Standards Conference Proceedings*, p. 189.

5. Monroe, Alfred J., "Forth Floating-Point Package," *Dr. Dobb's Journal*, 7/9, September 1982, pp. 16–29.

6. Petersen, Joel V., and Michael Lennon, "NIC-FORTH and Floating Point Arithmetic," *1981 Rochester Forth Standards Conference Proceedings*, pp. 213–17.

7. Duncan, Ray, and Martin Tracy, "The FVG Standard Floating-Point Extension," *Dr. Dobb's Journal*, 9/9, September 1984, pp. 110–15.

8. Redington, Dana, "Forth and Numeric Co-processors: An Extensible Way to Floating-Point Computation," *Conference Proceedings of the Eighth WCCF*, 3, pp. 368–73, March 18–20, 1983.

9. Redington, Dana, "Stack-Oriented Co-Processors and Forth," *Forth Dimensions*, 5/3 September–October 1983, pp. 20–22.

PROBLEMS

5-1. What's the difference between ⎡−1⎤ and ⎡1−⎤?

5-2. Translate the following algebraic expression into a Forth definition

$$-\frac{ab}{c}$$

given (a b c --)

5-3. Given four numbers on the stack, for example

(6 70 123 45 --)

write an expression that displays the largest value.

5-4. (a) Define the word 2ORDER to arrange two numbers already on the stack so that the greater is on top.

    (b) Now define the word 3ORDER to arrange three numbers already on the stack in order, with the largest on top.

    (c) Finally, remember the example called BOXTEST in Chapter 4? Rewrite it, using 3ORDER, so that the user may input the three dimensions in any order.

PRACTICE IN SCALING

5-5. A *histogram* is a graphic representation of a series of values, where each value is shown by the height or length of a bar. Define a word called PLOT which will serve as a component to the histogram application. Given a value between 0 and 100, PLOT will draw a horizontal row of stars on your video screen to represent the value.

    The catch? There are only 80 columns on your video screen. Thus, a value of 100 must be plotted as 80 stars; 50 must be plotted as 40 stars; 0 must be plotted as 0 stars, and so on. (Begin the definition with a ⎡CR⎤, and use your version of STARS from Chapter 4, Problem 4-7.)

5-6. In "calculator style," convert the following temperatures, using these formulas:

$$°C = \frac{°F - 32}{1.8}$$

$$°F = (°C \times 1.8) + 32$$

$$°K = °C + 273$$

(For now, express all arguments and results in whole degrees.)
a. 0°F in Centigrade
b. 212°F in Centigrade
c. −32°F in Centigrade
d. 16°C in Fahrenheit
e. 233°K in Centigrade

5-7. Now define words to perform the conversions in Problem 5-6. Use the following names:

F>C   F>K   C>F   C>K   K>F   K>C

Test them with the above values.

THROW IT
FOR A LOOP

In Chapter 4, we learned to program the computer to make "decisions" by branching to different parts of a definition depending on the outcome of certain tests. Conditional branching is one of the things that make computers as useful as they are.

In this chapter, we'll see how to write definitions in which execution can conditionally branch back to an earlier part of the same definition, so that some segment will repeat again and again. This type of control structure is called a *loop*. The ability to perform loops is probably the most significant thing that makes computers as powerful as they are. If we can program the computer to make out one payroll check, we can program it to make out a thousand of them.

For now, we'll write loops that do simple things like printing numbers on your screen. In later chapters, we'll learn to do much more with them.

DEFINITE LOOPS

One type of loop structure is called a *definite loop*. You, the programmer, specify the number of times the loop will loop. In Forth, you do this by specifying a beginning number and an ending number (in reverse order) before the word DO . Then you put the words that you want to have repeated between the words DO and LOOP . For example,

```
: TEST    10 0 DO  CR  ." Hello "  LOOP ;
```

will print a carriage return and "Hello" ten times, because zero from ten is ten.

```
TEST
Hello
Hello
Hello
Hello
Hello
Hello
Hello
Hello
Hello
Hello_ok
```

Like an IF THEN statement, which also involves branching, a DO LOOP statement must be contained within a (single) definition.

The ten is called the *limit* and the zero is called the *index*.

FORMULA:

limit index DO . . . LOOP

Here's what happens inside a DO LOOP :

First, DO removes the limit and the index from the data stack, using them to set the stage for LOOP .†

Then execution proceeds to the words inside the loop.

---

† DO is half-brother to the DODO bird; LOOP is sometimes called a "loophog" because he lives in a loophole.

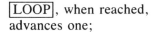

[LOOP], when reached, advances one;

then execution returns to [DO].

When [LOOP] crosses the finish line, the electric eye

switches the track and allows execution to continue past [LOOP].

The word [I] puts on the stack the current value of the *index* (where [LOOP] is standing) each time around. Try this:

```
: DECADE    10 0 DO  I .  LOOP ;
```

which executes like this:

```
DECADE 0 1 2 3 4 5 6 7 8 9 ok
```

Notice that the loop repeats a total of ten times, from 0 to 9. We don't see a 10, because [LOOP] crossed the boundary when it went from 9 to 10.

You can pick any range of numbers,† as long as the limit is higher than the index:

```
: SAMPLE    -243  -250  DO  I .  LOOP ;
```

```
SAMPLE -250 -249 -248 -247 -246 -245 -244 ok
```

Again, the limit (−243) is greater than the starting index (−250).

† **FORTH-83 Standard, For Experts:** The new [LOOP] and [+LOOP] allow any loop to have a full 64K range anywhere within the allowable range of single length signed or unsigned numbers. In earlier Forths, a loop could not range past 32K.

LOOP LIMITATIONS

There are several important things to remember about $\boxed{\text{DO}}$ loops. For one, with $\boxed{\text{DO}}$ the starting index and limit can never be the same. If you define

```
: STUCK   10 10 DO  I .  LOOP ;
```

you might expect this loop not to loop at all. But watch what happens:

Whoops! $\boxed{\text{LOOP}}$ is already past the finish line, and won't trigger the electric eye for a long, long time (until it comes back around 65,535 steps later)!†

If there's a chance that the limit and index might be the same in a definition, substitute the word $\boxed{\text{?DO}}$ for $\boxed{\text{DO}}$. This takes (limit index --) on the stack just like $\boxed{\text{DO}}$, but skips to $\boxed{\text{LOOP}}$ if the limit and index are equal.

Going back to our definition of STARS in Chapter 1, the right way to define it is

```
: STARS  ( #stars)  0 ?DO  42 EMIT  LOOP ;
```

If your system lacks $\boxed{\text{?DO}}$, use the definition

```
: STARS  ( #stars)  ?DUP IF  0 DO  42 EMIT  LOOP  THEN ;
```

Something else you should be aware of: In most Forth systems, $\boxed{\text{DO}}$ loops keep their internal counters on the return stack (introduced in Chapter 5). This implies a few restrictions.

First, the word $\boxed{\text{I}}$ can only be used validly in the same definition in which $\boxed{\text{DO}}$ and $\boxed{\text{LOOP}}$ appear. You cannot write

```
: TEST   I . ;
: DECADE   10 0 DO  TEST  LOOP ;
```

If the subdefinition (TEST) needs the index, you must pass it via the stack. For instance,

```
: TEST  ( index -- ) . ;
: DECADE   10 0 DO  I TEST  LOOP ;
```

---

† **For Pre-FORTH-83 Systems:** In older systems, the loop code will execute once, not 64K times. But that's still not what you want.

Some other restrictions: You can't put a temporary value on the return stack with $>$R before DO and access it from inside the loop, and if you put a value on the return stack inside a loop, you must remove it with R$>$ before encountering a LOOP (or a LEAVE, which we'll discuss later).

DO LOOP EXAMPLES

You can leave a number on the stack to serve as an argument to something inside a DO loop. For instance,

```
: MULTIPLES  ( n)   CR   11 1 DO   DUP I * . LOOP   DROP ;
```

will produce the following results:

```
7 MULTIPLES
7 14 21 28 35 42 49 56 63 70 ok
```

or

```
8 MULTIPLES
8 16 24 32 40 48 56 64 72 80 ok
```

Here we're simply multiplying the current value of the index by "n" each time around. Notice that we have to DUP "n" inside the loop so that a copy will be available each time, and that we have to DROP it after we come out of the loop.

A compound interest problem gives us the opportunity to demonstrate some trickier stack manipulations inside a DO loop. Given a starting balance, say $1,000, and an interest rate, say 6 percent, let's write a definition to compute and print a table such as this:

```
1000 6 COMPOUND
Year  1     Balance 1060
Year  2     Balance 1124
Year  3     Balance 1191
                          etc.
```

for twenty years.

First we'll load R%, our previously defined word from Chapter 5, then we'll define

```
: COMPOUND  ( amount interest -- )
   SWAP  21 1 DO
      CR ." Year "  I .  3 SPACES  2DUP R% + DUP ." Balance " .
   LOOP  2DROP ;
```

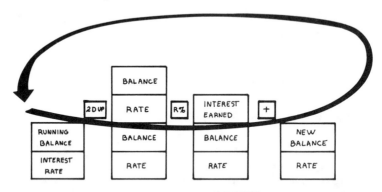

Each time through the loop, we do a 2DUP so that we always maintain a running balance and an unchanged interest rate for the next go-round. When we're finally done (outside the loop), we 2DROP them.

The index also can serve as a condition for an IF statement. In this way, you can make something special happen on certain passes through the loop but not on others. Here's a simple example:

```
: RECTANGLE   256 0 DO  I 16 MOD  0= IF
   CR THEN  ." *"  LOOP ;
```

RECTANGLE will print 256 stars, and at every sixteenth star it will also perform a carriage return at your terminal. The result should look like this:

NESTED LOOPS

Earlier, we defined a word called MULTIPLES which contained a $\boxed{\text{DO}}$ loop. If we wanted to, we could put MULTIPLES inside another $\boxed{\text{DO}}$ loop, like this:

```
: TABLE   CR 11 1 DO I MULTIPLES  LOOP ;
```

Now we'll get a multiplication table that looks like this:

```
1   2   3   4   5   6   7   8   9   10
2   4   6   8   10  12  14  16  18  20
3   6   9   12  15  18  21  24  27  30
                                        etc.
10  20  30  40  50  60  70  80  90  100
```

because the $\boxed{\text{I}}$ in the outer loop supplies the argument for MULTIPLES.

We also can nest $\boxed{\text{DO}}$ loops inside one another all in the same definition:

```
: TABLE   CR 11 1 DO
    11 1 DO I J *  4 .R  LOOP CR  LOOP ;
```

Notice this phrase in the inner loop:

```
I J *
```

While $\boxed{\text{I}}$ copies the index of the loop in which it appears, the word $\boxed{\text{J}}$ copies the index of the *next outer loop*. Thus the phrase "I J *" multiplies the two indexes to create the values in the table.

Now what about this phrase?

```
4 .R
```

This is nothing more than a fancy $\boxed{.}$ that is used to print numbers in table form so that they line up vertically. The four represents the number of spaces we've decided each column in the table should be. The output of the new table looks like this:

```
1     2     3     4     5     6     7     8     9     10
2     4     6     8     10    12    14    16    18    20
3     6     9     12    15    18    21    24    27    30 etc.
```

Each number takes four spaces, no matter how many digits it contains. $\boxed{.\text{R}}$ stands for "number-print, flush *right*."

$\boxed{+\text{LOOP}}$

If you want the index to go up by some number other than one each time around, you can use the word $\boxed{+\text{LOOP}}$ instead of $\boxed{\text{LOOP}}$. $\boxed{+\text{LOOP}}$ expects on the stack the number by which you want the index to change, called the *increment*. For example, in the definition

```
: PENTAJUMPS   50 0 DO  I .  5 +LOOP ;
```

the index will step by the increment five each time, with this result:

```
PENTAJUMPS 0 5 10 15 20 25 30 35 40 45 ok
```

(Imagine the loophog taking giant strides.)

A negative increment makes the loop go *downwards*. For instance

```
: FALLING   -10 0 DO  I .   -1 +LOOP ;
```

produces

```
FALLING 0 -1 -2 -3 -4 -5 -6 -7 -8 -9 -10 ok
```

Here's what happens:

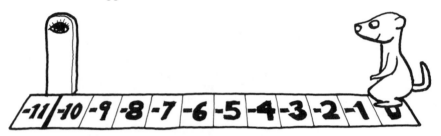

$\boxed{+\text{LOOP}}$ will start at zero, going back by steps of -1, until it crosses the finish line.

Notice that in this direction, we actually loop eleven times. This is because the boundary always lies between the limit and limit -1, regardless of which direction $\boxed{+\text{LOOP}}$ is going. It is the crossing of this boundary that causes the loop to terminate.

The increment can come from anywhere, but it must be put on the stack each time around. Consider this experimental example:

```
: INC-LOOP  ( increment limit index -- )
   DO I .  DUP +LOOP  DROP ;
```

There is no increment inside the definition; instead we will put it on the stack when we execute INC-LOOP, along with the limit and index. Watch what happens.

Step up by one:

```
1 5 0 INC-LOOP 0 1 2 3 4 ok
```

Step up by two:

```
2 5 0 INC-LOOP 0 2 4 ok
```

Step down by three:

```
-3 -10 10 INC-LOOP 10 7 4 1 -2 -5 -8 ok
```

In our next example, the increment changes each time through the loop.

```
: DOUBLING   CR   32767 1 DO   I .   I +LOOP ;
```

Here the index itself is used as the increment so that, starting with one, the index doubles each time:

```
DOUBLING
1 2 4 8 16 32 64 128 256 512 1024 2048 4096 8192 16384 ok
```

Notice that in this example we don't ever want the argument for $\boxed{+\text{LOOP}}$ to be zero, because if it were we'd never come out of the loop. We would have created what is known as an *infinite loop*.†

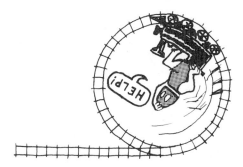

DOING IT—FORTH STYLE

We've said that $\boxed{\text{DO}}$ and $\boxed{\text{LOOP}}$ are branching commands, and as such they can only be executed inside a colon definition. This means that you cannot design/test your loop definitions in "calculator style" unless you simulate the loop yourself.

Let's see how a fledgling Forth programmer might go about design/testing the definition of COMPOUND (from the first section of this chapter). Before adding the $\boxed{."}$ messages, the programmer might begin by jotting down this version on a piece of paper:

```
: COMPOUND   ( amount interest -- )
  SWAP   21 1 DO   CR I .   2DUP R% +   DUP .   LOOP   2DROP ;
```

---

† **For Experts:** Some pre-FORTH-83 systems include the word $\boxed{/\text{LOOP}}$, which, like $\boxed{+\text{LOOP}}$, takes an increment, but the increment must be positive. This allows the index to safely exceed 32767, as might be done when indexing on addresses or block numbers, without these numbers appearing negative as they would in a signed comparison. The 83-Standard $\boxed{+\text{LOOP}}$ eliminates the problem.

The programmer might test this version at the keyboard, using $\boxed{.}$ or $\boxed{.S}$ to check the result of each step. The "conversation" might look like this:

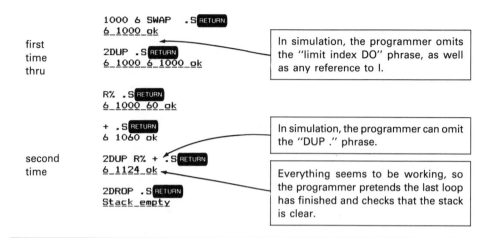

first
time
thru

```
1000 6 SWAP  .S RETURN
6 1000 ok
```

```
2DUP .S RETURN
6 1000 6 1000 ok
```

In simulation, the programmer omits the "limit index DO" phrase, as well as any reference to I.

```
R% .S RETURN
6 1000 60 ok
```

```
+ .S RETURN
6 1060 ok
```

In simulation, the programmer can omit the "DUP ." phrase.

second
time

```
2DUP R% + .S RETURN
6 1124 ok
```

Everything seems to be working, so the programmer pretends the last loop has finished and checks that the stack is clear.

```
2DROP .S RETURN
Stack empty
```

A HANDY HINT
HOW TO CLEAR THE STACK AND
VENT FRUSTRATION AT THE SAME TIME

Sometimes a beginner will unwittingly write a loop which leaves a whole lot of numbers on the stack. For example,

```
: FIVES  ( -- )  100 0 DO  I 5 .  LOOP ;
```

instead of

```
: FIVES  ( -- )  100 0 DO  I 5 *  .  LOOP ;
```

If you see this happen to anyone (surely it will never happen to you!), you may see the beginner typing in an endless succession of dots to clear the stack. Instead, recommend slapping the keyboard and pressing return. This will produce

```
ASDFKJ
```

or some such garbage, which, not being a Forth word, will cause the text interpreter to $\boxed{\text{ABORT}}$, which among other things clears both stacks.
(But discourage the beginner from striking the computer at *every* mistake!)

INDEFINITE LOOPS

While $\boxed{\text{DO}}$ loops are called definite loops, Forth also supports *indefinite* loops. This type of loop will repeat indefinitely or until some event occurs. One form of indefinite loop is

```
BEGIN ... UNTIL
```

The BEGIN UNTIL loop repeats until a condition is true.

The syntax is

```
BEGIN  xxx   ? UNTIL
```

where *xxx* stands for the words that you want repeated, and *?* stands for a flag. As long as the flag is false, the loop will continue to loop, but when the flag becomes true, the loop will end.

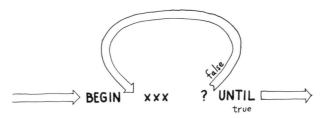

An example of a definition that uses a BEGIN UNTIL statement is one we mentioned earlier, in our washing machine example:

```
: TILL-FULL   BEGIN  ?FULL UNTIL ;
```

which we used in the higher-level definition

```
: FILL   FAUCETS OPEN   TILL-FULL   FAUCETS CLOSE ;
```

?FULL will be defined to electronically check a switch in the washtub that indicates when the water reaches the correct level, returning true when it does. TILL-FULL repeatedly makes this test (thousands of times per second) until the switch is finally activated, at which time execution will come out of the loop. The semicolon in TILL-FULL will return the flow of execution to the remaining words in FILL, and the water will be turned off.

Sometimes a programmer will deliberately want to create an infinite loop. In Forth, the best way is with the form

```
BEGIN  xxx   FALSE UNTIL
```

(The word FALSE is synonymous with the number zero; if your system doesn't have FALSE, use 0.) Since the flag to UNTIL will always be false, the loop will repeat eternally.

In some systems, the word AGAIN is synonymous with the phrase "FALSE UNTIL".

Beginners usually want to avoid infinite loops, because executing one means that they lose control of the computer (in the sense that only the words inside the loop are being executed). However, infinite loops do have their uses. For instance, the text interpreter is part of an infinite loop called QUIT, which waits for input, interprets it, executes it, prints "ok," then waits for input once again. In most microprocessor-controlled machines, the highest-level definition contains an infinite loop that defines the machine's behavior.

Another form of indefinite loop is used in this format:

```
BEGIN  xxx  ? WHILE  yyy  REPEAT
```

Here, the test occurs halfway through the loop rather than at the end. As long as the test is true, the flow of execution continues with the rest of the loop, then returns to the beginning again. If the test is false, the loop ends.

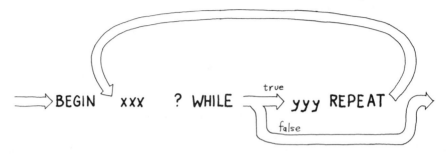

Notice that the effect of the test is opposite that in the BEGIN UNTIL construction. Here the loop repeats *while* something is true (rather than *until* it's true).

Suppose we have a database full of names. We've defined the word GET-NAME to push onto the stack the number of the next name in the list, or when there are no more names in the list, a "false" flag. And we have the word .NAME, which prints the person's name corresponding to the number on the stack.

```
: GET-NAME  ( -- name#-or-false )  ... ;
: .NAME  ( name# -- )  ... ;
```

Now suppose we want to print a list of all names. It happens that we don't know how many names there are on the list until we list them, so we can't use a DO LOOP. So we might define

```
: .ALL-NAMES
   BEGIN  GET-NAME DUP WHILE  CR .NAME  REPEAT   DROP ;
```

What if there are *no* names in the list? On the first pass, GET-NAME will return a zero; the second half of the loop will never be executed. WHILE eliminates the need for a special test.

LEAVES AND BRANCHES

There is a way to write a definite loop so that it stops short of the prescribed limit if a truth condition changes state, by using the word LEAVE within a DO loop. LEAVE causes execution to jump to the end of the loop immediately.†
Watch how we rewrite our earlier definition of COMPOUND.

---

† **For Pre-83 Systems:** Formerly, LEAVE caused the loop to end at the next LOOP or +LOOP.

Instead of just letting the loop run twenty times, let's get it to quit after twenty times *or* as soon as our money has doubled, whichever occurs first.

We'll simply add this phrase:

```
2000 > IF LEAVE THEN
```

like this:

```
: DOUBLED   ( amount interest -- )
    SWAP   21 1 DO
       CR ." Year "   I   2 .R   3 SPACES 2DUP   R% + DUP
       ." Balance "   .   DUP 2000 > IF
          CR ." More than doubled in " I .   ." years " LEAVE
       THEN
    LOOP   2DROP ;
```

The result will look like this:

```
1000 6 DOUBLED
Year   1     Balance 1060
Year   2     Balance 1124
Year   3     Balance 1191
Year   4     Balance 1262
Year   5     Balance 1338
Year   6     Balance 1418
Year   7     Balance 1503
Year   8     Balance 1593
Year   9     Balance 1689
Year  10     Balance 1790
Year  11     Balance 1897
Year  12     Balance 2011
More than doubled in 12 years
```

One of the problems at the end of this chapter asks you to rework DOUBLED so that it expects the arguments of interest and starting balance, and computes by itself the doubled balance that $\boxed{\text{LEAVE}}$ will try to reach.

$\boxed{\text{LEAVE}}$ behaves as you'd expect it to when you nest $\boxed{\text{DO}}$ loops: it only "leaves" the loops in which it appears. A single loop may contain multiple $\boxed{\text{LEAVE}}$s; whichever is first encountered will cause a jump to the end of the loop.

With the 83-Standard, remember that any code which appears after the "IF LEAVE THEN" statement will *not* be executed the last time. Usually it's best to make the "IF LEAVE THEN" statement the last thing before the $\boxed{\text{LOOP}}$.

Another warning: like all conditional operators, $\boxed{\text{LEAVE}}$ must appear in the same definition as the conditionals it relates to ($\boxed{\text{DO}}$ and $\boxed{\text{LOOP}}$). Remember not to factor $\boxed{\text{LEAVE}}$ into a word that is called from within the loop.

BAD example:

```
: DECIDE    SOMETHING IF SOMETHING-ELSE   LEAVE   THEN ;
: BAD-LOOP   1000 0 DO   CALCULATE   DECIDE   LOOP ;
```

The LEAVE is outside the loop. These words will compile but produce ''unpredictable results'' (a euphemism for ''eventual crash'').

TWO HANDY HINTS: PAGE AND QUIT

To give a neater appearance to your loop outputs (such as tables and geometric shapes), you might want to clear the screen first by using the word PAGE . You can execute PAGE interactively like this:

```
PAGE RECTANGLE
```

which will clear the screen before printing the rectangle that we defined earlier in this chapter. Or you could put PAGE at the beginning of the definition, like this:

```
: RECTANGLE   PAGE  256 0 DO
   I 16 MOD 0=  IF CR THEN  ." *" LOOP ;
```

If you don't want the "ok" to appear upon completion of execution, use the word QUIT . Again, you can use QUIT interactively:

```
RECTANGLE QUIT
```

or you can make QUIT the last word in the definition (just before the semicolon).

Here's a list of the Forth words we've covered in the chapter:

DO ... LOOP	DO: (limit index --) LOOP: (--)	Sets up a finite loop, given the index range.
DO ... +LOOP	DO: (limit index --) +LOOP: (n --)	Like DO LOOP except adds the value of *n* (instead of always one) to the index.
LEAVE	(--)	Terminates the loop at the next LOOP or +LOOP. (Must appear within the loop.)
BEGIN ... UNTIL	UNTIL: (? --)	Sets up an indefinite loop that ends when ? is true.
BEGIN xxx WHILE yyy REPEAT	WHILE: (? --)	Sets up an indefinite loop which always executes *xxx* and also executes *yyy* if ? is true. Ends when ? is false.
.R	(n width --)	Prints the number, right-justified within the field width.
PAGE	(--)	Clears the display screen and resets the cursor to the upper left-hand corner.
QUIT	(--)	Terminates execution for the current task and returns control to the terminal.

Key

n, n1 ... 16-bit signed numbers	? boolean flag

REVIEW OF TERMS

Definite loop — a loop structure in which the words contained within the loop repeat a definite number of times. In Forth, this number depends on the starting and ending counts (index and limit) which are placed on the stack prior to the execution of the word DO .

Infinite loop — a loop structure in which the words contained within the loop continue to repeat without any chance of an external event stopping them, except for the shutting down or resetting of the computer.

Indefinite loop — a loop structure in which the words contained within the loop continue to repeat until some truth condition changes state (true-to-false or false-to-true). In Forth, the indefinite loops begin with the word BEGIN .

PROBLEMS

In Problems 6-1 through 6-6, you will create several words which will display patterns of stars (asterisks). These will involve the use of DO loops and BEGIN   UNTIL loops.

6-1. First create a word named STARS as before (to display *n* stars on the same line, given *n* on the stack).

6-2. Next define BOX, which prints out a rectangle of stars given the width and height (number of lines), using the stack order (width height --).

```
10 3 BOX
**********
**********
********** ok
```

6-3. Now create a word named \STARS that will print a skewed array of stars (a rhomboid), given the height on the stack. Use a DO loop and, for simplicity, make the width a constant ten stars.

```
3 \STARS
**********
 **********
  ********** ok
```

6-4. Now create a word that slants the stars in the other direction; call it /STARS. It should take the height as a stack input and use a constant ten width. Use a DO loop.

6-5. Now redefine this last word, using a BEGIN   UNTIL loop.

6-6. Write a definition called DIAMONDS that will print out the given number of diamond shapes, as shown in this example:

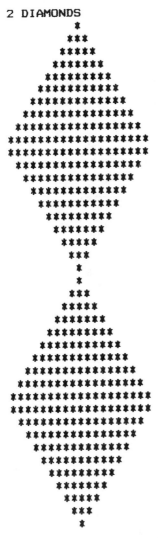

2 DIAMONDS

6-7. In Chapter 3, we introduced the word [THRU]. See if you can write its definition, invoking [LOAD]. If you want, add the feature whereby [THRU] displays the number of each block as it loads it.

6-8. In our discussion of [LEAVE], we gave an example that computed 6 percent compound interest on a starting balance of $1000 for twenty years or until the balance had doubled, whichever came first. Rewrite this definition so that it will expect a starting balance and interest rate on the stack and will [LEAVE] when this starting balance has doubled.

6-9. Define a word called ∗∗ that will compute exponential values, like this:

```
7 2 ** . _49_ok
( seven squared)

2 4 ** . _16_ok
( two to the fourth power)
```

For simplicity, assume nonnegative exponents only. But make sure ∗∗ works correctly when the exponent is 0 (the result should be one) or when the exponent is 1 (the result should be the number itself).

7

A NUMBER
OF KINDS
OF NUMBERS

So far, we've only talked about signed single-length numbers. In this chapter, we'll introduce unsigned numbers and double-length numbers, as well as a whole passel of new operators to go along with them.

The chapter is divided into two sections:

For beginners. This section explains how a computer looks at numbers and exactly what is meant by the terms *signed* or *unsigned* and by *single-length* or *double-length*.

For everyone. This section continues our discussion of Forth for beginners and experts alike, and explains how Forth handles signed and unsigned, single- and double-length numbers.

**SECTION 1
FOR BEGINNERS**

SIGNED VERSUS UNSIGNED NUMBERS

All digital computers store numbers in binary form.† In Forth, the stack is 16 bits‡ wide (a "bit" is a "*bi*nary digi*t*"). Below is a view of 16 bits, showing the value of each bit:

32768	16384	8192	4096	2048	1024	512	256	128	64	32	16	8	4	2	1

If every bit were to contain a 1, the total would be 65535. Thus, in 16 bits we can express any value between 0 and 65535. Because this kind of number does not let us express negative values, we call it an *unsigned number*. We have been indicating unsigned numbers with the letter *u* in our tables and stack notations.

But what about negative numbers? In order to be able to express a positive or negative number, we need to sacrifice one bit that will essentially indicate sign. This bit is the one at the far left, the *high-order bit*. In 15 bits, we can express a number as high as 32767. When the sign bit contains 1, we can go an equal distance back into the negative numbers. Thus, within 16 bits we can represent any number from −32768 to +32767. This should look familiar to you as the range of a single-length number, which we have been indicating with the letter *n*.

sign bit

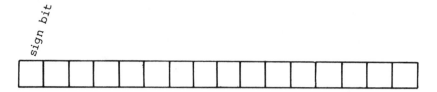

† **For Beginner Beginners:**   If you are unfamiliar with binary notation, ask someone you know who likes math, or find a book on computers for beginners.

‡ **For Users of 32-bit Machines:**   On processors such as the 68000, Forth's stack is often 32-bits wide. For such machines, the term *single length number* in this book typically refers to a 32-bit number.

Before we leave you with any misconceptions, we'd better clarify the way negative numbers are represented. You might think that it's a simple matter of setting the sign bit to indicate whether a number is positive or negative, but it doesn't work that way.

To explain how negative numbers are represented, let's return to decimal notation and examine a counter such as that found on many tape recorders.

Let's say the counter has three digits. As you wind the tape forward, the counter-wheels turn and the number increases. Starting once again with the counter at 0, now imagine you're winding the tape backwards. The first number you see is 999, which, in a sense, is the same as −1. The next number will be 998, which is the same as −2, and so on.

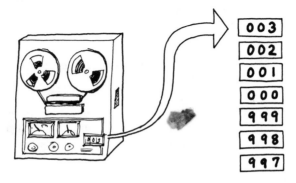

The representation of signed numbers in a computer is similar.
Starting with the number

0000000000000000

and going backwards one number, we get

1111111111111111   (sixteen ones)

which stands for 65535 in unsigned notation as well as for −1 in signed notation. The number

1111111111111110

which stands for 65534 in unsigned notation, represents −2 in signed notation.

(You can see why the numbers −1 and 0 are convenient representations for "true" and "false"; −1 is all bits on, and 0 is all bits off.)

The following chart shows how a binary number on the stack can be used either as an unsigned number or as a signed number:

as an unsigned number		as a signed number
65535	1111111111111111	
...	...	
32768	1000000000000000	
32767	0111111111111111	32767
...	...	...
0	0000000000000000	0
	1111111111111111	−1
	...	...
	1000000000000000	−32768

This bizarre-seeming method for representing negative values makes it possible for the computer to use the same procedures for subtraction as for addition.

To show how this works, let's take a very simple problem:

$$\begin{array}{r} 2 \\ -1 \\ \hline \end{array}$$

Subtracting one from two is the same as adding two plus negative one. In single-length binary notation, the two looks like this:

0000000000000010

while negative-one looks like this:

1111111111111111

The computer adds them up the same way we would on paper; that is, when the total of any column exceeds one, it carries a one into the next column. The result looks like this:

```
  0000000000000010
+ 1111111111111111
 10000000000000001
```

As you can see, the computer had to carry a one into every column all the way across, and ended up with a one in the seventeenth place. But since the stack is only 16 bits wide, the result is simply

0000000000000001

which is the correct answer, one.

We needn't explain how the computer converts a positive number to negative, but if you want to read more about it somewhere else, it's called *two's complementing*.

ARITHMETIC SHIFT

While we're on the subject of how a computer performs certain mathematical operations, we'll explain what is meant by the mysterious phrases back in Chapter 5: *arithmetic left shift* and *arithmetic right shift*.

A FORTH INSTANT REPLAY

2*	(n -- n*2)	Multiplies by two (arithmetic left shift).
2/	(n -- n/2)	Divides by two (arithmetic right shift).

To illustrate, let's pick a number—say, six—and write it in binary form:

0000000000000110

(4 + 2). Now let's shift every digit one place to the left, and put a zero in the vacant place in the one's column.

0000000000001100

This is the binary representation of twelve (8 + 4), which is exactly double the original number. This works in all cases, and it also works in reverse. If you shift every digit one place to the *right* and fill the vacant digit with a zero, the result will always be *half* of the original value.

In arithmetic shift, the sign bit does not get shifted. This means that a positive number will stay positive and a negative number will stay negative when you divide or multiply it by two. (When the high-order bit shifts with all the other bits, the term is *logical shift*.)

The important thing for you to know is that a computer can shift digits much more quickly than it can go through all the folderol of normal division or multiplication. When speed is critical, it's much better to say

2*

than

2 *

and it may even be better to say

2* 2* 2*

than

8 *

depending on your particular model of computer, but this topic is getting too technical for right now.

DOUBLE-LENGTH NUMBERS

A double-length number is just what you probably expected it would be: a number that is represented in thirty-two bits instead of sixteen. Signed double-length numbers have a range of ±2,147,483,647 (a range of over four billion).

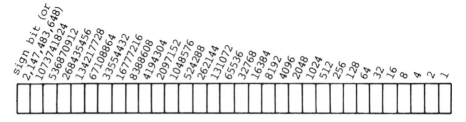

In Forth, a double-length number takes the place of two single-length numbers on the stack. Operators like 2SWAP and 2DUP are useful either for double-length numbers or for pairs of single-length numbers.

One more thing we should explain: To the non-Forth-speaking computer world, the term *word* means a 16-bit value, or two bytes. But in Forth, *word* means a defined command. So in order to avoid confusion, Forth programmers refer to a 16-bit value as a *cell*. A double-length number requires two cells.

THE JOY OF HEX
(AND OTHER NUMBER BASES)

As you get more involved in programming, you'll need to employ other number bases besides decimal and binary, particularly hexadecimal (base 16) and octal (base 8). Since we'll be talking about these two number bases later on in this chapter, we think you might like an introduction now.

Computer people began using hexadecimal and octal numbers for one main reason: computers think in binary and human beings have a hard time reading long binary numbers. For people, it's much easier to convert binary to hexadecimal than binary to decimal, because sixteen is an even power of two, while ten is not. The same is true with octal. So programmers usually use hex or octal to express the binary numbers that the computer uses for things like addresses and machine codes. Hexadecimal (or simply "hex") looks strange at first since it uses the letters A through F.

THE ASCII CHARACTER SET

DECIMAL	BINARY	HEXADECIMAL
0	0000	0
1	0001	1
2	0010	2
3	0011	3
4	0100	4
5	0101	5
6	0110	6
7	0111	7
8	1000	8
9	1001	9
10	1010	A
11	1011	B
12	1100	C
13	1101	D
14	1110	E
15	1111	F

Let's take a single-length binary number:

0111101110100001

To convert this number to hexadecimal, we first subdivide it into four units of four bits each:

| 0111 | 1011 | 1010 | 0001 |

then convert each 4-bit unit to its hex equivalent:

| 7 | B | A | 1 |

or simply 7BA1.

Octal numbers use only the numerals 0 through 7. Because nowadays most computers use hexadecimal representation, we'll skip an octal conversion example.

We'll have more on conversions in the section titled "Number Bases" later in this chapter.

THE ASCII CHARACTER SET

If the computer uses binary notation to store numbers, how does it store characters and other symbols? Binary, again, but in a special code that was adopted as an industry standard many years ago. The code is called the American Standard Code for Information Interchange code, usually abbreviated ASCII.

Table 7-1 shows each character in the system and its numerical equivalent, both in hexadecimal and in decimal form.

TABLE 7-1   ASCII Characters and Equivalents

CHAR	HEX	DEC	CHAR	HEX	DEC	CHAR	HEX	DEC	CHAR	HEX	DEC
NUL	00	0	SP	20	32	@	40	64	`	60	96
SOH	01	1	!	21	33	A	41	65	a	61	97
STX	02	2	"	22	34	B	42	66	b	62	98
ETX	03	3	#	23	35	C	43	67	c	63	99
EOT	04	4	$	24	36	D	44	68	d	64	100
ENQ	05	5	%	25	37	E	45	69	e	65	101
ACK	06	6	&	26	38	F	46	70	f	66	102
BEL	07	7	'	27	39	G	47	71	g	67	103
BS	08	8	(	28	40	H	48	72	h	68	104
HT	09	9	)	29	41	I	49	73	i	69	105
LF	0A	10	*	2A	42	J	4A	74	j	6A	106
VT	0B	11	+	2B	43	K	4B	75	k	6B	107
FF	0C	12	,	2C	44	L	4C	76	l	6C	108
CR	0D	13	−	2D	45	M	4D	77	m	6D	109
SM	0E	14	.	2E	46	N	4E	78	n	6E	110
SI	0F	15	/	2F	47	O	4F	79	o	6F	111
DLE	10	16	0	30	48	P	50	80	p	70	112
DC1	11	17	1	31	49	Q	51	81	q	71	113
DC2	12	18	2	32	50	R	52	82	r	72	114
DC3	13	19	3	33	51	S	53	83	s	73	115
DC4	14	20	4	34	52	T	54	84	t	74	116
NAK	15	21	5	35	53	U	55	85	u	75	117
SYN	16	22	6	36	54	V	56	86	v	76	118
ETB	17	23	7	37	55	W	57	87	w	77	119
CAN	18	24	8	38	56	X	58	88	x	78	120
EM	19	25	9	39	57	Y	59	89	y	79	121
SUB	1A	26	:	3A	58	Z	5A	90	z	7A	122
ESC	1B	27	;	3B	59	[	5B	91	{	7B	123
FS	1C	28	<	3C	60	\	5C	92			7C	124
GS	1D	29	=	3D	61	]	5D	93	}	7D	125
RS	1E	30	>	3E	62	^	5E	94	~	7E	126
US	1F	31	?	3F	63	_	5F	95	DEL (RB)	7F	127

The "Char" column shows the ASCII symbol or, in the case of the control characters, the standard abbreviated name. The other two columns give each character's numeric value, in hexadecimal and decimal.

    The characters in the first column (ASCII codes 0-1F hex) are called *control characters* because they indicate that the terminal or computer is supposed to do something like ring its bell, backspace, start a new line, etc. The remaining characters are called *printing characters* because they produce visible characters including letters, the numerals zero through nine, all available symbols and even the blank space (hex 20). The only exception is DEL (hex 7F), which is a signal to the computer to ignore the last character sent.

In Chapter 1 we introduced the word EMIT . EMIT takes an ASCII code on the stack and sends it to the terminal so that the terminal will print it as a character. For example,

```
65 EMIT A ok
66 EMIT B ok
```

and so on. (We're using the decimal, rather than the hex, equivalent because that's what your computer is most likely expecting right now.)†

Why not test EMIT "automatically" on *every* printing character.

```
: PRINTABLES    127 32 DO I EMIT SPACE LOOP ;
```

PRINTABLES will emit every printable character in the ASCII set; that is, the characters from decimal 32 to decimal 126. (We're using the ASCII codes as our DO loop index.)

```
PRINTABLES   _!_"_#_$_%_&_'_(_)_ ... ok
```

Beginners may be interested in some of the control characters as well. For instance, try this:

(BEEP!)

```
7 EMIT ok
```

You should have heard some sort of beep, which is the video terminal's version of the mechanical printer's "typewriter bell." (Some systems use EMIT to display odd characters on the screen rather than execute the command.)

Other control characters that are good to know include the following:

NAME	OPERATION	DECIMAL EQUIVALENT
BS	backspace	8
LF	line feed	10
CR	carriage return	13

Experiment with these control characters, and see what they do.

ASCII is designed so that each character can be represented by one byte. The tables in this book use the letter "c" to indicate a byte value that is being used as a coded ASCII character.

Some Forth systems feature a word called ASCII that makes for more readable definitions by translating a character into its ASCII value. For instance,

---

† **For Experts:** Why are you snooping on the beginner's section?

remember the definition:

```
: STAR    42 EMIT ;
```

If your system includes ASCII , you can also write

```
: STAR    ASCII * EMIT ;
```

The exact same dictionary entry is compiled in either case; the only difference is that the latter definition is more readable.

ASCII	(-- c)	Translates the next character in the input stream into its ASCII equivalent, leaving the value on the stack.

SECTION II
FOR EVERYBODY

BIT LOGIC

The words AND and OR (which we introduced in Chapter 4) use "bit logic"; that is, each bit is treated independently, and there are no "carries" from one bit-place to the next. For example, let's see what happens when we AND these two binary numbers:

```
0000000011111111
0110010110100010  AND
0000000010100010
```

For any result-bit to be "1," the respective bits in *both* arguments must be "1." Notice in this example that the argument on top contains all zeroes in the high-order byte and all ones in the low-order byte. The effect on the second argument in this example is that the low-order eight bits are kept but the high-order eight bits are all set to zero. Here the first argument is being used as a *mask,* to mask out the high-order byte of the second argument.

The word OR also uses bit logic. For example,

```
1000100100001001
0000001111001000  OR
1000101111001001
```

a "1" in either argument produces a "1" in the result. Again, each column is treated separately, with no carries.

By clever use of masks, we could even use a 16-bit value to hold sixteen separate flags. For example, we could find out whether this bit

```
1011101010011100
        ↑
```

is "1" or "0" by masking out all other flags, like this:

```
1011101010011100
0000000000010000  AND
0000000000010000
```

Since the bit was "1," the result is "true." Had it been "0," the result would have been "0" or "false."

We could set the flag to "0" without affecting the other flags by using this technique:

```
1011101010011100
1111111111101111  AND
1011101010001100
          ↑
```

We used an inverse mask that contains all "1"s except for the bit we wanted to set to "0." We can set the same flag back to "1" by using this technique:

```
1011101010001100
0000000000010000  OR
1011101010011100
          ↑
```

Here's a trick we can play using AND :

You'll notice in Table 7-1 that the ASCII code of each lowercase letter is exactly 32 (in decimal) higher than the same letter in uppercase. We could define a word that converts lowercase letters to uppercase as follows:

```
: UPPER  ( lower-case-letter -- upper-case-letter )
  32 - ;
```

Thus,

```
97 EMIT_a_ok
97 UPPER EMIT_A_ok
```

Unfortunately, this version of UPPER won't work if the letter is already uppercase, because we're subtracting.

But the ASCII character set was cleverly designed. The number 32 is not an accident; it's a binary bit-position. Here are the binary patterns for upper- and lowercase "A":

```
A  1000001
a  1100001
```

The only difference is one bit—the bit that represents the number 32. If we set that bit to 0, we can guarantee that any letter, whether it is uppercase or lowercase, will be set to uppercase. Here's how we can do this:

```
: UPPER  ( lower-case-letter -- upper-case-letter )
   95 AND ;
```

The number 95 is the decimal equivalent of the binary number

1011111

which is a mask for the "32" bit-position.

Thus,

```
97 UPPER EMIT_A_ok
65 UPPER EMIT_A_ok
```

(This UPPER does strange things to nonalphabetic characters, however. Try it with numerals, for example.)

The word $\boxed{\text{XOR}}$ is also a bit-wise operator. As you'll recall from Chapter 4, it produces "true" only when either of its inputs, but not both, are true. Compare the result of an $\boxed{\text{XOR}}$ operation with the $\boxed{\text{OR}}$ operation given earlier:

```
1000100100001001        1000100100001001
0000001111001000 [OR]    0000001111001000 [XOR]
1000101111001001        1000101011000001
```

When you $\boxed{\text{XOR}}$ a number with all 1's, you reverse all the bits!

```
1111111111111111
1000100100001001 [XOR]
0111011011110110
```

Thus, the phrase

```
-1 XOR
```

produces an inverse mask of a bit position or pattern. (Mathematically, this is called the *one's complement* of a number.)†

---

† **Forth-83 Standard and** $\boxed{\text{NOT}}$**:** The Forth-83 Standard has changed the definition of $\boxed{\text{NOT}}$ from its original meaning. On older systems $\boxed{\text{NOT}}$ reverses the meaning of the argument to $\boxed{\text{IF}}$; that is, nonzero (true) becomes false, and zero (false) becomes true. In other words, it was a synonym for $\boxed{\text{0=}}$ created for the purpose of better readability. In the 83 Standard, $\boxed{\text{NOT}}$ is equivalent to the phrase "−1 XOR". Thus it will *not* work if the original flag is true (non-zero) unless it is exactly −1.

Carefully ensure that any flag that may be reversed is logical, not arithmetic. Note that the phrase "0= NOT" ensures a valid boolean that is "true" when the value is non-zero.

SIGNED AND UNSIGNED NUMBERS

Back in Chapter 1, we introduced the word NUMBER .

If the word INTERPRET can't find an incoming string in the dictionary, it hands it over to the word NUMBER . NUMBER then attempts to convert the string into a number expressed in binary form. If NUMBER succeeds, it pushes the binary equivalent onto the stack.

NUMBER does not do any range-checking.† Because of this, NUMBER can convert either signed or unsigned numbers.

For instance, if you enter any number between 32768 and 65535, NUMBER will convert it as an unsigned number. Any value between −32768 and −1 will be stored as a two's-complement integer.

This is an important point: The stack can be used to hold either signed or unsigned integers. Whether a binary value is interpreted as signed or unsigned depends on the operators that you apply to it. You decide which form is better for a given situation, then stick to your choice.

We've introduced the word . , which prints a value on the stack as a *signed* number:

```
65535 . _-1_ok
```

The word U. prints the same binary representation as an *unsigned* number:

```
65535 U._65535_ok
```

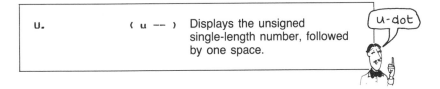

| U. | (u --) | Displays the unsigned single-length number, followed by one space. | u-dot |

----

† **For Beginners:** This means that NUMBER does not check whether the number you've entered as a single-length number exceeds the proper range. If you enter a giant number, NUMBER converts it but saves only the least significant 16 digits.

In this book, the letter "n" signifies *signed* single-length numbers, while the letter "u" signifies *unsigned* single-length numbers. Two more words that use unsigned numbers are:

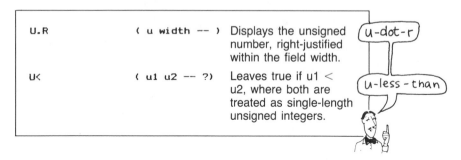

U.R	(u width --)	Displays the unsigned number, right-justified within the field width.
U<	(u1 u2 -- ?)	Leaves true if u1 < u2, where both are treated as single-length unsigned integers.

NUMBER BASES

When you first load Forth, all number conversions use base ten (decimal) for both input and output.

You can easily change the base by executing one of the following commands:

HEX	(--)	Sets the base to sixteen.
OCTAL	(--)	Sets the base to eight (available on some systems).†
DECIMAL	(--)	Returns the base to ten.

† **For Experts:** OCTAL is omitted unless the design of the particular processor compels its use.

When you change the number base, it stays changed until you change it again. So be sure to declare DECIMAL as soon as you're done with another number base.†

These commands make it easy to do number conversions in "calculator style." For example, to convert decimal 100 into hexadecimal, enter

```
DECIMAL 100 HEX . _64_ok
```

To convert hex F into decimal (remember you are already in hex), enter

```
ØF DECIMAL . _15_ok
```

Make it a habit, starting right now, to precede each hexadecimal value with a zero, as in

```
ØA   ØB   ØFF
```

This practice avoids mix-ups with predefined words (such as B in the editor.)

A HANDY HINT
A DEFINITION OF BINARY—OR *ANY*-ARY

Beginners who want to see what numbers look like in binary notation may enter this definition:

```
: BINARY    2 BASE ! ;
```

The new word BINARY will operate just like OCTAL or HEX but will change the number base to *two*. On systems which do not have the word OCTAL, experimenters may define

```
: OCTAL    8 BASE ! ;
```

DOUBLE-LENGTH NUMBERS

Double-length numbers provide a range of ±2,147,483,647. Most Forth systems support double-length numbers to some degree.‡ Normally, the way to enter a double-length number onto the stack (whether from the keyboard or from a block) is to include a decimal point in the number.

---

† **For People Using Multiprogrammed Systems:** When you change the number base, you change it for your terminal task only. Every terminal task uses a separate number base.

‡ **For polyFORTH Users:** polyFORTH includes double-length routines, but they are "electives," which means that they are written in the group of blocks that you must load each time the system is booted. This arrangement gives you the flexibility to either load these routines or to delete them from your load block, according to the needs of your application.

For example, when you type

200000. [RETURN]

[NUMBER] recognizes the period as a signal that this value should be converted to double-length. [NUMBER] then pushes the value onto the stack as two consecutive *cells* (cell is the Forth term for 16 bits), the high-order cell on top.†

The Forth word [D.] prints a double-length number without any punctuation.

D.	(d ––)	Prints the signed double-length number, followed by one space.	d-dot

In this book, the letter *d* stands for a double-length signed integer. For example, having entered a double-length number, if you were now to execute [D.], the computer would respond:

D._200000_ok

Some Forth systems allow another four punctuation marks to produce the same effect as a period:

, / - :

---

† **For Experts:** Most Forth systems save the position of the decimal point in a variable, for your own use. Consult your system documentation for details. We'll discuss this further in Chapter 10, under "Number Input Conversions."

Also, on some systems that use numeric coprocessors, an "X" suffix, not a decimal point, indicates extended integer precision. For example

123456789X

In such systems, all of the following numbers are converted in exactly the same way:

```
12345.  D._12345_ok
123.45 D._12345_ok
1-2345 D._12345_ok
1/23/45 D._12345_ok
1:23:45 D._12345_ok
```

However,

-12345

is not the same because this value would be converted as a negative, single-length number. (This is the only case in which a hyphen is interpreted as a minus sign and not as punctuation.)

In the next section, we'll show you how to define your own equivalents to $\boxed{\text{D.}}$, which will display whatever punctuation you want along with the number.

NUMBER FORMATTING—DOUBLE-LENGTH UNSIGNED

The numbers:

```
$200.00    12/31/86    372-8493    6:32:59    98.6
```

represent the kinds of output you can create by defining your own "number-formatting words" in Forth. This section will show you how.

The simplest number-formatting definition we could write would be

```
: UD.  ( ud -- )  <# #S #> TYPE ;
```

UD. will print an unsigned double-length number. The words $\boxed{<\#}$ and $\boxed{\#>}$ (respectively pronounced *bracket-number* and *number-bracket*) signify the beginning and the end of the number-conversion process. In this definition, the entire conversion is being performed by the single word $\boxed{\#S}$ (pronounced *numbers*). $\boxed{\#S}$ converts the value on the stack into ASCII characters. It will produce only as many digits as are necessary to represent the number; it will not produce leading zeroes. But it always produces at least one digit, which will be zero if the value was zero. For example,

```
12,345 UD._12345ok
12. UD._12ok
0. UD._0ok
```

The word $\boxed{\text{TYPE}}$ displays the characters that represent the number. Notice that there is no space between the number and the "ok." To get a space, you would simply add the word $\boxed{\text{SPACE}}$, like this:

```
: UD.  ( ud -- )  <# #S #> TYPE SPACE ;
```

Now let's say that we have a phone number on the stack, expressed as a 32-bit unsigned integer. For example, we may have typed in

372-8493

(Remember that the hyphen tells $\boxed{\text{NUMBER}}$ to treat this as a double-length value; your system may require a period.) We want to define a word that will format this value back as a phone number. Let's call it .PHONE# (for "display the phone number") and define it thus:

```
: .PHONE#   ( ud -- )
   <#  # # # #   45 HOLD   #S   #>   TYPE SPACE ;
```

Our definition of .PHONE# has everything that UD. has, and more. The Forth word $\boxed{\#}$ (pronounced *number*) produces a single digit only. A number-formatting definition is reversed from the order in which the number will be printed, so the phrase

```
# # # #
```

produces the right-most four digits of the phone number.

Now it's time to insert the hyphen. Looking up the ASCII value for hyphen in the table in the beginner's section of this chapter, we find that a hyphen is represented by decimal 45. The Forth word $\boxed{\text{HOLD}}$ takes this ASCII code and inserts it into the formatted number character string.

If your system includes the word $\boxed{\text{ASCII}}$, you can replace the mysterious "45 HOLD" in the foregoing definition with the more readable phrase

```
ASCII - HOLD
```

$\boxed{\text{ASCII}}$ (which we introduced in the beginner's section of this chapter) puts on the stack the numeric value of the next character in the input stream, in this case "hyphen."

We now have three digits left. We might use the phrase

```
# # #
```

but it's easier to simply use the word $\boxed{\#S}$, which will automatically convert the rest of the number for us.

The $\boxed{<\#}$ ... $\boxed{\#>}$ sequence is called a *pictured numeric output* phrase because it forms a picture (from right to left) of how you want the number to be formatted.

Now let's format an unsigned double-length number as a date, in the following form:

07/15/86

Here is the definition:

```
: .DATE   ( ud -- )
   <#  # # ASCII / HOLD  # # ASCII / HOLD  # #  #>
   TYPE SPACE ;
```

Let's follow this definition, remembering that it is written in reverse order from the output. The phrase

```
# #  ASCII / HOLD
```

(you can use "47" instead of "ASCII /") produces the right-most two digits (representing the year) and the right-most slash. The next occurrence of the same phrase produces the middle two digits (representing the day) and the left-most slash. Finally, "# #" produces the left-most two digits (representing the month).

We could have just as easily defined

```
: /nn   ( ud -- ud)  # # ASCII / HOLD ;
: .DATE   ( ud -- )  <#  /nn /nn  # #  #> TYPE SPACE ;
```

Since you have control over the conversion process, you can actually convert different digits in different number bases, a feature that is useful in formatting such numbers as hours and minutes. For example, let's say that you have the time in seconds on the stack, and you want a word that will print hh:mm:ss. You might define it this way:

```
: SEXTAL   6 BASE ! ;†
: :00   ( ud -- ud)  #  SEXTAL #  DECIMAL  ASCII : HOLD ;
: .SECONDS     ( ud -- )  <#  :00 :00  #S  #>  TYPE SPACE ;
```

We will use the word :00 to format the seconds and the minutes. Both seconds and minutes are modulo-60, so the right digit can go as high as nine, but the left digit can only go up to five. Thus, in the definition of :00 we convert the first digit (the one on the right) as a decimal number, then go into "sextal" (base 6) and convert the left digit. Finally, we return to decimal and insert the colon character. After :00 converts the seconds and the minutes, #S converts the remaining hours. For example, if we had 4,500 seconds on the stack, we would get

```
4500. .SECONDS 1:15:00 ok
```

(There are 86,400 seconds in a day, too many for a 16-bit number.)

---

† **For Beginners:** See the Handy Hint on page 149.

Table 7-2 summarizes the Forth words that are used in number formatting. The abbreviations are explained in the "key" at the bottom.

TABLE 7-2   Number Formatting

`<#`	Begins the number conversion process. Expects an *unsigned double-length* number on the stack.
`#`	Converts one digit and puts it into an output character string. # *always* produces a digit—if you're out of significant digits, you'll still get a zero for every #.
`#S`	Converts the number until the result is zero. Always produces at *least one digit* (0 if the value is zero).
`c HOLD`	Inserts, at the current position in the character string being formatted, a character whose ASCII value is on the stack.
`n SIGN`	Inserts a minus sign in the output string if *n* (which it consumes) is negative. (See footnote in next section.)
`#>`	Completes number conversion by leaving the character count and address on the stack (these are the appropriate arguments for TYPE).

less-Sharp

sharp

sharp-s

sharp-greater

Stack Effects for Number Formatting

PHRASE	STACK	TYPE OF ARGUMENTS
`<# ... #>`	(d -- a u) or	32-bit unsigned
	(u 0 -- a u)	16-bit unsigned
`<# ...` `n SIGN #>`	(¦d¦ -- a u) or	32-bit signed (where ¦d¦ is the absolute value of *d*, and *n* is the high-order cell of *d*).
	(¦n¦ 0 -- a u)	16-bit signed (where ¦n¦ is the absolute value).

Key

n, n1, ...	16-bit signed numbers	a	address
d, d1, ...	32-bit signed numbers	c	ASCII character
u, u1, ...	16-bit unsigned numbers		value

NUMBER FORMATTING—SIGNED AND SINGLE-LENGTH

So far, we have formatted only unsigned double-length numbers. The $\boxed{<\#}$ ... $\boxed{\#>}$ form expects only unsigned double-length numbers, but we can use it for other types of numbers by making certain arrangements on the stack. For instance, let's look at a simplified version of the system definition of $\boxed{\text{D.}}$ (which prints a *signed* double-length number):

```
: D.  ( d -- )
   DUP >R  DABS  <# #S  R> SIGN  #>  TYPE SPACE ;
```

The word $\boxed{\text{SIGN}}$, which must be situated with the pictured numeric output phrase, inserts a minus sign in the character string only if the top number on the stack is negative. So we'll have to save a copy of the high-order cell (the one with the sign bit) on the return stack for later use.

$\boxed{<\#}$ expects only *unsigned* double-length numbers; therefore, we must take the absolute value of our double-length *signed* number, with the word $\boxed{\text{DABS}}$. We now have the proper arguments for the pictured numeric output phrase.

Next, $\boxed{\#S}$ converts the digits, right to left.

Finally, we return the sign-indicator to the data stack. If it's negative, $\boxed{\text{SIGN}}$ will add a minus sign to the formatted string.†

Since we want our minus sign to appear at the left, we include $\boxed{\text{SIGN}}$ at the right of our $\boxed{<\#}$ ... $\boxed{\#>}$ phrase. In some cases, such as accounting, we may want a negative number to be written

12345-

in which case we would place the word $\boxed{\text{SIGN}}$ at the *left* side of our $\boxed{<\#}$ ... $\boxed{\#>}$ phrase, like this:

```
<#  SIGN #S  #>
```

---

† **For Older Systems:** The word $\boxed{\text{SIGN}}$ has had a confusing history. Originally, it used as its argument the *third* number on the stack. Thus, to define $\boxed{\text{D.}}$ one would write

```
: D.  ( d)
   SWAP OVER DABS  <#  #S SIGN  #>  TYPE SPACE ;
```

The phrase "SWAP OVER" puts a copy of the high-order cell (the one with the sign bit) at the bottom of the stack. By making $\boxed{\text{SIGN}}$ do the $\boxed{\text{ROT}}$ internally, the idea was to unclutter the pictured numeric output phrase.

You'll find this convention used in fig-Forth, in pre-83 Standard polyFORTH, and in old "Starting Forth" systems. But '79 and '83 Standard systems, as well as MVP and MMS Forths, use the "n-on-top" convention, which is more consistent with normal stack usage. So we'll join the crowd.

If you have the old version, define:

```
: SIGN  ( n)  0< IF  ASCII - HOLD  THEN ;
```

Let's define a word that will print a signed double-length number with a decimal point and two decimal places to the right of the decimal. Since this is the form most often used for writing dollars and cents, let's call it .$ and define it like this:

```
: .$   ( d -- )
   DUP >R   DABS   <#  # #   ASCII . HOLD   #S
   R> SIGN   ASCII $ HOLD   #> TYPE SPACE ;
```

Let's try it:

```
2000.00 .$ $2000.00
```

or even

```
2,000.00 .$ $2000.00
```

We recommend that you save .$, since we'll be using it in some future examples.

You can also write special formats for single-length numbers. For example, if you want to use an unsigned single-length number, simply put a zero on the stack before the word $<\#$. This effectively changes the single-length number into a double-length number which is so small that it has nothing (zero) in the high-order cell.

To format a *signed* single-length number, again you must supply a zero as a high-order cell. But you also must save a copy of the signed number for SIGN, and you must leave the absolute value of the number in the second stack position:

```
( n -- )   DUP >R   ABS 0   <#   #S   R> SIGN   #>
```

The following "set-up" phrases are needed to print various kinds of numbers:

NUMBER TO BE PRINTED	PRECEDE $<\#$ by
32-bit number, unsigned	(nothing needed)
31-bit number and sign bit	DUP >R DABS (to save the sign on the return stack, for removal just before SIGN)
16-bit number, unsigned	0 (to give a dummy high-order part)
15-bit number and sign bit	DUP >R ABS 0 (to save the sign)

DOUBLE-LENGTH OPERATORS

Here is a list of double-length math operators. Not all Forths support all these words. Some systems provide these double-length routines as electives; you must first load them.

D+	(d1 d2 -- d-sum)	Adds two 32-bit numbers.	d-plus
D-	(d1 d2 -- d-diff)	Subtracts two 32-bit numbers (*d1 – d2*).	d-minus
DNEGATE	(d -- -d)	Changes the sign of a 32-bit number.	d-negate
DABS	(d -- ¦d¦)	Returns the absolute value of a 32-bit number.	d-absolute
DMAX	(d1 d2 -- d-max)	Returns the maximum of two 32-bit numbers.	d-max
DMIN	(d1 d2 -- d-min)	Returns the minimum of two 32-bit numbers.	d-min
D=	(d1 d2 -- ?)	Returns true if *d1* and *d2* are equal.	d-equal
D0=	(d -- ?)	Returns true if *d* is zero.	d-zero-equal
D<	(d1 d2 -- ?)	Returns true if *d1* is less than *d2*.	d-less
DU<	(ud1 ud2 -- ?)	Returns true if *ud1* is less than *ud2*. Both numbers are unsigned.	d-u-less
D.R	(d width --)	Displays the signed 32-bit number, right-justified within the field width.	d-dot-r

The initial "D" signifies that these operators may be used only for double-length operations, whereas the initial "2," as in 2SWAP and 2DUP, signifies that these operators may be used either for double-length numbers or for pairs of single-length numbers.

Here's an example using ⟨D+⟩ :

```
200000. 300000. D+ D. 500000 ok
```

MIXED-LENGTH OPERATORS

The following table lists Forth words that operate on useful combinations of single- and double-length numbers.

UM*	(u1 u2 -- ud)	Multiplies two 16-bit numbers. Returns a 32-bit result. All values are unsigned. (Formerly called U*.)	*u-m-star*
UM/MOD	(ud u1 -- u2 u3)	Divides a 32-bit by a 16-bit number. Returns a 16-bit remainder and quotient (quotient on top). Quotient is floored.† All values are unsigned. (Formerly called U/MOD.)	*u-m-slash-mod*
M*	(n1 n2 -- d-prod)	Multiplies two 16-bit numbers. Returns a 32-bit result. All values are signed.	*m-star*
M+	(d n -- d-sum)	Adds a 32-bit number to a 16-bit number. Returns a 32-bit result.	*m-plus*
M/	(d n -- n-quot)	Divides a 32-bit number by a 16-bit number. Returns a 16-bit result. All values are signed.	*m-slash*
M*/	(d n u -- d)	Multiplies a 32-bit number by a 16-bit number and divides the triple-length result by a 16-bit number ($d*n/u$). Returns a 32-bit result.	*m-star-slash*

⟨UM*⟩ is a fast form of multiplication that allows full precision in the double-length result, and can be used in defining all other multiplications. Similarly, all division operators can be defined in terms of ⟨UM/MOD⟩.

Here's an example using ⟨M+⟩ :

```
200,000 7 M+ D. 200007 ok
```

Or, using ⟨M*/⟩, we can redefine our earlier version of % so that it will accept a double-length argument:

```
: % ( d n% -- d)  100 M*/ ;
```

† See footnote under "The Division Operators" in Chapter 2.

as in

```
200.50 15 % D._3007_ok
```

If you have loaded the definition of .$ (which we gave a few pages back), you can enter

```
200.50 15 % .$_$30.07
```

We can redefine our earlier definition of R% to get a rounded double-length result, like this:

```
: R% ( d n% -- d)  10 M*/  5 M+  1 10 M*/ ;
```

then

```
200.50 15 R% .$_$30.08
```

Notice that M*/ is the only ready-made Forth word which performs multiplication on a double-length argument. To multiply 200,000 by 3, for instance, we must supply a "1" as a dummy denominator:

```
200,000 3 1 M*/ D._600000_ok
```

since

$$\frac{3}{1}$$

is the same as 3.

M*/ is also the only ready-made Forth word that performs division with a double-length result. So to divide 200,000 by 4, for instance, we must supply a "1" as a dummy numerator:

```
200,000 1 4 M*/ D._50000_ok
```

NUMBERS IN DEFINITIONS

When a definition contains a number, such as

```
: SCORE-MORE ( n -- n+20)  20 + ;
```

the number is compiled into the dictionary in binary form, just as it looks on the stack.

The number's binary value depends on the number base at the time you *compile* the definition. For example, if you were to enter

```
HEX    : SCORE-MORE   ( n -- n+20)   14 + ;   DECIMAL
```

the dictionary definition would contain the hex value 14, which is the same as the decimal value 20 (16 + 4). Henceforth, SCORE-MORE will always add the equivalent of decimal 20 to the value on the stack, regardless of the current number base.

If, on the other hand, you were to put the word $\boxed{\text{HEX}}$ *inside* the definition, you would change the number base when you *execute* the definition. For example, if you were to define

```
DECIMAL
: EXAMPLE   HEX 20 .   DECIMAL ;
```

the number would be compiled as the binary equivalent of decimal 20, since $\boxed{\text{DECIMAL}}$ was current at compile time.

At run time, here's what happens:

```
EXAMPLE_14_ok
```

The number is output in hexadecimal.

For the record, a number that appears inside a definition is called a *literal*. (Unlike the words in the rest of the definition which allude to other definitions, a number must be taken literally.)

The following table lists the Forth words that were covered in this chapter:

ASCII	(-- c)	Translates the next character in the input stream into its ASCII equivalent, leaving the value on the stack.
Unsigned Operators		
U.	(u --)	Prints the unsigned single-length number, followed by one space.
U.R	(u width --)	Displays the unsigned number, right-justified within the field width.
U<	(u1 u2 -- ?)	Leaves true if $u1 < u2$, where both are treated as single-length unsigned integers.
Number Bases		
HEX	(--)	Sets the base to sixteen.
OCTAL	(--)	Sets the base to eight (available on some systems).
DECIMAL	(--)	Returns the base to ten.
Number Formatting Operators		
<#		Begins the number conversion process. Expects an *unsigned double-length* number on the stack.
#		Converts one digit and puts it into an output character string. # *always* produces a digit—if you're out of significant digits, you'll still get a zero for every #.
#S		Converts the number until the result is zero. Always produces *at least one digit* (0 if the value is zero).
c HOLD		Inserts, at the current position in the character string being formatted, a character whose ASCII value is on the stack. HOLD (or a word that uses HOLD) must be used between <# and #>.
n SIGN		Inserts a minus sign in the output string if *n* (which it consumes) is negative. (See footnote in the section "Number Formatting—Signed and Single-length.")
#>		Completes number conversion by leaving the character count and address on the stack (these are the appropriate arguments for TYPE).

Stack Effects for Number Formatting

PHRASE	STACK	TYPE OF ARGUMENTS
`<# ... #>`	`( d -- a u)` or	32-bit unsigned
	`( u 0 -- a u)`	16-bit unsigned
`<# ...` `  n SIGN #>`	`( !d! -- a u)` or	32-bit signed (where |d| is the absolute value of d, and n is the high-order cell of d).
	`( !n! 0 -- a u)`	6-bit signed (where |n| is the absolute value).

Double-Length Operators

D+	`( d1 d2 -- d-sum)`	Adds two 32-bit numbers
D-	`( d1 d2 -- d-diff)`	Subtracts two 32-bit numbers (d1 − d2).
DNEGATE	`( d -- -d)`	Changes the sign of a 32-bit number.
DABS	`( d -- !d!)`	Returns the absolute value of a 32-bit number.
DMAX	`( d1 d2 -- d-max)`	Returns the maximum of two 32-bit numbers.
DMIN	`( d1 d2 -- d-min)`	Returns the minimum of two 32-bit numbers.
D=	`( d1 d2 -- ?)`	Returns true if d1 and d2 are equal.
D0=	`( d -- ?)`	Returns true if d is zero.
D<	`( d1 d2 -- ?)`	Returns true if d1 is less than d2.
DU<	`( ud1 ud2 -- ?)`	Returns true if ud1 is less than ud2. Both numbers are unsigned.
D.	`( d -- )`	Prints the signed 32-bit number, followed by one space.
D.R	`( d width -- )`	Prints the signed 32-bit number, right-justified within the field width.

Mixed-Length Operators

UM*	(u1 u2 -- ud)	Multiplies two 16-bit numbers. Returns a 32-bit result. All values are unsigned. (Formerly called U*.)
UM/MOD	(ud u1 -- u2 u3)	Divides a 32-bit by a 16-bit number. Returns a 16-bit remainder and quotient (quotient on top). Quotient is floored. All values are unsigned. (Formerly called U/MOD.)
M*	(n1 n2 -- d-prod)	Multiplies two 16-bit numbers. Returns a 32-bit result. All values are signed.
M+	(d n -- d-sum)	Adds a 32-bit number to a 16-bit number. Returns a 32-bit result.
M/	(d n -- n-quot)	Divides a 32-bit number by a 16-bit number. Returns a 16-bit result. All values are signed.
M*/	(d n u -- d)	Multiplies a 32-bit number by a 16-bit number and divides the triple-length result by a 16-bit number ($d \times n/u$). Returns a 32-bit result.

Key

n, n1, ...	16-bit signed numbers	b	8-bit byte
d, d1, ...	32-bit signed numbers	?	Boolean flag
u, u1, ...	16-bit unsigned numbers	c	ASCII character value
ud, ud1, ...	32-bit unsigned numbers	a	address

REVIEW OF TERMS

Arithmetic left and right shift	the process of shifting all bits in a number, except the sign bit, to the left or right, in effect doubling or halving the number, respectively, while maintaining the correct sign.
ASCII	a standardized system of representing input/output characters as byte values. Acronym for American Standard Code for Information Interchange. (Pronounced *ask-key*.)
Binary	number base 2.
Byte	the standard term for an 8-bit value.
Cell	the Forth term for a 16-bit value.
Decimal	number base 10.
Hexadecimal	number base 16.
Literal	in general, a number or symbol which represents only itself; in Forth, a number that appears inside a definition.
Mask	a value that can be "superimposed" over another, hiding certain bits and revealing only those bits that we are interested in.
Number formatting	the process of converting a binary number to displayable characters, usually in a special form such as 3/13/85 or $47.93.
Octal	number base 8.
Sign bit	the bit that, for a signed number, indicates whether it is positive or negative and, for an unsigned number, represents the bit of the highest magnitude (*most significant bit*).
Two's complement	for any number, the number of equal absolute value but opposite sign. To calculate $10 - 4$, the computer first produces the two's complement of 4 (i.e., -4), then computes $10 + (-4)$.
Unsigned number	a number that is assumed to be positive.
Unsigned single-length number	an integer which falls within the range 0 to 65535.
Word	in Forth, a defined dictionary entry; elsewhere, a term for a 16-bit value.

PROBLEMS

FOR BEGINNERS

7-1. Veronica Wainwright couldn't remember the upper limit for a signed single-length number, and she had no book to refer to, only a Forth system. So she wrote a definition called N-MAX, using a $\boxed{\text{BEGIN}}\ \boxed{\text{UNTIL}}$ loop. When she executed it, she got

    32767_ok

What might have been her definition?

7-2. (This problem gives practice in bit-manipulation).

Before beginning, define the word BINARY if you don't already have it.

(a) Bit-positions within a 16-bit cell are usually numbered from 0 on the right (the "least significant bit"—LSB) to 15 on the left (the "sign bit" or "most significant bit"—MSB). Define a word called BIT which converts such a number (from 0 to 15) into a mask corresponding to that bit; for example, 0 BIT produces 1, 1 BIT produces 2, 2 BIT produces 4, and so on. (Hint: A $\boxed{\text{DO}}$ loop is easiest.)

(b) Suppose you have a value on the stack that represents an array of 16 bits (call it "bits1"). Define a word called SET-BIT which turns on (sets to "1") a specified bit in "bits1". The stack effect will be (bits1 bit# — bits2). For instance, if you have the bit pattern 1000 (in binary) on the stack, and you execute 1 SET-BIT (in decimal), you'll get binary 1010.

(c) Next, define CLEAR-BIT, which turns off the specified bit. The stack arguments are the same as in SET-BIT. For example,

    BINARY 111111111

    DECIMAL 5 CLEAR-BIT 7 CLEAR-BIT
    BINARY U._101011111

(d) Define GET-BIT, which puts on the stack the single bit specified (masked out from "bits"), suitable as an argument to IF (i.e., any bit "on" means "true", no bits "on" means "false"). The stack comment will be (bits bit# — bit). For example,

    BINARY 1001 DECIMAL
    DUP 0 GET-BIT ._1_ok
    DUP 1 GET-BIT ._0_ok
    3 GET-BIT ._8_ok

(e) Define TOGGLE-BIT with the same stack effect as SET-BIT and CLEAR-BIT, but have it toggle the bit (turn it on if it's off and vice versa).

(f) Given an old copy of a bit mask and a second copy with some bits changed, define a word called CHANGED that produces a bit-mask showing which bits have changed.

7-3. Write a definition that "rings" your display's bell three times. Make sure that there is enough of a delay between the bells so that they are distinguishable. Each time the bell rings, the word "BEEP" should appear on the terminal screen.

(Problems 7-4 and 7-5 are practice in double-length math.)

7-4. (a) Rewrite the temperature conversion definitions that you created for the problems in Chapter 5. This time assume that the input and resulting temperatures are to be double-length signed integers that are scaled (i.e., multiplied) by ten. For example, if 10.5 degrees is entered, it is a 32-bit integer with a value of 105.

(b) Write a formatted output word named .DEG that will display a 32-bit signed integer scaled by ten as a string of digits, a decimal point, and one decimal digit. For example:

```
12.3 .DEG RETURN 12.3 ok
```

(c) Solve the following conversions:

0.0°F in Centigrade

212.0°F in Centrigrade

20.5°F in Centigrade

16.0°C in Fahrenheit

−40.0°C in Fahrenheit

100.0°K in Centigrade

100.0°K in Fahrenheit

233.0°K in Centigrade

233.0°K in Fahrenheit

7-5. (a) Write a routine that evaluates the quadratic equation

$$7x^2 + 20x + 5$$

given x, and returns a double-length result.

(b) How large an x will work without overflowing thirty-two bits as a signed number?

FOR EVERYONE

7-6. A new user experimenting with HEX numbers attempted to change back to decimal by typing DEC. Although Forth responded "ok," it seemed to remain in hex. What happened?

7-7. Write a word that prints the numbers 0 through 16 (decimal) in decimal, hexadecimal, and binary form in three columns. For example,

```
DECIMAL  0    HEX  0    BINARY      0
DECIMAL  1    HEX  1    BINARY      1
DECIMAL  2    HEX  2    BINARY     10
          . . .
DECIMAL 16    HEX 10    BINARY  10000
```

7-8. Enter 3.7 and execute ⌞.⌟ (dot) twice. Explain why you get what you get. Enter 65536. and execute dot twice; explain the significance. Try 65538. (with the decimal point).

7-9. If you enter

.. RETURN

(two periods *not* separated by a space) and the system responds ''ok,'' what does this tell you?

7-10. Write a definition for a phone-number formatting word that will also print the area code with a slash *if and only if* the number includes an area code. For example,

```
555-1234 .PH# 555-1234 ok
213/372-8493 .PH# 213/372-8493 ok
```

(Depending on your system, you may have to *enter* the numbers using decimal points in the place of the hyphen and slash.)

8

VARIABLES, CONSTANTS, AND ARRAYS

As we have seen throughout the previous seven chapters, Forth programmers use the stack to pass arguments from one word to another. When programmers need to store numbers more permanently, they use variables and constants.

In this chapter, we'll learn how Forth treats variables and constants, and in the process we'll see how to directly access locations in memory.

VARIABLES

Let's start with an example of a situation in which you'd want to use a variable—to store the day's date.† First we'll create a variable called DATE. We do this by saying

    VARIABLE DATE ‡

If today is the twelfth, we now say

    12 DATE !

---

† **For Beginners:** Suppose your computer generates bank statements all day, and every statement must show the date. You don't want to keep the date on the stack all the time, and you don't want the date to be part of a definition that you'd have to redefine every day. You want to use a variable.

‡ **For fig-Forth Systems:** To make your version of $\boxed{\text{VARIABLE}}$ compatible with the one described here, define

    : VARIABLE   0 VARIABLE ;

that is, we put a twelve on the stack, then give the name of the variable, then finally execute the word [!], which is pronounced *store*. This phrase stores the number twelve into the variable DATE.

Conversely, we can say

```
DATE @
```

that is, we can name the variable, then execute the word [@], which is pronounced *fetch*. This phrase fetches the twelve and puts it on the stack. Thus the phrase

```
DATE @ . 12 ok
```

prints the date.

To make matters even easier, there is a Forth word whose definition is this:

```
: ?   @ . ;
```

So instead of "DATE-fetch-dot," we could simply type

```
DATE ? 12 ok
```

The value of DATE will be twelve until we change it. To change it, we simply store a new number:

```
13 DATE ! ok
DATE ? 13 ok
```

Conceivably, we could define additional variables for the month and year:

```
VARIABLE DATE   VARIABLE MONTH   VARIABLE YEAR
```

then define a word called !DATE (for "store-the-date") like this:

```
: !DATE   ( month day year -- )   YEAR !  DATE !  MONTH ! ;
```

to be used like this:

```
7 31 86 !DATE ok
```

then define a word called .DATE (for "print-the-date") like this:

```
: .DATE   MONTH ?  DATE ?  YEAR ? ;
```

Your Forth system already has a number of variables defined; one is called [BASE]. [BASE] contains the number base that you're currently working in. In fact, the definitions of [HEX] and [DECIMAL] (and [OCTAL], if your system has it) are simply

```
: DECIMAL   10 BASE ! ;
: HEX   16 BASE ! ;
: OCTAL    8 BASE ! ;
```

You can work in any number base by simply storing it into $\boxed{\text{BASE}}$.†

Somewhere in the definitions of the system words that perform input and output number conversions, you will find the phrase

> BASE @

because the current value of $\boxed{\text{BASE}}$ is used in the conversion process. Thus, a single routine can convert numbers in *any* base. This leads us to make a formal statement about the use of variables: In Forth, variables are appropriate for any value that is used inside a definition which may need to change at any time after the definition has already been compiled.

A CLOSER LOOK AT VARIABLES

When you create a variable such as DATE by using the phrase

> VARIABLE DATE

you are really compiling a new word, called DATE, into the dictionary. A simplified view would look like this:

```
|----------------------------|‡
|            DATE            |
|----------------------------|
|      instruction code      |
|       appropriate for      |
|          variables         |
|----------------------------|
|       space for the        |
|       actual value         |
|       to be stored         |
|----------------------------|
```

DATE is like any other word in your dictionary except that you defined it with the word $\boxed{\text{VARIABLE}}$ instead of the word $\boxed{:}$. As a result, you didn't have to define what your definition would *do*; the word $\boxed{\text{VARIABLE}}$ itself spells out what is supposed to happen. And here *is* what happens:

When you say

> 12 DATE !

---

† **For Experts:** A three-letter code such as an airport terminal name, can be stored as a single-length unsigned number in base 36. For example:

```
: ALPHA    36 BASE ! ;
ALPHA_ok
ZAP U._ZAP_ok
```

‡ **For Experts:** In the next chapter, we'll show you what a dictionary entry really looks like in memory.

Twelve goes onto the stack,

then the text interpreter looks up DATE in the dictionary,

and, finding it, points it out to EXECUTE .

EXECUTE executes a variable by copying the address of the variable's "empty" cell (where the value will go) onto the stack.†

The word ! takes the address (on top) and the value (underneath), and stores the value into that location. Whatever number used to be at that address is replaced by the new number.

† **For Beginners:**   In computer terminology, an address is a number that identifies a location in computer memory. For example, at address 2076 (addresses are usually expressed as hexadecimal, unsigned numbers), we can have a 16-bit representation of the value 12. Here 2076 is the "address"; 12 is the "contents."

(To remember the order in which the arguments belong, think of setting down your parcel, then sticking the address label on top.)

The word @ expects one argument only: an address, which in this case is supplied by the name of the variable, as in

DATE @

Using the value on the stack as an address, the word @ pushes the contents of that location onto the stack, consuming the address. (The contents of the location remain intact.)

USING A VARIABLE AS A COUNTER

In Forth, a variable is ideal for keeping a count of something. To reuse our egg-packer example, we might keep track of how many eggs go down the conveyor belt in a single day. (This example will work at your display, so enter it as we go.)

First, we can define

VARIABLE EGGS

to keep the count in. To start with a clean slate every morning, we would store a zero into EGGS by executing a word whose definition looks like this:

: RESET   0 EGGS ! ;

Then somewhere in our egg-packing application, we would define a word which executes the following phrase every time an egg passes an electric eye on the conveyor:

```
1 EGGS +!
```

The word $\boxed{+!}$ adds the given value to the contents of the given address.† (It doesn't bother to tell you what the contents are.) Thus the phrase

```
1 EGGS +!
```

increments the count of eggs by one. To illustrate, let's put this phrase inside a definition, like this:

```
: EGG    1 EGGS +! ;
```

At the end of the day, we would say

```
EGGS ?
```

to find out how many eggs went by since morning.
   Let's try it:

```
RESET_ok
EGG_ok
EGG_ok
EGG_ok
EGGS ?_3_ok
```

---

† **For the Curious:** $\boxed{+!}$ is usually defined in assembly language, but an equivalent high-level definition is

```
: +! ( increment a -- )  DUP @  ROT +  SWAP ! ;
```

Here's a review of the words we've covered in the chapter so far:

VARIABLE xxx	(--)	Creates a variable named *xxx*;	variable
	xxx: (-- a)	the word *xxx* returns its address when executed.	
!	(n a --)	Stores a single-length number into the address.	store
@	(a -- n)	Replaces the address with its contents.	fetch
?	(a --)	Prints the contents of the address, followed by one space.	question
+!	(n a --)	Adds a single-length number to the contents of the address.	plus-store

CONSTANTS

While variables are normally used for values that may change, constants are used for values that *won't* change. In Forth, we create a constant and set its value at the same time, like this:

LIMIT
instruction code appropriate for constants
220

    220 CONSTANT LIMIT

Here, we have defined a constant named LIMIT, and given it the value 220. Now we can use the word LIMIT in place of the value, like this:

    : ?TOO-HOT (temperature --)
      LIMIT > IF ." Danger -- Reduce Heat! " THEN ;

If the number on the stack is greater than 220, the warning message will be printed.

Notice that when we say

    LIMIT

we get the *value*, not the address. We don't need the "fetch."

This is an important difference between variables and constants.† The reason for the difference is that with variables, we need the address to have the option of fetching or storing. With constants, we always want the value; we never store.

One use for constants is to name a hardware address. For example, a microprocessor-controlled camera application might contain this definition:

```
: PHOTOGRAPH    SHUTTER OPEN   TIME EXPOSE   SHUTTER CLOSE ;
```

Here the word SHUTTER has been defined as a constant so that it returns the hardware address of the camera's shutter. It might, for example, be defined:

```
HEX
3E27 CONSTANT SHUTTER
DECIMAL
```

The words OPEN and CLOSE might be defined simply as

```
: OPEN  ( a -- )  1 SWAP ! ;
: CLOSE ( a -- )  0 SWAP ! ;
```

so that the phrase

```
SHUTTER OPEN
```

writes a "1" to the shutter address, causing the shutter to open.

Using constants in definitions instead of "hard-coded" numbers is an important element of good style. For one thing, using constants makes your code more readable. All Forth definitions should be as self-documenting as the one of PHOTOGRAPH.

Even more importantly, the value may change (because, for instance, the hardware might get changed). If you can make the correction in one place only—the definition of the constant—you won't have to worry about changing it everywhere and probably missing an instance.

A third benefit is that, in the compiled form of a definition, reference to a constant requires less memory space than reference to a number literal. If a number is used several times, the savings will outweigh the expenditure of defining the constant. For this reason, many Forth systems define these often-used numbers as constants:

```
0 CONSTANT 0
1 CONSTANT 1
etc.
```

In the rest of this book, we'll assume that your system contains these definitions

---

† **For People Who Intend to Use polyFORTH's Target Compiler℗:** In your case, the difference is more profound. A constant's *value* will be compiled into PROM; a variable compiles into PROM a reference to a location in RAM.

of FALSE and TRUE :

```
Ø CONSTANT FALSE
-1 CONSTANT TRUE
```

CONSTANT xxx	(n --) xxx: (-- n)	Creates a constant named *xxx* with the value *n*; the word *xxx* returns *n* when executed.
FALSE	(-- f)	Returns logical false (0).
TRUE	(-- t)	Returns logical true (−1).

DOUBLE-LENGTH VARIABLES AND CONSTANTS

You can define a double-length variable by using the word 2VARIABLE . For example,

```
2VARIABLE DATE
```

Now you can use the Forth words 2! (pronounced *two-store*) and 2@ (*two-fetch*) to access this double-length variable. You can store a double-length number into it by simply saying

```
800000. DATE 2!
```

and fetch it back with

```
DATE 2@ D._800000_ok
```

Or you can store the full month/date/year into it, like this:

```
7/16/86 DATE 2!
```

and fetch it back with

```
DATE 2@ .DATE_07/16/86_ok
```

assuming that you've loaded the version of .DATE we gave in the last chapter.

You can define a double-length constant by using the Forth word 2CONSTANT , like this:

```
200000. 2CONSTANT APPLES
```

Now the word APPLES will place the double-length number on the stack.

```
APPLES D._200000_ok
```

As the prefix "2" reminds us, we can also use 2CONSTANT to define a *pair* of single-length numbers. The reason for putting two numbers under the same name is a matter of convenience and of saving space in the dictionary.

As an example, recall (from Chapter 5) that we can use the phrase

        355 113 */

to multiply a number by an approximation of *pi*. We could store these two integers as a 2CONSTANT as follows:

        355 113 2CONSTANT PI

then simply use the phrase

        PI */

as in

        10000 PI */ . _31415_ok

Let's review the double-length data-structure words:

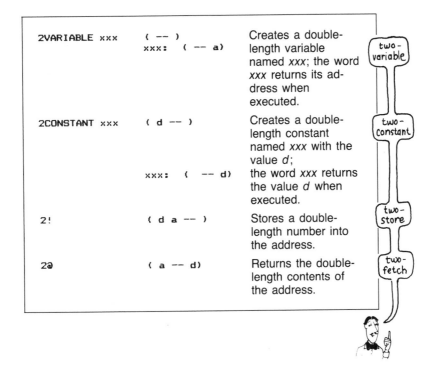

2VARIABLE xxx	(--) xxx: (-- a)	Creates a double-length variable named *xxx*; the word *xxx* returns its address when executed.
2CONSTANT xxx	(d --) xxx: (-- d)	Creates a double-length constant named *xxx* with the value *d*; the word *xxx* returns the value *d* when executed.
2!	(d a --)	Stores a double-length number into the address.
2@	(a -- d)	Returns the double-length contents of the address.

ARRAYS

As you know, the phrase

        VARIABLE DATE

creates a definition and leaves room for one single-length value:

DATE
code
room for a single-length value

What if we want to leave room for ten or twenty single-length values, under the same name? Such a structure is called an *array*; here's how we build it in Forth:

First, we define the array using a different defining word, CREATE†, like this:

```
CREATE MY-ARRAY
```

Like VARIABLE, CREATE compiles a new name (whatever you call your array) into the dictionary, along with some code that specifies what this name will do. But it does *not* leave any room for data.

MY-ARRAY
code

How then do you make room for the array? With the word ALLOT, which takes as its argument the number of *bytes* to reserve for the array.

---

† **For fig-Forth Users:** Your system has a word called CREATE that is different and rarely needed. To follow this discussion, redefine it as:

```
: CREATE   <BUILDS DOES> ;
```

If we need room for 10 single-length values, we say

`20 ALLOT`

(A single-length value fills two bytes.)

MY-ARRAY
code
value
value
value
value
value
value
value
value
value
value

room for ten
single-length values

When you execute a word defined as a variable, Forth pushes the address of the data onto the stack. In the same way, when you execute a word defined by CREATE , Forth pushes the address of the beginning of the array (where the first value is) onto the stack.

To illustrate the use of an array, let's say that in our laboratory we have not just one, but *five* burners that heat various kinds of liquids.

We can make our word ?TOO-HOT check that all five burners have not exceeded their individual limit if we define LIMIT using an array rather than a constant.

Let's give the array the name LIMITS, like this:

```
CREATE LIMITS  10 ALLOT
```

LIMITS	addresses
code	↓
room for burner-0's limit	3162
room for burner-1's limit	3164
room for burner-2's limit	3166
room for burner-3's limit	3168
room for burner-4's limit	316A

Suppose we want the limit for burner 0 to be 220. We can store this value by simply saying

```
220 LIMITS !
```

because LIMITS returns the address of the first cell in the array. Suppose we want the limit for burner 1 to be 340. We can store this value by adding 2 bytes to the address of the original cell, like this:

```
340 LIMITS 2+ !
```

We can store limits for burners 2, 3, and 4 by adding the *offsets* 4, 6, and 8, respectively, to the original address. Since the offset is always double the burner number, we can define the convenient word

```
: LIMIT  ( burner# -- adr-of-limit)  2* LIMITS + ;
```

to take a burner number on the stack and compute an address that reflects the appropriate offset.†

This technique increases the usefulness of the word LIMIT, so that we can redefine ?TOO-HOT as:

```
: ?TOO-HOT  ( temperature burner# -- )
   LIMIT @ >  IF ." Danger -- Reduce heat! " THEN ;
```

which works like this:

```
210 0 ?TOO-HOT_ok
230 0 ?TOO-HOT_Danger_--_Reduce_heat!_ok
300 1 ?TOO-HOT_ok
350 1 ?TOO-HOT_Danger_--_Reduce_heat!_ok
```

etc.

CREATE xxx	(--) xxx: (-- a)	Creates a dictionary header named *xxx*; the word *xxx* returns its address when executed.
ALLOT	(n --)	Reserves *n* additional bytes for the parameter field of the most recently defined word.

ANOTHER EXAMPLE—USING AN ARRAY FOR COUNTING

Meanwhile, back at the egg ranch:

Here's another example of an array. In this example, each element of the array is used as a separate counter. Thus we can keep track of how many cartons of "extra large" eggs the machine has packed, how many "large," and so forth.

† **For Beginners:** (a) In this case the burner number is called an *index* into the array. The index is a relative pointer to a logical element. When we multiply the index by 2, we get an *offset* into the array. The offset is the actual number of bytes between the beginning of the array and the element we want. (b) The reason we number our burners 0 through 4 instead of 1 through 5 is so that we can use the burner number itself as the index. What most people would call the "first" in a series, programmers think of as the "zeroth." If the users insist that your program number the burners 1 through 5, that's okay. Add the conversion (a simple 1 −) to the definitions of the highest-level words in the application, the ones the users use.

Recall from our previous definition of EGGSIZE (in Chapter 4) that we used four categories of acceptable eggs, plus two categories of "bad eggs."

```
0 REJECT
1 SMALL
2 MEDIUM
3 LARGE
4 EXTRA LARGE
5 ERROR
```

So let's create an array that is six cells long:

```
CREATE COUNTS   12 ALLOT
```

The counts will be incremented using the word $\boxed{+!}$, so we must be able to set all the elements in the array to zero before we begin counting. The phrase

```
COUNTS 12 0 FILL
```

will fill twelve bytes, starting at the address of COUNTS, with zeros. If your Forth system includes the word $\boxed{\text{ERASE}}$ it's better to use it in this situation. $\boxed{\text{ERASE}}$ fills the given number of bytes with zeroes. Use it like this:

```
COUNTS 12 ERASE
```

FILL	(a u b --)	Fills *u* bytes of memory, beginning at the address, with value *b*.
ERASE	(a u --)	Fills *u* bytes of memory, beginning at the address, with zeroes.

For convenience, we can put the phrase inside a definition, like this:

```
: RESET   COUNTS   12 ERASE ;
```

Now let's define a word that will give us the address of one of the counters, depending on the category number it is given (0 through 5), like this:

```
: COUNTER  ( category# -- a)   2*   COUNTS + ;
```

and another word that will add one to the counter whose number is given, like this:

```
: TALLY   ( category# -- )   COUNTER   1 SWAP +! ;
```

The "1" serves as the increment for $\boxed{+!}$, and $\boxed{\text{SWAP}}$ puts the arguments for $\boxed{+!}$ in the order they belong, i.e., (n adr --).

Now, for instance, the phrase

```
3 TALLY
```

will increment the counter that corresponds to large eggs.

Now let's define a word that converts the weight per dozen into a category number:

```
: CATEGORY   ( weight-per-dozen -- category#)†
    DUP 18 < IF   0   ELSE
    DUP 21 < IF   1   ELSE
    DUP 24 < IF   2   ELSE
    DUP 27 < IF   3   ELSE
    DUP 30 < IF   4   ELSE
                  5
    THEN THEN THEN THEN THEN   SWAP DROP ;
```

(By the time we get to the phrase "SWAP DROP," we will have two values on the stack: the weight that we have been $\boxed{\text{DUP}}$ing and the category number, which will be on top. We want only the category number; "SWAP DROP" eliminates the weight.)

For instance, the phrase

```
25 CATEGORY
```

will leave the number 3 on the stack. The foregoing definition of CATEGORY resembles our old definition of EGGSIZE, but, in the true Forth style of keeping words as short as possible, we have removed the output messages from the definition. Instead, we'll define an additional word that expects a category number and prints an output message, like this:

```
: LABEL   ( category# -- )‡
    DUP   0= IF   ." Reject "           ELSE
    DUP   1 = IF  ." Small "            ELSE
    DUP   2 = IF  ." Medium "           ELSE
    DUP   3 = IF  ." Large "            ELSE
    DUP   4 = IF  ." Extra Large "      ELSE
                  ." Error "
    THEN THEN THEN THEN THEN   DROP ;
```

for example,

```
1 LABEL_Small_ok
```

Now we can define EGGSIZE using three of our own words:

```
: EGGSIZE   ( weight-per-dozen -- )
    CATEGORY  DUP LABEL   TALLY ;
```

---

† **For Experts:** We'll see a simpler definition at the end of this chapter.

‡ **For Experts:** We'll see a more elegant version of this definition in Chapter 10.

Thus, the phrase

```
23 EGGSIZE
```

will display

```
Medium ok
```

and update the counter for medium eggs.

How will we read the counters at the end of the day? We could check each cell in the array separately with a phrase such as

```
3 COUNTER ?
```

(which would tell us how many "large" cartons were packed). But let's get a little fancier and define our own word to print a table of the day's results in this format:

Quantity	Size
1	Reject
112	Small
132	Medium
143	Large
159	Extra Large
0	Ostrich

Since we have already devised category numbers, we can simply use a |DO| loop and index on the category number, like this:

```
: REPORT    PAGE  ." Quantity    Size"  CR CR
    6 0 DO  I COUNTER @  5 U.R
    7 SPACES  I LABEL  CR   LOOP ;
```

(The phrase

```
I COUNTER @  5 U.R
```

takes the category number given by |I|, indexes into the array, and prints the contents of the proper element in a five-column field.)

FACTORING DEFINITIONS

This is a good time to talk about factoring as it applies to Forth definitions. We've just seen an example in which factoring simplified our problem.

Our first definition of EGGSIZE, from Chapter 4, categorized eggs by weight and printed the name of the categories. In our present version, we factored out the "categorizing" and the "printing" into two separate words. We can use the word CATEGORY to provide the argument either for the printing word or the counter-tallying word (or both). And we can use the printing word, LABEL, in both EGGSIZE and REPORT.

As Charles Moore, the inventor of Forth, has written:

A good Forth vocabulary contains a large number of small words. It is not enough to break a problem into small pieces. The object is to isolate words that can be reused.

For example, in the recipe

Get can of tomato sauce.
Open can of tomato sauce.
Pour tomato sauce into pan.
Get can of mushrooms.
Open can of mushrooms.
Pour mushrooms into pan.

you can *factor out* the getting, opening, and pouring, since they are common to both cans. Then you can give the factored-out process a name and simply write:

```
TOMATOES ADD
MUSHROOMS ADD
```

and any chef who's graduated from the Postfix School of Cookery will know exactly what you mean.

Not only does factoring make a program easier to write and maintain, it saves memory space, too. A reusable word such as ADD gets defined only once. The more complicated the application, the greater the savings.

Here's another thought about Forth style before we leave the egg ranch. Recall our definition of EGGSIZE

```
: EGGSIZE   ( weight-per-dozen -- )
   CATEGORY  DUP LABEL   TALLY ;
```

CATEGORY gave us a value that we wanted to pass on to both LABEL and TALLY, so we include the DUP. To make the definition "cleaner," we might have been tempted to take the DUP out and put it inside the definition of LABEL, at the beginning. Thus we might have written

```
: LABEL   ( category# -- category#)   etc. ;
: EGGSIZE   ( weight-per-dozen -- )
   CATEGORY  LABEL   TALLY ;
```

where CATEGORY passes the value to LABEL, and LABEL passes it on to TALLY. Certainly this approach would have worked. But then, when we defined REPORT, we would have had to say

```
I LABEL DROP
```

instead of simply

```
I LABEL
```

Forth programmers tend to follow this convention: when possible, words should destroy their own parameters. In general, it's better to put the DUP inside the "calling definition" (EGGSIZE, here) than in the "called" definition (LABEL, here).

ANOTHER EXAMPLE—"LOOPING"
THROUGH AN ARRAY

We'd like to introduce a little technique that is relevant to arrays. We can best illustrate this technique by writing our own definition of a word called DUMP. DUMP is used to print out the contents of a series of memory addresses. The usage is

```
adr count DUMP
```

For instance, we could enter

```
COUNTS 12 DUMP
```

to print out the contents of our egg-counting array called COUNTS. Since DUMP is primarily designed as a programming tool to print out the contents of memory locations, it prints either byte-by-byte or cell-by-cell, depending on the need. Our version of DUMP will print cell-by-cell.

Obviously, our DUMP will involve a DO loop. The question is: What should we use for an index? Although we might use the count itself (0 − 6) as the loop index, it's faster to use the *address* as the index.

The address of COUNTS will be the starting index for the loop, while the address plus the count will serve as the limit, like this:

```
: DUMP  ( a # -- )
   OVER + SWAP  DO  CR I @  5 U.R  2 +LOOP ;
```

The key phrase here is

```
OVER + SWAP
```

which immediately precedes the DO.

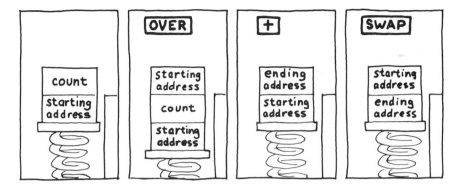

The ending and starting addresses are now on the stack, ready to serve as the limit and index for the |DO| loop. A phrase such as

    OVER + SWAP

is called a *cliché*, because it takes on a higher-level meaning. This particular cliché converts an address and count into suitable arguments for |DO|.

Since we are "indexing on the addresses," once we are inside the loop we merely have to say

    I @ 5 U.R

to print the contents of each element in the array. Since we are examining bytes in pairs (because |@| fetches a 16-bit value), we increment the index by *two* each time, by using

    2 +LOOP

BYTE ARRAYS

Forth lets you create an array in which each element consists of a single byte rather than a full cell. This is useful any time you are storing a series of numbers whose range fits into eight bits.

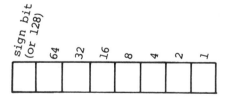

The range of an unsigned 8-bit number is 0 to 255. Byte arrays are also used to store ASCII character strings. The benefit of using a byte array instead of a cell array is that you can get the same amount of data in half the memory space.

The mechanics of using a byte array are the same as using a cell array except that

1. you don't have to double the index, since each element corresponds to one address, and

2. you must use the words C! and C@ instead of ! and @. These words, which operate on byte values only, have been given the prefix "C" because their typical use is accessing ASCII characters.

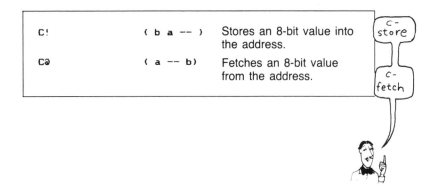

| C! | (b a --) | Stores an 8-bit value into the address. | c-store |
| C@ | (a -- b) | Fetches an 8-bit value from the address. | c-fetch |

INITIALIZING AN ARRAY

Many situations call for an array whose values never change during the operation of the application and which may as well be stored into the array at the same time that the array is created, just as CONSTANTs are. Forth provides the means to accomplish this through the word , (pronounced *comma*).

Suppose we want permanent values in our LIMITS array. Instead of saying

```
CREATE LIMITS  10 ALLOT
```

we can say

```
CREATE LIMITS  220 , 340 , 170 , 100 , 190 ,
```

Usually the above line would be loaded from a disk block, but it also works interactively.

Remember that CREATE puts a new name in the dictionary at compile time and returns the address of that definition when it is executed. But it does not "allot" any bytes for a value.

The word $\boxed{,}$ takes a number off the stack and stores it into the array. So each time you enter a number and follow it with $\boxed{,}$, you add one cell to the array.†

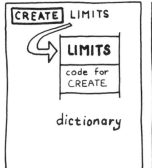  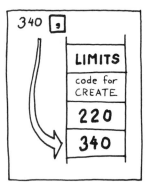

You can access the elements in this array just as you would the elements in an $\boxed{\text{ALLOT}}$ ted array. For example,

```
LIMITS 2+ ?_340_ok
```

You can even store new values into the array, just as you would into an $\boxed{\text{ALLOT}}$ ted array.

To create a byte-array, you can use the word $\boxed{\text{C,}}$ (*c-comma*). For instance, we could store each of the values used in our egg-sorting definition CATEGORY as follows:

```
CREATE SIZES  18 C,  21 C,  24 C,  27 C,  30 C,  255 C,
```

This would allow us to redefine CATEGORY using a $\boxed{\text{DO}}$ loop rather than a series of nested $\boxed{\text{IF}}$ $\boxed{\text{THEN}}$ statements, as follows‡

```
: CATEGORY  ( weight-per-dozen -- category# )
   6 0 DO  DUP  SIZES I + C@
   < IF  DROP  I LEAVE  THEN  LOOP ;
```

---

† **For Newcomers:** Ingrained habits, learned from English writing and BASIC programming, lead some newcomers to forget to type the final $\boxed{,}$ in the line. Remember that $\boxed{,}$ does not separate the numbers, it *compiles* them.

‡ **For People Who Don't Like Guessing How It Works:** The idea here is this: since there are five possible categories, we can use the category numbers as our loop index. Each time around, we compare the number on the stack against the element in SIZES, offset by the current loop index. As soon as the weight on the stack is less than one of the elements in the array, we leave the loop and use $\boxed{\text{I}}$ to tell us how many times we had looped before we "left." Since this number is our offset into the array, it will also be our category number.

Notice that we have added a maximum (255) to the array to simplify our definition regarding category 5.

This new version is more elegant and more compact than the earlier version.

Here is a list of Forth words we've covered in this chapter:

CONSTANT xxx	(n --) xxx: (-- n)	Creates a constant named *xxx* with the value *n*; the word *xxx* returns *n* when executed.
VARIABLE xxx	(--) xxx: (-- a)	Creates a variable named *xxx*; the word *xxx* returns its address when executed.
CREATE xxx	(--) xxx: (-- a)	Creates a dictionary header named *xxx*; the word *xxx* returns its address when executed.
!	(n a --)	Stores a single-length number into the address.
ə	(a -- n)	Replaces the address with its contents.
?	(a --)	Prints the contents of the address, followed by one space.
+!	(n a --)	Adds a single-length number to the contents of the address.
ALLOT	(n --)	Adds *n* bytes to the parameter field of the most recently defined word.
,	(n --)	Compiles *n* into the next available cell in the dictionary.
C,	(b --)	Compiles *b* into the next available byte in the dictionary.
C!	(b a --)	Stores an 8-bit value into the address.
Cə	(a -- b)	Fetches an 8-bit value from the address.
FILL	(a u b --)	Fills *u* bytes of memory, beginning at the address, with value *b*.
ERASE	(a u --)	Stores zeroes into *n* bytes of memory, beginning at *adr*.
BASE	(-- a)	A variable that contains the value of the number base being used by the system.
DUMP	(a u --)	Displays *u* bytes of memory, starting at the address.

Double-length Operators		
2VARIABLE xxx	(--) xxx: (-- a)	Creates a double-length variable named *xxx*; the word *xxx* returns its address when executed.
2CONSTANT xxx	(d --) xxx: (-- d)	Creates a double-length constant named *xxx* with the value *d*; the word *xxx* returns the value *d* when executed.
2!	(d a --)	Stores a double-length number into the address.
2@	(a -- d)	Returns the double-length contents of the address.
Constants		
0	(-- 0)	Returns the constant zero.
1	(-- 1)	Returns the constant one.
0.	(-- 0 0)	Returns the double-length constant zero.
FALSE	(-- f)	Returns logical false (0).
TRUE	(-- t)	Returns logical true (-1).
Key		
n, n1, ...	single-length signed numbers	b	8-bit byte
d, d1, ...	double-length signed numbers	?	Boolean flag
u, u1, ...	single-length unsigned numbers	c	ASCII character value
ud, ud1, ...	double-length unsigned numbers	a	address

REVIEW OF TERMS

Array a series of memory locations with a single name. Values can be stored and fetched into the individual locations by giving the name of the array and adding an offset to its address.

Constant a value that has a name. The value is stored in memory and usually never changes.

Factoring as it applies to programming in Forth, simplifying a large job by extracting those elements which might be reused and defining those elements as operations.

Fetch to retrieve a value from a given memory location.

Index in reference to an array, a number that indicates the relative position of a particular element in the array. The index is multiplied by the width of each element to produce the "offset," which is then added to the base address of the array to produce the "absolute address" of the element.

Initialize   to give a variable (or array) its initial value(s) before the rest of the program begins.

Offset   a number that can be added to the address of the beginning of an array to produce the address of the desired location within the array.

Store   to place a value in a given memory location.

Variable   a location in memory which has a name and in which values are frequently stored and fetched.

PROBLEMS

8-1. (a) Write two words called BAKE-PIE and EAT-PIE. The first word increases the number of available PIES by one. The second decreases the number by one and thanks you for the pie. If there are no pies, it types "What pie?" (Make sure you start out with no pies.)

```
EAT-PIE_What_pie?
BAKE-PIE_ok
EAT-PIE_Thank_you!_ok
```

(b) Write a word called FREEZE-PIES that takes all the available pies and adds them to the number of pies in the freezer. Remember that frozen pies cannot be eaten.

```
BAKE-PIE BAKE-PIE FREEZE-PIES_ok
PIES ?_0_ok
FROZEN-PIES ?_2_ok
```

8-2. Define a word called .BASE that prints the current value of the variable [BASE] in decimal. Test it by first changing [BASE] to some value other than ten. (This one's trickier than it may seem.)

```
DECIMAL .BASE_10_ok
HEX .BASE_16_ok
```

8-3. Define a number-formatting word called M. that prints a double-length number with a decimal point. The position of the decimal point within the number is movable and depends on the value of a variable. If your system has the variable [DPL], or some other variable to indicate the position of the decimal of the number just input, use it here; for instance,

```
2000.00 M._2000.00_ok
```

Otherwise define the variable PLACES and store values into it by hand; for example,

```
2 PLACES !
2000.00 M._2000.00_ok
```

(If using DPL , at first ignore the possibility of entering a number with no decimal point. This causes "−1" to appear in DPL and pushes a single-length number on the stack. For extra credit, make M. handle this possibility.)

8-4. In order to keep track of the inventory of colored pencils in your office, create a four-cell array, each cell of which contains the count of a different colored pencil. Define a set of words so that, for example, the phrase

```
RED PENCILS
```

returns the address of the cell that contains the count of red pencils, and so on. Then set these variables to indicate the following counts:

23 red pencils

15 blue pencils

12 green pencils

 0 orange pencils

8-5. Create an array of values and print a histogram (see Chapter 5 Problems) which displays a line of "*"s for each value. First, create an array with ten cells. Initialize each element of the array with a value in the range of zero to seventy. Then define a word PLOT that will print a line for each value. On each line, print the number of the cell followed by a number of "*"s equal to the contents of that cell.

8-6. In this exercise, we'll be using single-length variables as flag-arrays, and constants as bit-masks.

Begin by defining as constants the following adjectives, each representing a different bit position (from among the four least-significant bits of a 16-bit value):

```
FEMALE  MARRIED  EMPLOYED  CITIZEN
```

Now define as constants the following adjectives, each of which returns zero in all bits:

```
MALE  SINGLE  UNEMPLOYED  NON-CITIZEN
```

Now define two persons as variables; for example,

```
VARIABLE JOHN
VARIABLE MARY
```

Later, these variables will contain our attributes.

Now define a word called DESCRIBES that takes (on the stack) four of the eight adjectives defined, and the person's field, like this:

```
FEMALE SINGLE EMPLOYED CITIZEN  MARY DESCRIBES
```

DESCRIBES will store into the person's field the bit pattern representing the attributes.

Finally, define the word REPORT that, when preceded by the person's name, gives

```
MARY REPORT female single emplyed citizen ok
```

8-7. Create an application that displays a tic-tac-toe board, so that two human players can make their moves by entering them from the keyboard. For example, the phrase

```
4 X!
```

puts an "X" in box 4 (counting starts with 1) and produces this display:

```
  :   :
---------
X :   :
---------
  :   :
```

Then the phrase

```
3 O!
```

puts an "o" in box 3 and prints the display:

```
  :   : O
---------
X :   :
---------
  :   :
```

Use a byte array to remember the contents of the board, with the value 1 to signify an "X," a −1 to signify a "0," and a 0 to signify an empty box.

Since some computers don't allow the cursor to be positioned at a given location on the display, we'll simply regenerate a new board on each move using [CR], [SPACE], and so on.

(*Note*: Until we explain more about vocabularies, avoid naming anything "X," because this may conflict with the editor's [X].)

9

UNDER THE HOOD

Let's stop for a chapter to lift Forth's hood and see what goes on inside.

We've already given some of the information contained herein, but at the risk of redundancy we're now going to view the Forth "engine" as a whole, and see how it all fits together.

SEARCHING THE DICTIONARY

Back in Chapter 1, we learned that the text interpreter, whose name is INTERPRET, picks words out of the input stream and tries to find their definitions in the dictionary. If it finds a word, INTERPRET has it executed.

Let's look at the components of INTERPRET, beginning with words for searching the dictionary.

The word ⌐'⌐ (an apostrophe, but pronounced *tick*) finds a definition in the dictionary and returns its *address*. If we have defined GREET as we did in Chapter 1, we can now say

    ' GREET U. _25520_ok

and discover the address of GREET (whatever it happens to be). (Actually, ⌐INTERPRET⌐ and *tick* both use the primitive for dictionary searching, called ⌐FIND⌐.)

The word ⌐'⌐ has several uses. For instance, you can use the phrase

    ' GREET .

to find out whether GREET has been defined without actually having to execute it (the foregoing phrase will either print an address or respond "?").

You can also use the address to ⌐DUMP⌐ the contents of the definition, like this:

    ' GREET   12 DUMP

Or you can use tick in conjunction with the word ⌐EXECUTE⌐. Remember that the text interpreter, having found a word, passes its address to ⌐EXECUTE⌐. Well, you can, too. ⌐EXECUTE⌐ will execute a definition, given its address on the stack. Thus, we can say (in 83-Standard)

    ' GREET EXECUTE_Hello_I_speak_Forth_ok

and accomplish the same thing as if we had merely said GREET, only in a more roundabout way.

⌐EXECUTE⌐ does not check whether the address you give it is valid; that's your responsibility. An invalid address will almost certainly cause the system to crash.

In the 83 Standard, *tick* returns the appropriate address for ⌐EXECUTE⌐. Unfortunately, the relationship between *tick* and ⌐EXECUTE⌐ has changed from dialect to dialect through the years. The following chart shows the syntax required to compute the address of a word appropriate for ⌐EXECUTE⌐. Column 1 demonstrates the interpretive use of *tick*, as we've just demonstrated. For instance, in fig-Forth one would enter

    ' GREET CFA EXECUTE

We'll explain the remaining columns shortly.

Computing "EXECUTE address" (address required by EXECUTE)

	1. interpretively get EXECUTE address	2. get EXECUTE adr of word in input stream (from within definition)	3. compile EXECUTE adr of next word in the definition	tick returns:
fig-Forth	' name CFA	[COMPILE] ' CFA	' name CFA	pfa
MMS Forth	' name 2 –	[COMPILE] ' 2 –	' name 2 –	pfa
79-Stand.	' name CFA or FIND name	[COMPILE] ' CFA	' name CFA	pfa
polyForth	' name	'	['] name	pfa
83-Stand.	' name	'	['] name	cfa

VECTORED EXECUTION

While it may *sound* hairy, the idea of vectored execution is really quite simple. Instead of executing a definition *directly*, as we did with the phrase

```
' GREET EXECUTE
```

we can execute it *indirectly* by keeping its address in a variable, then executing the contents of the variable, like this:

```
VARIABLE POINTER   ( place to hold execution vector)
' GREET POINTER !  ( make pointer point to GREET)
POINTER @ EXECUTE  ( execute what POINTER points to)
```

(Use the appropriate phrase from column 1 to compute the address to store into POINTER.) Some systems include the word $\boxed{@EXECUTE}$, which is equivalent to, but more efficient than, the phrase "@ EXECUTE."

You can try the following example yourself:

```
1 VARIABLE 'ALOHA   ( vector)
2 : ALOHA   'ALOHA @ EXECUTE ;   ( vectorable definition)
3 : HELLO   ." Hello " ;
4 : GOODBYE   ." Goodbye " ;
5
6 ' HELLO   'ALOHA !  ( initialize the vector)
```

On Line 1, we've defined a variable called 'ALOHA. This will be our pointer. On Line 2, we've defined the word ALOHA to execute the definition whose address is in 'ALOHA. On Lines 3 and 4, we've created words that display the messages "Hello" and "Goodbye." In Line 6, we store the address of HELLO into 'ALOHA (using column 1 syntax).

Now if we execute ALOHA, we will get

```
ALOHA Hello ok
```

Alternatively, if we execute the phrase

```
' GOODBYE 'ALOHA !
```

to store the address of GOODBYE into 'ALOHA, we will get

```
ALOHA_Goodbye_ok
```

We named our pointer 'ALOHA (which we would pronounce *tick-aloha*) to obey a Forth naming convention for vectored execution pointers. Since *tick* provides an address, we use it as a prefix to suggest "the address of" ALOHA.

Notice that we can make the single word ALOHA do anything we want it to, even execute words (HELLO and GOODBYE) that are defined *after* ALOHA. Thus, *tick* provides one way in Forth to accomplish a *forward reference*. A forward reference occurs when, in defining a word, you refer to another word that hasn't been defined yet. Forth doesn't let you do that naturally, and in most cases you can simply rearrange the order in which the definitions are loaded. But sometimes rearrangement is impractical, and you need a forward reference. In our example, line 6 completes the forward reference.

Vectored execution is more commonly used to change the operation of some word *after it has been compiled*. Definitions that communicate with the outside world, such as words to control the video display, printer, and disk drives, are often vectored. Vectoring allows names for these functions to exist in the precompiled Forth system, while at the same time allowing you to define your own versions of what they do. Since the Forth system itself uses these vectors, your changes will affect the Forth system itself; you can make Forth say "ok" and do a carriage return on any terminal or printer you can find.

USING TICK IN DEFINITIONS

In the 83 Standard, *tick* always tries to find the next word in the *input stream*. What if we put tick inside a definition? When we execute the definition, tick will find the next word in the input stream. Thus, we could define

```
: SAY   ( name   ( -- )    ' 'ALOHA ! ;
```

(For other systems, refer to column 2 of the previous chart.) The unusual comment indicates that SAY will scan ahead in the input stream for the next word.

We can now enter

```
SAY HELLO_ok
ALOHA_Hello_ok
```

or

```
SAY GOODBYE_ok
ALOHA_Goodbye_ok
```

The *tick* in SAY finds the names of the defined words HELLO or GOODBYE in the input stream when you *execute* SAY; it does nothing (except get compiled) when you *define* SAY.

So how *can* we "tick" the next word in the definition? We must use the word ['] (*bracket-tick-bracket*) instead of tick.† For example,

```
: COMING   ['] HELLO  'ALOHA ! ;
: GOING    ['] GOODBYE 'ALOHA ! ;
```

Now we can say

```
COMING_ok
ALOHA_Hello_ok
GOING_ok
ALOHA_Goodbye_ok
```

Column 3 of the preceding table shows the syntax for doing this in each dialect.

Here are the commands we've covered so far:

' xxx	(-- a)	Attempts to find the dictionary address of *xxx* (the word that follows in the input stream). **(tick)**
[']	compile-time: (--) run-time: (-- a)	Used only in a colon definition, compiles the address of the next word in the definition as a literal. **(bracket-tick-bracket)**
EXECUTE	(a --)	Executes the dictionary entry whose parameter field address is on the stack.
@EXECUTE	(a --)	Executes the dictionary entry whose parameter field address is pointed to by the contents of *a*. If the address contains zero, @EXECUTE does nothing. **(fetch-execute)**

† **For Some Small-System Users:** If your keyboard doesn't have a "[" or a "]" key, the documentation that came with your Forth system should indicate substitutes.

THE STRUCTURE OF A DICTIONARY ENTRY†

All definitions, whether they have been defined by $\boxed{:}$, by $\boxed{\text{VARIABLE}}$, by $\boxed{\text{CREATE}}$, or by any other *defining word,* share these basic parts:

> name field
> link field
> code pointer field
> parameter field

The precise arrangement of these parts in memory is considered implementation-dependent. Although the 83 Standard specifies "natural-length" name fields (all the characters of a name are saved in the dictionary, up to a maximum of 31), we'll use a three-character-maximum version as our example because it's the easiest to explain.

For the sake of discussion, here's how these components are arranged, using the variable DATE as an example. In this diagram, each horizontal line represents one cell in the dictionary:

NAME

In our example, the first byte contains the number of characters in the full name of the defined word (there are four letters in DATE). The next three bytes contain the ASCII representations of the first three letters in the name of the defined word. In a three-character system, this is all the information that tick or bracket-tick-bracket have to go on in matching up the name of a definition with a word in the input stream.

(Notice in the diagram that the sign bit of the "count" byte is called the *precedence bit.* This bit is used during compilation to indicate whether the word

---

† **For Systems Running on Direct Forth Engines:** The following discussion of dictionary-entry formats and subroutine nesting applies to those Forths being emulated as a virtual machine on a typical processor via indirect threaded code, not to those running on a true Forth engine that implements the virtual machine directly in silicon. (But understanding these sections will be helpful in learning how the Forth engines work.)

is supposed to be executed during compilation, or to simply be compiled into the new definition. More on this matter in Chapter 11.)

LINK

The *link* cell contains the address of the previous definition in the dictionary list. The link cell is used in searching the dictionary. To simplify things a bit, imagine that it works this way:

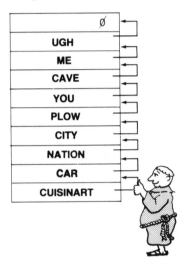

Each time the compiler adds a new word to the dictionary, he sets the link field to point to the address of the previous definition. Here he is setting the link field of CUISINART to point to the definition of CAR.

At search time, tick (or bracket-tick-bracket, etc.) starts with the most recent word and follows the "chain" backwards, using the address in each link cell to locate the next definition back.

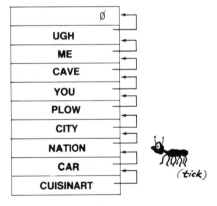

(tick)

The link field of the first definition in the dictionary contains a zero, which tells tick to give up; the word is not in the dictionary.

CODE POINTER

Next is the *code pointer*. The address contained in this pointer is what distinguishes a variable from a constant or a colon definition. When Forth executes a word, it does so by running the machine-language routine pointed to by this field.

For example, in the case of a variable, the pointer points to code that pushes the address of the variable onto the stack. In the case of a constant, the pointer points to code that pushes the contents of the constant onto the stack. In the case of a colon definition, the pointer points to code that executes the rest of the words in the colon definition.

The code that is pointed to is called the *run-time code* because it's used when a word of that type is executed (not when a word of that type is defined or compiled).

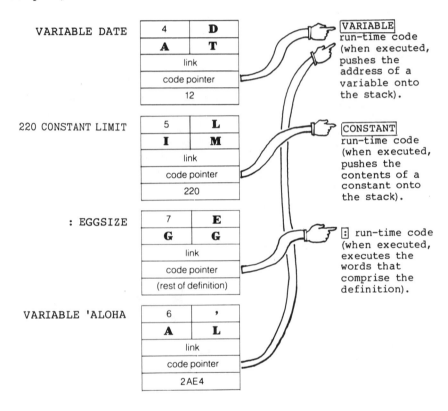

All variables have the same code pointer; all constants have the same code pointer of their own; all colon definitions have their own; and so on.

PARAMETER FIELD

Following the code pointer is the parameter field. In variables and constants, the parameter field is only one cell. In a 2CONSTANT or 2VARIABLE, the parameter field is two cells. In an array, the parameter field can be as long as you want it. In a colon definition, the length of the parameter field depends on the length of the definition, as we'll explain in the next section.

ADDRESSING THE FIELDS

In discussing the parts of dictionary structures, it's important to distinguish between the *addresses* of the parts and their *contents*. By convention, the address that contains the code pointer is called the "code field address" (written *cfa*). Thus, a word's cfa contains a pointer to its run-time code.

The address of the first cell that contains the parameter(s) is called the "parameter field address" (written *pfa*).

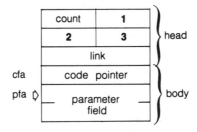

The specific address returned by *tick* is the cfa in some implementations, the pfa in others. In the 83 Standard, it is the cfa. The Standard includes the word >BODY , which converts a cfa to a pfa.

Thus, it's possible (though not "Standard," and not normally recommended) to change the value of an existing constant, like this:

```
n ' LIMIT >BODY !
```

For all other systems, refer to Column 4 of the chart on page 197.

By the way, the name and link fields are often called the "head" of the entry; the code pointer and parameter fields are called the "body."

THE STRUCTURE OF A COLON DEFINITION

While the format of the head and code pointer is the same for all types of definitions within a given system, the format of the parameter field varies from type to type. Let's look at the parameter field of a colon definition.

The parameter field of a colon definition contains the *addresses* of the previously defined words that comprise the definition.† Here is the dictionary entry for the definition of PHOTOGRAPH, which we defined as:

```
: PHOTOGRAPH    SHUTTER OPEN   TIME EXPOSE   SHUTTER CLOSE ;
```

When PHOTOGRAPH is executed, the definitions that are located at the successive addresses are executed in turn. The mechanism which reads the list of addresses and executes the definitions at each address is called the *address interpreter*.

---

† **For Experts:** The addresses that comprise the body of a colon definition usually point to code fields rather than parameter fields (i.e., they are cfas, not pfas).

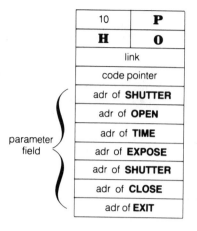

The word $;$ at the end of the definition compiles the address of a word called EXIT. As you can see in the figure, the address of EXIT resides in the last cell of the dictionary entry. The address interpreter will execute EXIT when it gets to this address, just as it executes the other words in the definition. EXIT terminates execution of the address interpreter, as we will see in the next section.

NESTED LEVELS OF EXECUTION

The function of EXIT is to return the flow of execution to the next higher-level definition that refers to the current definition. Let's see how this works in simplified terms.

Suppose that DINNER consists of three courses:

    : DINNER   SOUP ENTREE DESSERT ;

and that tonight's ENTREE consists simply of

    : ENTREE   CHICKEN RICE ;

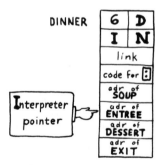

We are executing DINNER and we have just finished the SOUP. The pointer that is used by the address interpreter is called the *interpreter pointer* (I). Since the next course after SOUP is the EN-TREE, our interpreter pointer is pointing to the cell that contains the address of ENTREE.

Before we go off and execute ENTREE, we first increment the interpreter pointer so that when we come back it will be pointing to DESSERT.

Now we begin to execute ENTREE. The first thing we execute is ENTREE's "code" that is, the code that is pointed to by the "code field," common to all colon definitions.

This code does two things: First, it saves the contents of the interpreter pointer on the return stack . . .

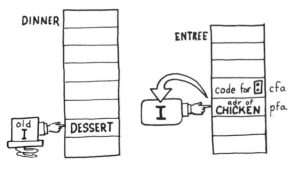

. . . then it puts the address of its own parameter field (pfa) into the interpreter pointer. Now the interpreter pointer is pointing to CHICKEN. So the address interpreter gets ready to serve up the chicken.

But first, as we did with ENTREE, we increment the pointer so that when we return it will be pointing to RICE. Then CHICKEN's code saves *this* pointer on the return stack and puts CHICKEN's own pfa into the interpreter pointer.

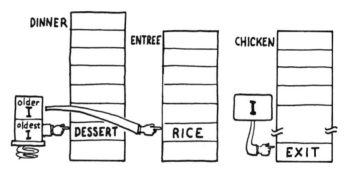

Finally, we have our chicken, as the foregoing process continues all down the line to the lowest-level definition involved in the making of the succulent poultry. Sooner or later, we come to the EXIT in CHICKEN.

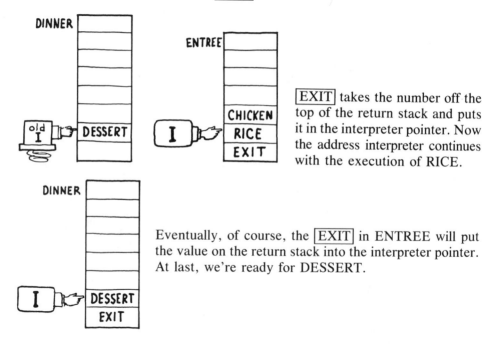

EXIT takes the number off the top of the return stack and puts it in the interpreter pointer. Now the address interpreter continues with the execution of RICE.

Eventually, of course, the EXIT in ENTREE will put the value on the return stack into the interpreter pointer. At last, we're ready for DESSERT.

OTHER USES OF THE RETURN STACK

After learning how Forth keeps return addresses on the return stack, you can now see why it's so important to be careful using the return stack to hold temporary values. If you execute this definition:

```
: TEST   3 >R   CR CR CR ;
```

you'll put a "3" on the return stack, execute three carriage returns, and then return to—what? Odds are there's no word at address 3, so you'll probably crash.

In most Forth systems, $\boxed{\text{DO}}$ loops keep their information about the index and limit on the return stack as well (though not always in a way that you'd expect). This explains why the use of $\boxed{>R}$ and $\boxed{R>}$ must be symmetric around $\boxed{\text{DO}}$ and $\boxed{\text{LOOP}}$. In other words, you can write

```
... >R ... DO ... LOOP ... R> ... ;
```

but not

```
... >R ... DO ... R> ... LOOP ... ;
```

Also, the loop-index-fetch word $\boxed{\text{I}}$ is not valid if you have placed a temporary value on the return stack inside the loop:

```
... DO ... >R ... I ... R> ... LOOP ... ;
```

ONE STEP BEYOND

Perhaps you're wondering what happens when we finally execute the $\boxed{\text{EXIT}}$ in DINNER? Whose return address is on the stack? What do we return to?

Well, DINNER has just been executed by $\boxed{\text{EXECUTE}}$. $\boxed{\text{EXECUTE}}$ is a component of $\boxed{\text{INTERPRET}}$. $\boxed{\text{INTERPRET}}$ is a loop that checks the entire input stream. Assuming that we entered after DINNER, then there is nothing more to interpret. So when we exit $\boxed{\text{INTERPRET}}$, where does that leave us? In the outermost definition, called $\boxed{\text{QUIT}}$.

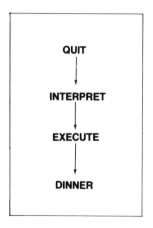

$\boxed{\text{QUIT}}$, in simplified form, looks like this:

```
: QUIT   BEGIN   RESET   QUERY   INTERPRET   ." ok" CR
   FALSE UNTIL ;
```

where

        RESET   clears the return stack, and
        QUERY   accepts input from the keyboard.

($\boxed{\text{QUIT}}$'s definition may be different in your system.) We can see that after the word $\boxed{\text{INTERPRET}}$ comes a dot-quote message, "ok," and a $\boxed{\text{CR}}$, which of course are what we see after interpretation has been completed.

Next is the phrase

```
FALSE UNTIL
```

which unconditionally returns us to the beginning of the loop, where we clear the return stack and once again wait for input.

If we execute [QUIT] at any level of execution, we will immediately cease execution of our application and re-enter [QUIT]'s loop. The return stack will be cleared (regardless of how many levels of return addresses we had there, since we could never use any of them now), and the system will wait for input. You can see why [QUIT] can be used to keep the message "ok" from appearing.

MORE WAYS TO QUIT

Two other useful words invoke [QUIT]. One is [ABORT], which has the added effect of clearing the data stack. The other is [ABORT"], which also

1. consumes a flag on the stack to determine whether it should abort (true = abort), and
2. displays whatever message you want associated with the error condition before aborting.

(We introduced [ABORT"] at the end of Chapter 4.)

A common use of [ABORT"] is right at the beginning of a user (highest level) word, to determine whether there are at least enough values on the stack for the operation. For instance, you might define

```
: LIST  ( n -- )  DEPTH 1 < ABORT" Needs block# "  LIST ;
```

or, the more general

```
: ARGUMENTS  ( n -- )  DEPTH < NOT ABORT" Values?" ;
```

which can be used like this:

```
: LIST  ( n -- )  1 ARGUMENTS  LIST ;
```

ABANDONING THE NEST

It's possible to skip one level of execution simply by removing one return address from the return stack. For example, consider the three levels of execution associated with DINNER, shown here:

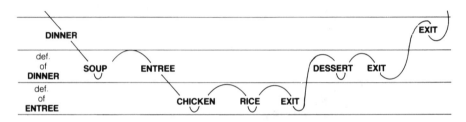

Now suppose that the definition ENTREE is changed to

```
: ENTREE   CHICKEN RICE   R> DROP ;
```

The phrase "R> DROP" will drop from the return stack the return address of DESSERT, which was put on just prior to the execution of ENTREE. If we reload these definitions and execute DINNER, the EXIT on the third level will take us directly back to the first level. We'll get SOUP, CHICKEN, and RICE, but we'll skip DESSERT, as you can see here:

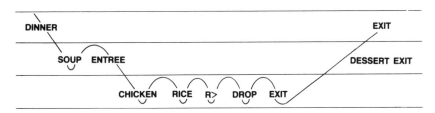

Using "R> DROP" in applications is dangerous stuff; it violates the principles of structured programming. Nevertheless it can sometimes simplify problems. We won't discuss the pros and cons here, just beware.

We've mentioned that the word EXIT removes a return address from atop the return stack and puts it into the interpreter pointer. The address interpreter, which gets its bearings from the interpreter pointer, begins looking at the next level up. It's possible to include EXIT in the middle of a definition. For example, suppose we were to redefine ENTREE as follows:

```
: ENTREE   RICE   VEGETARIAN IF EXIT THEN   CHICKEN ;
```

Then if we were vegetarian, we'd exit right after rice, skipping the ckicken, going straight to DESSERT.

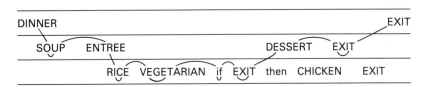

The foregoing definition is functionally equivalent to

```
: ENTREE   RICE   VEGETARIAN NOT   IF CHICKEN THEN ;
```

You can't use EXIT inside a DO loop—instead of removing a return address from the return stack, it will remove one of the arguments saved there by DO !

We've just seen the effects of removing a return address from the return stack. Another interesting experiment involves putting an extra address *onto* the return stack.

Try the following experiment (you may have to adjust the cfas and pfas to make this work on your system):

```
: HELLO    ." Hello " ;
: GOODBYE    ." Goodbye " ;
' GOODBYE >BODY >R    HELLO
```

First, we "tick" the address of GOODBYE and push it onto the return stack, making Forth think that it's a return address. Then we invoke HELLO, which displays its greeting. Eventually, Forth goes back to the return stack for its next address, and finding it, executes GOODBYE—after the HELLO!

>BODY	(cfa -- pfa)	Computes the parameter field address of the definition whose "compilation address" is on the stack.
EXIT	(--)	Removes a return address from atop the return stack, restoring it to the address interpreter pointer. When compiled within a colon definition, terminates execution of that definition at that point.
QUIT	(--)	Clears return stack and returns control to the terminal, awaiting input. No message is given.
ABORT	(--)	Clears the data stack and performs the function of QUIT. No message is given.

RECURSION

Recursion is a technique whereby a routine calls itself. By default, Forth prevents this. For instance, when you write

```
: LOAD  ( n -- )  DUP .  LOAD ;
```

you are defining a new version of LOAD which displays the number of the block being loaded, then invokes the *original* version of LOAD . To allow this type of construction, Forth deliberately hides the header during compilation of a definition so that it will not be found, letting the address of the original version be compiled into the new definition.

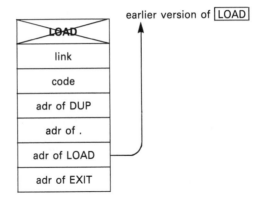

earlier version of LOAD

name, hidden during
compilation

```
LOAD
link
code
adr of DUP
adr of .
adr of LOAD
adr of EXIT
```

Nevertheless, recursion is easy to accomplish in Forth (since all that's involved is getting around Forth's defenses). The word RECURSE will compile the address of the word currently being defined. (In some systems, this word is known as MYSELF.)†

Here's an example of recursion:

```
VARIABLE COUNTER
: WHY   CR ." Why do you ask? "  -1 COUNTER +!
    COUNTER @ IF  RECURSE   THEN ;
5 COUNTER !
```

Invoking WHY will produce

```
WHY
Why do you ask?
Why do you ask?
Why do you ask?
Why do you ask?
Why do you ask? ok
```

Notice that there are no loops anywhere. With the counter starting at 5, WHY will invoke itself as long as the counter is nonzero. (Don't execute WHY with the counter set to zero, or to too large a number, or your return stack will overflow.)

---

† **For fig-Forth Systems:** The definition is

```
: RECURSE   LATEST  PFA CFA , ; IMMEDIATE
```

For older polyFORTH Systems:

```
: RECURSE   LAST @ @ 2+ , ; IMMEDIATE
```

FORTH GEOGRAPHY

HIGH MEMORY
BLOCK
BUFFERS
USER VARIABLES
RETURN STACK
TEXT INPUT BUFFER
DATA STACK
PAD
USER DICTIONARY ←H
ELECTIVE DEFINITIONS
SYSTEM VARIABLES
PRECOMPILED FORTH NUCLEUS
LOW MEMORY

This is a *memory map*† of a typical single-user Forth system. Multiprogrammed systems such as polyFORTH are more complicated, as we will explain later on. For now let's take the simple case and explore each region of the map, one at a time.

PRECOMPILED PORTION

In low memory resides the only precompiled portion of the system (already compiled into dictionary form). On some systems this code is kept on disk (often blocks 1–8) and automatically loaded into low RAM when you start up or "boot" the computer. On other systems, the precompiled portion resides permanently in PROM, where it is active as soon as you power up the computer.

The precompiled portion usually includes most of the single-length math operators and number-formatting words, single-length stack manipulation operators, editor commands, branching and structure-control words, the assembler, all the defining words we've covered so far, and, of course, the text and address interpreters.‡

SYSTEM VARIABLES

The next section of memory contains *system variables* which are created by the precompiled portion and used by the entire system. They are not generally used by the user.

---

† **For Beginners:** A "memory map" depicts how computer memory is divided up for various purposes in a particular system.

Memory space is measured in groups of 1,024 bytes. This quantity is called a "K" (from "kilo-," meaning a thousand, which is close enough).

‡ **For Experts:** To give you an idea of how compact Forth can be, all of polyFORTH's precompiled portion resides in less than 8K bytes.

ELECTIVE DEFINITIONS

The portion of the Forth system that is not precompiled is kept on disk in source-text form. You can elect to load or not to load any number of these definitions to better control use of your computer's memory space. The load block for all *electives* is called the *electives block*.

USER DICTIONARY

The dictionary will grow into higher memory as you add your own definitions within the portion of memory called the *user dictionary*. The next available cell in the dictionary at any time is pointed to by a variable called [H] (or [DP]). During the process of compilation, the pointer [H] is adjusted cell-by-cell (or byte-by-byte) as the entry is being added to the dictionary. Thus [H] is the compiler's bookmark; it points to the place in the dictionary where the compiler can next compile.

[H] is also used by the word [ALLOT], which advances [H] by the number of bytes given. For example, the phrase

    10 ALLOT

adds ten to [H] so that the compiler will leave room in the dictionary for a ten-byte (or five-cell) array.

A related word is [HERE], which is simply defined as

    : HERE   (-- here)   H @ ;

to put the value of [H] on the stack. The word [,] (comma), which stores a single-length value into the next available cell in the dictionary, is simply defined

    : ,   (n --)   HERE !   2 ALLOT ;

that is, it stores a value into [HERE] and advances the dictionary pointer two bytes to leave room for it.

You can use [HERE] to determine how much memory any part of your application requires, simply by comparing the [HERE] from before with the [HERE] after compiling. For example,

    HERE   220 LOAD   HERE SWAP - . 196 ok

indicates that the definitions loaded by block 220 filled 196 bytes of memory space in the dictionary.

THE PAD

At a certain distance from [HERE] in your dictionary, you will find a small region of memory called the *pad*. Like a scratch pad, it is usually used to hold character strings that are being manipulated prior to being displayed. For example, the number-formatting words use the pad to hold the ASCII numerals during the conversion process, prior to [TYPE].

The size of the pad is indefinite. In most systems there are hundreds or even thousands of bytes between the beginning of the pad and the top of the data stack.

Since the pad's beginning address is defined relative to the last dictionary entry, it moves every time you add a new definition or execute FORGET or EMPTY . This arrangement proves safe, however, because the pad is never used when any of these events are occurring. The word PAD returns the current address of the beginning of the pad. It is defined simply as

        : PAD (-- a)   HERE   34 + ;

that is, it returns an address that is a fixed number of bytes beyond HERE . (The actual number may vary.)

DATA STACK

Far above the pad in memory is the area reserved for the data stack. Although we like to imagine that values actually move up and down somewhere as we "pop them off" and "push them on," in reality nothing moves. The only thing that changes is a pointer to the "top" of the stack.

As you can see below, when we "put a number on the stack," what really happens is that the pointer is "decremented" (so that it points to the next location toward low memory), then our number is stored where the pointer is pointing. When we "remove a number from the stack," the number is fetched from the location where the pointer is pointing, then the pointer is incremented. Any numbers above the stack pointer on our map are meaningless.

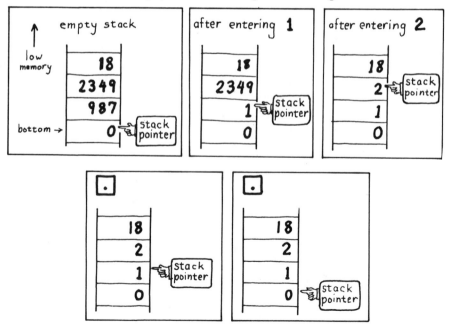

As new values are added to the stack, it "grows toward low memory."

The stack pointer is fetched by the word SP@ (pronounced *s-p-fetch*).†
Since SP@ provides the address of the top stack location, the phrase

    SP@ @

fetches the contents of the top of the stack. This operation, of course, is identical
to that of DUP. If we had five values on the stack, we could copy the fifth
one down with the phrase

    SP@ 8 + @

(but this is not considered good programming practice).

The bottom of the stack is pointed to by a variable
called S0 (*S-zero*). S0 always contains the address of
the next cell *below* the "empty stack" cell.

Notice that with double-length numbers, the high-
order cell is stored at the lower memory address whether
on the stack or in the dictionary. The operators 2! and
2@ keep the order of cells consistent, as you can see
here.

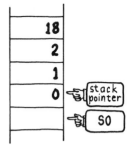

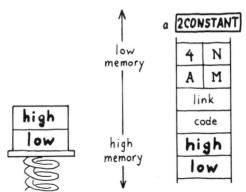

TEXT INPUT BUFFER

The *text input buffer* is the region of memory, usually 80 bytes wide, that receives
the characters you type in from the keyboard prior to pressing "return." It is
here that they will be scanned by the text interpreter.

Don't confuse this with the *input stream* (Chapter 3). The input stream is
the sequence of words being interpreted; they may reside in the text input buffer
(during interpretation) or in a source block (during a load).

The text input buffer grows toward *high* memory (the same direction as
the pad). The word TIB fetches the starting address of this buffer. (In fig-Forth,
you must say "TIB @"; in polyFORTH you would say "S0 @").

† **For polyFORTH Users:** This word is called 'S .

RETURN STACK

Above the text input buffer resides the return stack, which operates identically to the data stack and grows toward low memory.

USER VARIABLES

The next section of memory contains "user variables." These variables include BASE , S0 , and many others that we'll cover in an upcoming section.

BLOCK BUFFERS

At the high end of memory reside the block buffers. Each buffer provides 1,024 bytes for the contents of a disk block. Whenever you access a block (by listing or loading it, for example) the system copies the block from the disk into the buffer, where it can be modified by the editor or interpreted by LOAD . We'll discuss the block buffers in Chapter 10.

This completes our journey across the memory map of a typical single-user Forth system. Here are the words we've just covered that relate to memory regions in the Forth system.

H or DP	(-- a)	Returns the address of the dictionary pointer.
HERE	(-- a)	Returns the next available dictionary location.
PAD	(-- a)	Returns the beginning address of a scratch area used to hold character strings for intermediate processing.
SP@ or 'S	(-- a)	Returns the address of the top of the data stack before SP@ is executed.
S0	(-- a)	Contains the address of the bottom of the data stack.
TIB	(-- a)	Returns the starting address of the text input buffer.

s-p-fetch

s-zero

t-i-b

THE GEOGRAPHY OF A MULTI-TASKED FORTH SYSTEM

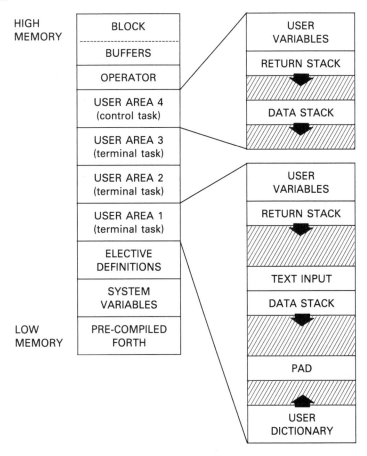

Some Forth systems (such as polyFORTH) can be multitasked,† so that any number of additional tasks can be added. A task may be either a *terminal task,* which puts the full interactive power of Forth into the hands of a human at a terminal, or a *control task,* which controls a hardware device that has no terminal.

Either type of task requires its own *user area.* The size and contents of a user area depend on the type of task, but typical configurations for the two types of tasks are shown in the figure.

Each terminal task has its own private dictionary, pad, data stack, text input buffer, return stack, and user variables. This means that any words that

---

† **For Beginners:** The term *multitasked* describes a system in which numerous tasks operate concurrently on the same computer without interference from one another.

you define are normally *not* available to other tasks. Similarly, each task has its own copies of the user variables, such as $\boxed{\text{BASE}}$.

Each control task has a pair of stacks and a small set of user variables. Since a control task uses no terminal, it doesn't need a dictionary of its own; nor does it need a pad or a message buffer.

USER VARIABLES

User variables are not like ordinary variables. With an ordinary variable (one defined by the word $\boxed{\text{VARIABLE}}$), the value is kept in the parameter field of the dictionary entry.

Each user variable, on the other·hand, consists of two parts. The actual data is kept in an array called the *user table*. The dictionary entry for each user variable is located elsewhere; it contains an offset into the user table. When you execute the name of a user variable, such as $\boxed{\text{H}}$, this offset is added to the beginning address of the user table. This gives you the address of $\boxed{\text{H}}$ in the array, allowing you to use $\boxed{@}$ or $\boxed{!}$ in the normal way.

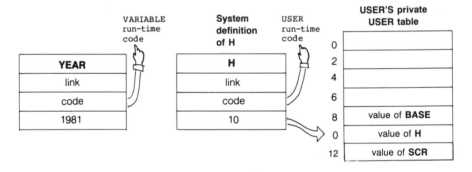

The main advantage of user variables is that any number of tasks can use the same *definition* of a variable and each get its own *value*. Each task that executes

BASE ə

gets the value for $\boxed{\text{BASE}}$ from its own user table. This saves a lot of room in the system while still allowing each task to execute independently.

The sequence of user variables in the table and their offset values vary from one system to another.

To summarize, there are three kinds of variables: System variables contain values used by the entire Forth system. User variables contain values that are unique for each task, even though the definitions can be used by all tasks in the system. Regular variables can be accessible either system-wide or within a single task only, depending upon whether they are defined within $\boxed{\text{OPERATOR}}$ or within a private task.

VOCABULARIES

In a simple Forth system there are three standard vocabularies: Forth, the editor, and the assembler.

All the words that we've covered so far belong to the Forth vocabulary, except for the editor commands which belong to the editor vocabulary. The assembler vocabulary contains commands that are used to write assembly-language code for your particular computer.

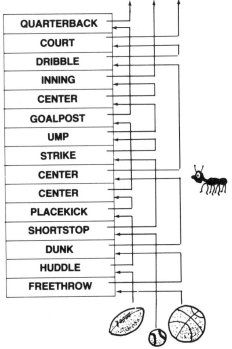

All definitions are added to the same dictionary in the order in which they are compiled, regardless of which vocabulary they belong to. So vocabularies are not subdivisions of the dictionary; instead, they are independently linked lists that weave through it.

For example, in the figure shown here, there are three vocabularies: football, baseball, and basketball. All three are co-resident in the same dictionary, but when tick follows the basketball chain, for instance, it only finds words in the basketball vocabulary. Even though each vocabulary has a word called CENTER, tick will find whichever version is appropriate for the context.

There is another advantage besides exclusivity, and that is speed of searches. If we are talking about basketball, why waste time hunting through the football and baseball words?

You can change the context in which the dictionary is searched by executing any of the three commands FORTH , EDITOR , or ASSEMBLER . For example, if you enter

FORTH

you know for sure that the search context is the Forth vocabulary.

Ordinarily, however, the Forth system automatically changes the context for you. Here's a typical scenario:

The system starts out with Forth being the context. Let's say you start entering an application into a block. Certain editor commands switch the context to the editor vocabulary. You will stay in the editor vocabulary until you load the block and begin compiling definitions. The word : will automatically reset the context to what it was before—Forth.

Different versions of Forth have different ways of implementing vocabularies. Still, we can make a few general statements that will cover most systems.

The vocabulary to be searched is specified by a user variable called $\boxed{\text{CONTEXT}}$. As we said, the commands $\boxed{\text{FORTH}}$, $\boxed{\text{EDITOR}}$, and $\boxed{\text{ASSEMBLER}}$ change the search context.

There is another kind of vocabulary "context": the vocabulary to which new definitions will be linked. The link vocabulary is specified by another variable called $\boxed{\text{CURRENT}}$. Since $\boxed{\text{CURRENT}}$ normally specifies the Forth vocabulary, new definitions are normally linked to the Forth vocabulary.

But how does the system compile words into the editor and assembler vocabularies? By using the word $\boxed{\text{DEFINITIONS}}$, as in

```
EDITOR DEFINITIONS
```

We know that the word $\boxed{\text{EDITOR}}$ sets $\boxed{\text{CONTEXT}}$ to "EDITOR." The word $\boxed{\text{DEFINITIONS}}$ copies whatever is in $\boxed{\text{CONTEXT}}$ into $\boxed{\text{CURRENT}}$. The definition of DEFINITIONS is simply

```
: DEFINITIONS   CONTEXT @ CURRENT ! ;
```

Having entered

```
EDITOR DEFINITIONS
```

any words that you compile henceforth will belong to the editor vocabulary until you enter

```
FORTH DEFINITIONS
```

to reset $\boxed{\text{CURRENT}}$ to "FORTH."†

The handling of vocabularies is highly system-dependent and controversial. The 83 Standard wisely skirts the details. And so will we. Check your system documentation.

---

† **For Curious polyFORTH Users:** polyFORTH allows several vocabularies to be chained in sequence. $\boxed{\text{CONTEXT}}$ specifies the search order.

The polyFORTH dictionary is comprised of eight "linked lists" which do not correspond with the vocabularies. At compile time a hashing function, based on (usually) the first letter of the word being defined, computes a "hashing index." This index is combined with the "current" vocabulary to produce an index into one of the eight lists.

Thus, a single list may contain words from many vocabularies, but any words with identical names belonging to separate vocabularies will be linked to separate lists. The distribution of entries in each chain is balanced, and an entire vocabulary can be searched by searching only one-eighth of the dictionary.

' xxx	(-- a)	Attempts to find the dictionary address of *xxx* (the word that follows in the input stream).
[']	compile-time: (--) run-time: (-- a)	Used only in a colon definition, compiles the address of the next word in the definition as a literal.
EXECUTE	(a --)	Executes the dictionary entry whose parameter field address is on the stack.
@EXECUTE	(a --)	Executes the dictionary entry whose pfa is pointed to by the contents of adr. If address contains zero, @EXECUTE does nothing.
>BODY	(cfa -- pfa)	Computes the parameter field address of the definition whose *compilation address* is on the stack.
EXIT	(--)	Removes a return address from atop the return stack, restoring it to the address interpreter pointer. When compiled within a colon definition, terminates execution of that definition at that point.
QUIT	(--)	Clears the return stack and returns control to the monitor, awaiting input. No message is given.
ABORT	(--)	Clears the data stack and performs the function of QUIT. No message is given.
H or DP	(-- a)	Returns the address of the dictionary pointer.
HERE	(-- a)	Returns the next available dictionary location.
PAD	(-- a)	Returns the beginning address of a scratch area used to hold character strings for intermediate processing.
SP@ or 'S	(-- a)	Returns the address of the top of the data stack before SP@ is executed.
SØ	(-- a)	Contains the address of the bottom of the data stack.
TIB	(-- a)	Returns the starting address of the text input buffer.
FORTH	(--)	Makes Forth the context vocabulary.
EDITOR	(--)	Makes the editor vocabulary the context vocabulary.
ASSEMBLER	(--)	Makes the assembler vocabulary the context vocabulary.
CONTEXT	(-- a)	Returns the address of a variable that specifies the dictionary search order.

CURRENT	(-- a)	Returns the address of a variable that specifies the vocabulary in which new word definitions are linked.
DEFINITIONS	(--)	Sets the "current" vocabulary to the "context" vocabulary so that subsequent definitions will be linked to the "context" vocabulary.

REVIEW OF TERMS

Address interpreter
the second of Forth's two interpreters, the one that executes the list of addresses found in the dictionary entry of a colon definition.

Body
the code and parameter fields of a Forth dictionary entry.

Boot
simply, to load the precompiled portion of Forth into the computer so that you can talk to the computer in Forth. This happens automatically when you turn the computer on or press "Reset."

Cfa
code field address; the address of a dictionary entry's code pointer field.

Control task
on a multitasked system, a task which cannot converse with a terminal. Control tasks usually run hardware devices.

Code pointer field
the cell in a dictionary entry that contains the address of the run-time code for that particular type of definition.

Defining word
a Forth word that creates a dictionary entry. Examples include [:], [CONSTANT], [VARIABLE], and so on.

Electives
the set of Forth definitions that come with a system but not in the precompiled portion. The *electives block* loads the blocks that contain the elective definitions; the block can be modified as the user desires.

Forward reference
in general, a reference to a word that has not yet been defined. In Forth, a technique such as vectored execution must be used.

Head
the name and link fields of a Forth dictionary entry.

Link field
the cell in a dictionary entry that contains the address of the previous definition, used in searching the dictionary. (On systems which use multiple chains, the link field contains the address of the previous definition in the same chain.)

Name field	the area of a dictionary entry that contains the name (or abbreviation thereof) of the defined word, along with the number of characters in the name.
Pad	the region of memory within a terminal task that is used as a scratch area to hold character strings for intermediate processing.
Parameter field	the area of a dictionary entry that contains the "contents" of the definition: for a $\boxed{\text{CONSTANT}}$, the value of the constant; for a $\boxed{\text{VARIABLE}}$, the value of the variable; for a colon definition, the list of addresses of words that are to be executed in turn when the definition is executed. Depending on its use, the length of a parameter field varies.
Pfa	parameter field address; the address of the first cell in a dictionary entry's parameter field (or, if the parameter field consists of only one cell, its address).
Precompiled portion	the part of the Forth system that is resident in object form immediately after the power-up or boot operation. The precompiled portion usually includes the text interpreter and the address interpreter; defining, branching, and structure-control words; single-length math and stack operators; single-length number conversion and formatting commands; the editor; and the assembler.
Run-time code	a routine, compiled in memory, that specifies what happens when a member of a given class of words is executed. The run-time code for a colon definition performs a "nest" and invokes the address interpreter; the run-time code for a variable pushes the address of the variable's parameter field onto the stack.
System variable	one of a set of variables provided by Forth which are referred to system-wide (by any task). Contrast with *user variable*.
Task	in Forth, a partition in memory that contains at minimum a data stack, a return stack, and a set of user variables.
Terminal task	on a multitasked system, a task that can converse with a human being using a terminal; that is, one that has a text interpreter, dictionary, and so on.
Text input buffer	the region of memory within a terminal task that is used to store text as it arrives from a terminal. Incoming source text is interpreted here.
User variable	one of a set of variables provided by Forth, whose values are unique for each task. Contrast with *system variable*.

Vectored execution	the method of specifying code to be executed by providing not the address of the code itself but the address of a location which contains the address of the code. This location is often called the *vector*. As circumstances change within the system, the vector can be reset to point to some other piece of code.
Vocabulary	an independently linked subset of the Forth dictionary.

PROBLEMS

9-1. Define the word EQUALS such that its behavior can be changed by the words ADDING and MULTIPLYING, as seen in this example:

```
ADDING 2 3 EQUALS_5_ok
MULTIPLYING 2 3 EQUALS_6_ok
```

9-2. What is the beginning address of your private dictionary?

9-3. In your system, how far is the pad from the top of your private dictionary?

9-4. Assuming that DATE has been defined by ⌈VARIABLE⌉, what is the difference between these two phrases:

```
DATE .
```

and

```
' DATE >BODY .
```

What is the difference between these two phrases:

```
BASE .
```

and

```
' BASE >BODY .
```

9-5. In this exercise you will create a *vectored execution array,* that is, an array which contains addresses of Forth words.

Define a one-dimensional array of two-byte elements that will return the nth element's address when given a preceding index *n*. Define several words which output something at your display and take no inputs. Store the addresses of these output words in various elements of the array. Store the address of a do-nothing word in any remaining elements of the array.

Define a word that will take a valid array index and execute the word whose address is stored in the referenced element. For example,

```
0 DO-SOMETHING Hello, I speak Forth. ok
1 DO-SOMETHING 1 2 3 4 5 6 7 8 9 10  ok
2 DO-SOMETHING
**********
**********
**********
**********
**********
3 DO-SOMETHING ok
4 DO-SOMETHING ok
```

10

I/O AND YOU

In this chapter, we'll explain how Forth handles I/O (input-output); how text is input through the keyboard and output to the screen, and how data is written-to and read-from mass storage.

Specifically, we'll discuss disk-access commands, output commands, string-manipulation commands, input commands, and number-input conversion.

BLOCK BUFFER BASICS

The Forth system is designed so that—ordinarily—you don't need to think about the mechanics of the block buffers. But nothing in Forth is too complicated to understand, control, and, if necessary, change. So here's how the block buffers work.

As we mentioned earlier, each buffer is large enough to hold the contents of one block (1024 bytes) in RAM so that it can be edited, loaded, or generally accessed in any way. While we can imagine that we're communicating directly to the disk, in reality the system brings the data from the disk into the buffer where we can read it. We can also write data to the buffer, letting the system send it along to the disk.

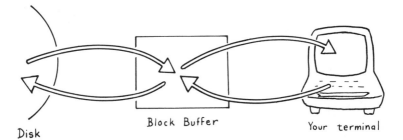

Disk   Block Buffer   Your terminal

This arrangement is called *virtual memory* because the mass storage memory is made to act like computer memory.

Many Forth systems use as few as two block buffers, even when the system is multiprogrammed. Let's see how this is possible.

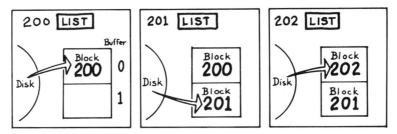

Suppose there are two buffers in your system. Now imagine the following scenario:

First, you list block 200. The system reads the disk and transfers the block to buffer 0, from which LIST displays it.

Now you list block 201. The system copies block 201 from the disk into the other buffer.

Now you list block 202. The system copies block 202 from the disk into the less-recently used buffer, namely buffer 0.

What happened to the former contents of buffer 0? They were simply overwritten (erased) by the new contents. This is no loss because block 200 is still on the disk. But what if you had *edited* block 200? Would your changes be lost? No. Here's what would happen when you listed block 202:

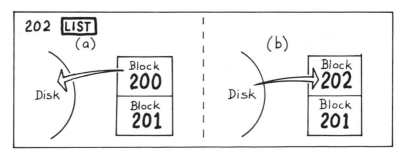

First, the modified contents of block 200 would be sent to the disk to update the former contents of 200 there, *then* the contents of 202 would be brought into the buffer.

The magic word is UPDATE, which sets a flag (the *update flag*), associated with each buffer. This flag indicates that the current block (the one most recently accessed) has been changed since it was read from disk. All editor commands that change the contents of a block, whether adding or deleting, include UPDATE in their definitions. When a buffer is needed to host a different block, its contents will be copied back to disk, rather than erased, if its update flag has been set.

The basic word that brings a block in from the disk is BLOCK. For instance, if you say

205 BLOCK

the system will copy block 205 from disk into one of the buffers. BLOCK also leaves on the stack the address of the beginning of this buffer. Using this address as a base, you can access any byte in the block.† BLOCK is invoked every time you list or load a block.

Here's what BLOCK does in more detail: First, it checks whether the requested block is already in a buffer. If it is, fine; BLOCK returns the address of that buffer. If not, it finds another buffer (in most systems, this is the buffer least-recently accessed). If this buffer has been updated, the system copies its contents back onto disk, then finally copies the requested block into the buffer.

This arrangement lets you modify the contents of the block any number of times without activating the disk drive each time. Since conversing with the disk takes longer than conversing with RAM, this can save a lot of time.

On the other hand, when several users are on a single system, this arrangement allows all of them to get by with as few as two buffers (2K of memory), even though each may be accessing a different block.

Many Forth systems give their owners the option to specify the number of block buffers, making the trade-off based on available memory size versus frequency of the application's disk transfers.

The word FLUSH forces all updated buffers to be written to disk immediately. (Now that you know about the buffers, you can see why we need FLUSH: merely updating a buffer doesn't get it written to disk.) Also, when you FLUSH, the system "forgets" that it has any blocks in the buffers (it unassigns all buffers). If you list or load one of these blocks again, BLOCK will have to read it from the disk again.

In the 83 Standard, the word SAVE-BUFFERS does less than FLUSH; it saves the contents of updated buffers on disk but it leaves the buffers assigned.

---

† **On Some fig-Forth Systems:** 1024-byte blocks may be read into several noncontiguous buffers, making it more difficult to index into a block. Refer to the fig-Forth listing.

If you request a block again that is already in a buffer, Forth will *not* have to access the disk.

Ordinarily, you needn't worry about these words; $\boxed{\text{BLOCK}}$ ensures that blocks are written out before buffers are reused. In an editing session, however, you'd want to use $\boxed{\text{SAVE-BUFFERS}}$ or $\boxed{\text{FLUSH}}$ before trying new code that may not work (to make sure the disk is actually rewritten before the system crashes). $\boxed{\text{SAVE-BUFFERS}}$ writes the blocks to disk, but keeps them handy for later access. This cuts down on disk access (saving wear and tear and time). $\boxed{\text{FLUSH}}$ is necessary only when changing disks, because it effectively "empties" the buffers of their previous contents, or when you want to verify what was *really* written to the disk.

Unfortunately, these words and their functions play musical chairs from dialect to dialect. The following scorecard shows how they work in various systems:

	FLUSH	SAVE-BUFFERS
fig-Forth	Copies all updated buffers to mass storage and unassigns them.	(Not defined.)
79 Standard	(Not defined; renamed SAVE-BUFFERS.)	Copies all updated buffers to mass storage and unassigns them.
83 Standard	Copies all updated buffers to mass storage and unassigns them.	Copies all updated buffers to mass storage, un-updates them, but keeps them assigned.

In all dialects, the word $\boxed{\text{EMPTY-BUFFERS}}$ makes the system "forget" any blocks it has in buffers and clears all the update flags, without writing anything to disk. $\boxed{\text{EMPTY-BUFFERS}}$ is useful if you've accidentally got "garbage"† in a buffer (e.g., you've deleted some important lines and forgotten what you had originally, or generally messed up) and you *don't* want it to get forced onto the disk. When you list your block again, after entering $\boxed{\text{EMPTY-BUFFERS}}$, the

---

† **For Beginners:** "Garbage" is computer jargon for data which is wrong, meaningless, or irrelevant for the use to which it is being put.

system won't know it ever had your block in memory and will bring it off the disk anew.†

In the 83-Standard, FLUSH can be defined simply as

```
: FLUSH   SAVE-BUFFERS  EMPTY-BUFFERS ;
```

To write data to the disk without reading what's on the disk already (e.g., to initialize a disk, write raw data, transfer tape to disk, etc.), use the word BUFFER. BUFFER is used by BLOCK to assign a block number to the next available buffer. BUFFER does not necessarily read the contents of the disk into the buffer (although it may on some systems). Also, BUFFER doesn't check to see whether the block number has already been assigned to a buffer, so you have to make sure that no two buffers get assigned to the same number.

UPDATE	(--)	Marks the most recently referenced block as modified. The block will later be automatically transferred to mass storage if its buffer is needed to store a different block or if FLUSH is executed.
SAVE-BUFFERS	(--)	Writes the contents of all updated buffers to their corresponding mass-storage blocks. All buffers are un-updated, but may still be assigned.
FLUSH	(--)	Performs SAVE-BUFFERS then unassigns all block buffers. Useful for mounting or changing mass storage media.
EMPTY-BUFFERS	(--)	Marks all block buffers as empty without necessarily affecting their actual contents. Updated blocks are not written to mass storage.
BLOCK	(u -- a)	Leaves the address of the first byte in block *u*. If the block is not already in memory, it is transferred from mass storage into whichever memory buffer has been least recently accessed. If the block occupying that buffer has been updated (i.e., modified), it is rewritten onto mass storage before block *u* is read into the buffer.
BUFFER	(u -- a)	Functions like BLOCK, except that the block is not necessarily read from mass storage.

† **For Those Using a Multiprogrammed System:** Careful! EMPTY-BUFFERS empties *everyone's* buffers. A data base application with extensive error-recovery features would not rely on EMPTY-BUFFERS for this purpose; but Forth's block-handling routines are easily extended to do whatever the application requires.

OUTPUT OPERATORS

The word EMIT takes a single ASCII representation on the stack, using the low-order byte only, and displays the character. For example, in decimal,

```
65 EMIT_Aok
66 EMIT_Bok
```

The word TYPE displays an entire *string* of characters, given the starting address of the string and the count, in this form:

```
( a # -- )
```

We've already seen TYPE in our number-formatting definitions without worrying about the address and count, because they are automatically supplied by #> .

Let's give TYPE an address that we know contains a character string. Remember that the starting address of the input message buffer is given by the word TIB (see Chapter 9 for dialect variations). Suppose we enter the following:

```
TIB 11 TYPE
```

This will type eleven characters from the text input buffer, which contains the command we just entered:

```
TIB 11 TYPE RETURN TIB_11_TYPEok
```

TYPE	(a # --)	Transmits # characters, beginning at address, to the current output device.

OUTPUTTING STRINGS FROM DISK

We mentioned before that the word BLOCK copies a given block into an available buffer and leaves the address of the buffer on the stack. Using this address as a starting point, we can index into one of the buffer's 1,024 bytes and type any string we care to. For example, to print line 0 of block 214, we could say

```
CR  214 BLOCK  64 TYPE RETURN
( THIS IS BLOCK 214)_____ok
```

To print line 8, we could add 512 (8 × 64) to the address, like this:

```
CR  214 BLOCK  512 +  64 TYPE
```

Before we give a more interesting example, it's time to introduce two words that are closely associated with TYPE .

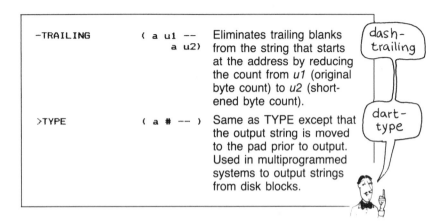

−TRAILING	(a u1 −− a u2)	Eliminates trailing blanks from the string that starts at the address by reducing the count from *u1* (original byte count) to *u2* (shortened byte count).
>TYPE	(a # −−)	Same as TYPE except that the output string is moved to the pad prior to output. Used in multiprogrammed systems to output strings from disk blocks.

−TRAILING can be used immediately before the TYPE command to adjust the count so that trailing blanks will not be printed. For instance, inserting it into our first example would give us

```
CR  214 BLOCK  64 −TRAILING TYPE RETURN
(THIS_IS_BLOCK_214)ok
```

(−TRAILING removes trailing blanks [ASCII 32]; it will not remove other non-printing characters such as ASCII 0 which are also displayed as blanks.)

The word >TYPE is used only on multiprogrammed systems to print strings from disk buffers. Instead of typing the string directly from the address given, it first moves the entire string into the pad, then types it from there. Since all users share the same block buffers, the system cannot guarantee that by the time TYPE has finished typing, the buffer will still contain the same block. It *can* guarantee, however, that the buffer will contain the same block during the move to the pad.† Since each task has its own pad, >TYPE can safely type from there.

The following example uses TYPE , but you may substitute >TYPE if need be. The random number generator appears in the Handy Hint at the end of this section.

---

† **For Experts:** In a multiprogrammed system, a task only releases control of the CPU to the next task during I/O or upon explicit command, a command that is deliberately left out of the definition of the word which moves strings.

```
Block# 231
  0 ( Buzzphrase generator)
  1 : BUZZWORDS  ( -- a)   232 BLOCK ;
  2 : BUZZWORD  ( row# column# -- a)
  3    20 * SWAP  64 * +  BUZZWORDS + ;
  4 : .BUZZWORD  ( row# col# -- )  BUZZWORD  20 -TRAILING TYPE ;
  5 : 1ADJECTIVE    10 CHOOSE  0 .BUZZWORD ;
  6 : 2ADJECTIVE    10 CHOOSE  1 .BUZZWORD ;
  7 : NOUN          10 CHOOSE  2 .BUZZWORD ;
  8 : PHRASE   1ADJECTIVE  SPACE  2ADJECTIVE  SPACE  NOUN ;
  9 : PARAGRAPH
 10    CR  ." By using " PHRASE  ." coordinated with "
 11    CR  PHRASE  ." it is possible for even the most "
 12    CR  PHRASE  ." to function as "
 13    CR  PHRASE  ." within the constraints of "
 14    CR  PHRASE  ." . " ;
 15 PARAGRAPH
```

```
Block# 232
  0 integrated          management          criteria
  1 total               organization        flexibility
  2 systematized        monitored           capability
  3 parallel            reciprocal          mobility
  4 functional          digital             programming
  5 responsive          logistical          concepts
  6 optimal             transitional        time phasing
  7 synchronized        incremental         projections
  8 compatible          third generation    hardware
  9 qualified           policy              through-put
 10 partial             decision            engineering
 11
 12
 13
 14
 15
```

Upon loading the application block (in this case block 231), we get something like the following output, although some of the words will be different every time we execute PARAGRAPH.

```
By using integrated policy through-put coordinated with
compatible organization capability it is possible for even the most
optimal third generation programming to function as
systematized monitored criteria within the constraints of
responsive policy hardware.
```

As you can see, the definition of PARAGRAPH consists of a series of ." strings interspersed with the word PHRASE. If we execute PHRASE alone, we get

```
PHRASE systematized management mobility ok
```

that is, one word chosen randomly from column 0 in block 232, one word from column 1, and one from column 2.

Looking at the definition of PHRASE, we see that it invokes three application words: 1ADJECTIVE, 2ADJECTIVE and NOUN. Each of these parts-of-speech in turn invoke the word .BUZZWORD, which requires a row-number (0–9) and column-number (0–2) on the stack representing the word or phrase to be displayed.

We provide the row number by choosing a random number between 0 and 9 with the phrase "10 CHOOSE". Each part of speech provides its unique column number.

.BUZZWORD invokes BUZZWORD to compute the address of the requested buzzword, passing this address, with the maximum count of 20, to TYPE. But first, the word − TRAILING reduces the count of 20 to the actual number of non-blank characters in the string, eliminating trailing blanks from the output.

BUZZWORD does the arithmetic to offset into the block, multiplying the column# by 20 (since each column is 20 characters wide) and the row# by 64 (since each line is 64 characters wide), then adds this offset to the base address supplied by BUZZWORDS. It's generally good technique to factor out routines that calculate addresses from routines that operate on those addresses (because the address will often be needed for another purpose).

The base address is supplied by BUZZWORDS, which simply invokes BLOCK. Here again we have factored out a meaningful address, in this case because we may want to change the location of the buzzword database. For instance, we might change the block number, or—given this factoring—we can even move the database to the dictionary, simply by redefining BUZZWORDS as

```
CREATE BUZZWORDS  64 10 * ALLOT
```

A HANDY HINT
A RANDOM NUMBER GENERATOR

This simple random number generator can be useful for games, although for more sophisticated applications such as simulations, better versions are available.

```
( Random number generator -- High level )
VARIABLE RND    HERE RND !
: RANDOM  ( -- )  RND @    31421 *   6927 +  DUP RND ! ;
: CHOOSE  ( u1 -- u2)  RANDOM UM*   SWAP DROP ;

( where CHOOSE returns a random integer within the range
   0 <= u2 < u1      )
```

Here's how to use it:
To choose a random number between zero and ten (but exclusive of ten) simply enter

```
10 CHOOSE
```

and CHOOSE will leave the random number on the stack.

INTERNAL STRING OPERATORS

The commands for moving character strings or data arrays are very simple. Each
requires three arguments: a source address, a destination address, and a count.

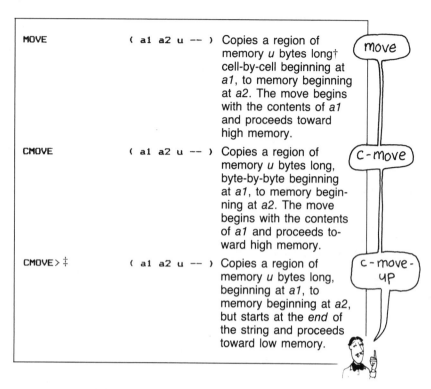

MOVE	(a1 a2 u --)	Copies a region of memory *u* bytes long† cell-by-cell beginning at *a1*, to memory beginning at *a2*. The move begins with the contents of *a1* and proceeds toward high memory.
CMOVE	(a1 a2 u --)	Copies a region of memory *u* bytes long, byte-by-byte beginning at *a1*, to memory beginning at *a2*. The move begins with the contents of *a1* and proceeds toward high memory.
CMOVE> ‡	(a1 a2 u --)	Copies a region of memory *u* bytes long, beginning at *a1*, to memory beginning at *a2*, but starts at the *end* of the string and proceeds toward low memory.

Notice that these commands follow certain conventions we've seen before:

1. When the arguments include a source and a destination (as they do with COPY), the source precedes the destination.
2. When the arguments include an address and a count (as they do with TYPE), the address precedes the count.

And so with these three words the arguments are

    (source destination count --)

To move the entire contents of a buffer into the pad, for example, we would write

    210 BLOCK PAD 1024 CMOVE

although on cell-address machines the move might be made faster if it were cell-by-cell, like this:

    210 BLOCK PAD 1024 MOVE

---

† **Forth-79 Standard:** The 79 Standard's MOVE expects a cell count.
‡ **Pre-83 Standard:** CMOVE> was named <CMOVE .

The word CMOVE> lets you move a string to a region that is higher in memory but that overlaps the source region.†

To blank an array, we can use the word BLANK .‡ For example, to store blanks (ASCII 32) into 1,024 bytes of the pad, we say

```
PAD 1024 BLANK
```

This is equivalent to the phrase

```
PAD   1024 BL FILL
```

BL is a constant defined as 32 in most systems.)

BLANK	(a u —)	Fill *u* bytes of memory beginning at *a* with ASCII blank.

A cute, but non-Standard trick: To fill memory with a multiple-byte pattern, use CMOVE . The following phrase fills a 20-byte array with 10 copies of the 16-bit address of the word NOOP:

```
CREATE TABLE  ' NOOP ,  18 ALLOT  \  10 cells
TABLE  DUP 2+ 18 CMOVE  \  initialize all to adr of NOOP
```

INPUT FROM THE KEYBOARD

The word KEY awaits the entry of a single key from your keyboard and leaves the character's ASCII equivalent on the stack in the low-order byte.

† **For Beginners:** Let's say that you want to move a string one byte to the "right" in memory (e.g., when the editor inserts a character).

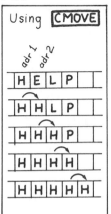

If you were to use CMOVE , the first letter of the string would get copied to the second byte, but that would "clobber" the second letter of the string. The final result would be a string composed of a single character.

Using CMOVE> in this situation keeps the string from clobbering itself during the move.

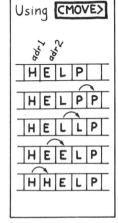

‡ **For fig-Forth Users:** Your system calls this word BLANKS .

Type

KEY ⟨RETURN⟩

The cursor will advance a space, but Forth will *not* print "ok"; it is waiting for your input. Press the letter "A," for example, and Forth will respond "ok." The ASCII value is now on the stack, so enter

. ⟨RETURN⟩ _65_ok

This saves you from having to look in the table to determine a character's ASCII code.

You can also include ⎡KEY⎤ inside a definition. Execution of the definition will stop when ⎡KEY⎤ is encountered, until an input character is received. For example, the following definition will list a given number of blocks in series, starting with the current block, and wait for you to press any key before it lists the next one:

```
: BLOCKS  ( # -- )
   SCR @ +  SCR @ DO  I LIST  KEY DROP  LOOP ;
```

In this case, we ⎡DROP⎤ the value left by ⎡KEY⎤ because we do not care what it is.

We'll see ⎡KEY⎤ being used in an input routine later in this chapter.

Some systems support a non-standard word called ⎡KEY?⎤ (or in older systems ⎡?TERMINAL⎤). The word returns "true" if a key has been pressed, without halting execution or awaiting input.

Suppose we have this endlessly incrementing loop:

```
: FOREVER   O BEGIN  DUP . 1+  FALSE UNTIL   DROP ;
```

We can add an escape by replacing ⎡FALSE⎤ with ⎡KEY?⎤

```
: SAY-WHEN   O BEGIN  DUP . 1+  KEY? UNTIL  DROP
   KEY DROP ;
```

⎡KEY?⎤ does not actually read the key from the keyboard; it merely senses that a key was pressed. To read the key, you must subsequently invoke ⎡KEY⎤. At this time, you may want to test to see what key was pressed. Or, in this case, we invoke "KEY DROP" since we don't care. (On some systems with type-ahead buffers, failure to invoke ⎡KEY⎤ after ⎡KEY?⎤ in effect clogs the keyboard-input path, causing system-dependent maladies.)

While ⎡KEY⎤ awaits a single character, the word ⎡EXPECT⎤ awaits a complete line of text from the keyboard. In effect, it is ⎡KEY⎤ in a loop. The loop ends when a given number of keystrokes has been input (usually 80), or the return key pressed.

In addition, ⎡EXPECT⎤ is smart enough to recognize the backspace key, and back up both your cursor and its internal pointer. ⎡EXPECT⎤ is the word that Forth uses to await your input commands.

EXPECT takes two stack arguments; the address to store the received text and the maximum count. For instance, the phrase

```
TIB 80 EXPECT
```

awaits up to eighty characters, or the return key, and stores them in the text input buffer as they are typed. This phrase appears in the definition of QUERY , which as we've seen, is used by QUIT .

You can use EXPECT to request input under control of a definition.†
Here is a word which, when invoked, prompts the user to type in his or her name, then types it back in a greeting:

```
CREATE USER-NAME   40 ALLOT
: .USER    USER-NAME 40 -TRAILING TYPE ;
: GET-NAME   USER-NAME 40 BLANK   USER-NAME 40 EXPECT ;
: GREET    CR   ." Please type your name: "   GET-NAME
     CR   ." Hello, " .USER   ." , I speak Forth. " ;
```

This produces:

```
GREET_                                                        ‡
Please type your name: TRAVIS MC GEE
Hello, TRAVIS MC GEE, I speak Forth.
```

† **For Experts:**   You can use EXPECT to accept data from a serial line, such as a measuring device. Since you supply the address and count, such data can be read directly into an array. In a single-user environment, you may read data into a buffer for storage on disk. In a multiuser environment, however, you must use TIB and later move the data into the buffer, since another task may use ''your'' block buffer. polyFORTH includes STRAIGHT which behaves like EXPECT but ignores control characters.

‡ **Pre-83 Standard Systems:**   Before the 83 Standard, EXPECT was required to insert a null at the end of the input text. On such a system, the above example may show a blank space between the user's name and the comma. − TRAILING interprets the null as a non-blank character and allows it to be typed. A solution is to EXPECT the name at PAD , then copy into USER-NAME only as many characters as were received, by using SPAN :

```
: GET-NAME    USER-NAME  40 BLANK  PAD 40 EXPECT
    PAD USER-NAME  SPAN @ CMOVE ;
```

SPAN is a user variable that contains the number of characters actually received by EXPECT.

KEY	(-- c)	Returns the ASCII value of the next available character from the current input device.
EXPECT	(a u --)	Awaits *u* characters (or a carriage return) from the keyboard and stores them starting at *a* and continuing towards high memory; responds to the backspace by backing up the cursor.
SPAN	(-- a)	Contains the number of characters received by EXPECT.

INPUT FROM THE INPUT STREAM

We've just seen how to await input from the keyboard. Forth also allows input from the input stream. The input stream, you'll recall, is the sequence of characters that are about to be scanned by the text interpreter. These characters may reside in the text input buffer (during interpretation) or in a block (during a LOAD).

Suppose we want to allow the user to give his codename with the word I'M, like this:

I'M TRAVIS RETURN

The user will type the words "I'M TRAVIS" together on a line before pressing return. We want I'M to save the name in the array USER-NAME. However, the string "TRAVIS" lies ahead in the input stream. The word I'M, therefore, can't EXPECT the characters—they've already been entered. Instead, we need some way to *scan* ahead in the input stream.

The word WORD scans the input stream for a string of characters bound by the character whose ASCII value is on the stack. For instance, the phrase

BL WORD

will scan the input stream for a string of characters delimited by blanks. WORD then moves this sub-string to a temporary buffer of its own, placing the count in the first byte of the buffer. In Forth, this structure—a string of characters preceded by a one-byte count of characters—is called a *counted string*.

Finally, WORD leaves the address of this temporary buffer on the stack.†

WORD is an important element of Forth's text interpreter, which uses the phrase "BL WORD" to scan the input stream for words and numbers.

† **For fig-Forth Users:** Your version of WORD does *not* return anything on the stack. For compatibility with this book, simply define

```
: WORD  ( -- a)  WORD HERE ;
```

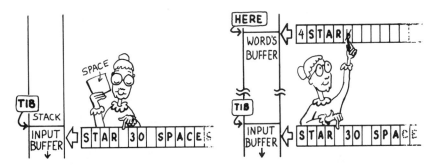

When WORD moves the substring, it includes a blank at the end but does not include it in the count.

Here's how we might define I'M (using the array we created earlier for GREET):†

```
: I'M    (    user-name    ( -- )
     USER-NAME 40 BLANK  BL WORD  COUNT  USER-NAME  SWAP CMOVE ;
```

We can use the previously defined .USER to see the entered name.

What's this word COUNT ? This useful Forth word converts an address of a counted string into an address and a count. The new address points to the start of the actual text, not to the count byte. For instance, given the address of the counted string "HELLO" on the stack,

the word COUNT puts the count on the stack and increments the address, like this:

leaving the stack with a string address and a count as appropriate arguments for TYPE , CMOVE , and so on.

In our definition of I'M, WORD leaves the address of the counted string, and COUNT converts it to an address and count. USER-NAME provides the

† **For the Curious:** To allow I'M to accept first and last names separated by a space, change "BL WORD" to "1 WORD." We'll explain why in the next section.

destination address, and $\boxed{\text{SWAP}}$ places the arguments in the proper order—source destination count—for $\boxed{\text{CMOVE}}$.

Notice the unusual stack notation for I'M. By convention, a description preceding the stack-effect comment specifies what the definition is scanning the input stream for. The "skip-line" character can also be used:

```
: I'M  \    user-name    ( -- )
   USER-NAME 40 BLANK  BL WORD  COUNT  USER-NAME  SWAP CMOVE ;
```

One peculiarity of $\boxed{\text{WORD}}$ that arises from its use by Forth's text interpreter is this: anything that you scan for with $\boxed{\text{WORD}}$ will be clobbered the next time a string is scanned for in the input stream. Try entering the phrase

```
BL WORD HI COUNT TYPE
```

The phrase "BL WORD" scans for the string "HI" and moves it to the temporary buffer, but when $\boxed{\text{COUNT}}$ is interpreted, it has already overwritten "HI", storing a count of five—not two—in the first byte. The execution of $\boxed{\text{COUNT}}$ puts a count of five on the stack. Finally, when $\boxed{\text{TYPE}}$ is interpreted it overwrites $\boxed{\text{COUNT}}$, causing the string "TYPE" (including a fifth character, the space) to be displayed.

$\boxed{\text{WORD}}$ is typically used within a definition, and you must move the scanned string from $\boxed{\text{WORD}}$'s buffer to a more permanent location before anything else is interpreted.

Another feature of $\boxed{\text{WORD}}$: It ignores initial occurrences of the delimiting character. When you type several spaces at the beginning of a line, or between words, the phrase "BL WORD" seaches until it finds a nonblank character, then scans the word until it finds the next blank. Only the sequence of nonblank characters is counted and moved to the temporary buffer.

This feature can cause some problems when you use $\boxed{\text{WORD}}$ with nonblank delimiters. For instance, in Chapter 3 we introduced the word $\boxed{.(}$, which immediately displays the string following in the input stream, up to the delimiting right parenthesis. It might be defined like this:

```
: .(  \     text)  ( -- )
   ASCII ) WORD COUNT TYPE ;
```

The comment indicates that the definition scans for text, up to the delimiter ")".

But this definition fails in the case of an "empty string" (no characters):

```
.( )  CR CR
```

Our definition will ignore the right parenthesis because it is the first character it sees; instead, it will assume "CR CR" is the string we want displayed.

To solve this problem, some Forth-83 systems offer the word $\boxed{\text{PARSE}}$, which works like $\boxed{\text{WORD}}$ except it doesn't skip initial appearances of the delimiter.

But beware, it returns the string-address and count, not the address of the packed string as WORD does.

Here's a word you may find useful:

```
: TEXT   ( c)   PAD 80 BLANK   WORD COUNT   PAD SWAP CMOVE> ;
```

TEXT, like WORD, takes a delimiter and scans the input stream until it finds the string delimited by it. It then moves the string to the pad. What is especially nice about TEXT is that before it moves the string, it blanks the pad for a line's-worth of spaces. This makes it very convenient for use with TYPE in conjunction with −TRAILING.

| WORD | (c -- a) | Reads one word from the input stream, using the character as a delimiter. Moves the string to the address returned, with the count in the first byte. |
| COUNT | (a -- a+1 #) | Converts the address of a counted string (whose length is contained in the first byte) into the form appropriate for TYPE by leaving the address of the first character and the length on the stack. |

APPLICATIONS OF WORD

Besides the text interpreter, many other Forth words use WORD. For instance, CREATE scans ahead for the name of the word to be created. FORGET scans ahead for the name of the word to be forgotten.

Let's apply WORD to our earlier example of the buzzphrase generator. In programming the generator, it would be nice to have a convenient way to enter the buzzwords into the data base (the Forth editor doesn't show us where the 20th or 40th columns begin). Suppose we could define the word "add," to add the next word in the input stream to the database, like this:

```
start
add integrated
add management
add criteria
add total
etc...
```

Here's an approach to this problem:

```
\ buzzphrase data base loader
VARIABLE ROW
VARIABLE COLUMN
: start    O ROW !  O COLUMN ! ;
: +ROW    1 ROW +! ;
: +COLUMN    COLUMN @  1+  3 /MOD  ROW +!  COLUMN ! ;
: add    \   buzzword   ( -- )
   1 WORD COUNT  ROW @ COLUMN @ BUZZWORD  DUP 20 BLANK
   SWAP CMOVE  UPDATE  +COLUMN ;
```

Observe how these routines compute the appropriate row and column positions each time. Also notice how we were able to benefit from the factoring of the word BUZZWORD, which simply returns a block-buffer address indexed by the given row and column positions.

Finally, notice that we use the phrase "1 WORD" rather than "BL WORD." The reason is that some of the phrases consist of two words separated by spaces. We don't want to scan for the first word only; we want everything the user types up to the end of the line. ASCII 1 is a control character that typically is never sent from the keyboard and therefore won't appear in the input buffer. Thus, "1 WORD" is a convention used to read the entire input buffer, up to where the user pressed return.

Other delimiters, such as quotation marks and parentheses, can be used with WORD. The Forth word .″ uses the phrase

```
ASCII " WORD
```

to scan ahead for the string to be displayed. The word ((uses the phrase

```
ASCII ) WORD
```

to scan ahead for the string to be ignored.

By scanning for commas or other separators, we can even parse a series of strings on the same line into different fields.

Having the word TEXT , which we introduced earlier, would simplify the definition of add:

```
: add    \   buzzword   ( -- )
   1 TEXT  PAD  ROW @ COLUMN @ BUZZWORD  20 CMOVE UPDATE
   +COLUMN ;
```

WORD'S INPUT-STREAM POINTERS

WORD relies on two pointers to tell it where and what to scan. The first of these is called >IN† (which stands for "into the input"). >IN is a *relative*

---

† **For fig-Forth Users:** Your system calls this word IN . For compatibility with this book, simply define

```
: >IN  ( -- a)  IN ;
```

pointer; it indicates how far into the input stream (in bytes) the interpreter has gotten.

Suppose we type the string

STAR 30 SPACES

and press return. Initially, the variable $\boxed{>IN}$ is set to zero. After $\boxed{WORD}$ has scanned the string "STAR," the value of $\boxed{>IN}$ is five.

Input Message Buffer

For some applications, you can even change $\boxed{>IN}$, to play with the order in which words are interpreted.

The second pointer is called $\boxed{BLK}$. Recall that the input stream is the sequence of characters that may be either in the input message buffer or in a block being loaded. $\boxed{BLK}$ specifies which one. It acts as both a flag and a pointer. If it contains zero, then $\boxed{WORD}$ scans the text input buffer. But if $\boxed{BLK}$ contains a nonzero number, then $\boxed{WORD}$ scans the block whose number it contains. (This explains why you can't load block 0.)

The following table shows the address at which text is actually being interpreted at any one time:

CONTENTS OF BLK	ADDRESS CURRENTLY USED BY WORD:
0	TIB >IN ə + (>IN bytes into the text input buffer)
non-zero	BLK ə BLOCK >IN ə + (>IN bytes into the block buffer)

Or, restated in Forth, the address being scanned by $\boxed{WORD}$ is

... BLK ə ?DUP IF BLOCK ELSE TIB THEN >IN ə + ...

Notice that $\boxed{WORD}$ invokes $\boxed{BLOCK}$ so that, if interpreting from a block, the block is always guaranteed to reside in a buffer.

>IN	(-- a)	User variable containing the present character off-set within the input stream.
BLK	(-- a)	User variable containing the number of the mass storage block being interpreted as the input stream. If the value of BLK is zero the input stream is taken from the text input buffer.

to-in

b-l-k

NUMBER INPUT CONVERSIONS

In Chapter 7, we learned how <#| and |#> can be used to convert a binary number on the stack into an ASCII string. The word |CONVERT| does the opposite: It converts a string of ASCII characters representing a number into a binary number on the stack.

CONVERT	(ud1 a1 -- ud2 a2)	Beginning at $a1+1$ (the byte containing the count is ignored), CONVERT converts the string to a binary value with regard to BASE. The new value is accumulated into $ud1$, being left as $ud2$. It continues until it encounters a character that can't be converted in the current number base; this address is left on the stack as $a2$.

A simple example is:

```
: PLUS  \   n2   ( n1 -- sum )
   0  0  BL WORD   CONVERT 2DROP   + ;
```

which is used like this:

```
12 PLUS 23 ._35_ok
```

PLUS can prove to any skeptic that Forth could use infix notation if it wanted to. With a "12" already on the stack in binary, PLUS is executed: First, a double-length 0 is pushed onto the stack as an accumulator. Then |WORD| scans the input stream for "n2", leaving the address of this string on the stack. |CONVERT| translates the string at the given address (skipping the first byte, the count byte) into a double-length number which it leaves on the stack in place of the zero. |2DROP| gets rid of the ending address returned by |CONVERT|, along with the high-order cell of the converted number to make it single-length. Finally, |+| adds the two numbers.

The reason $\boxed{\text{CONVERT}}$'s stack effect is not simply this:

```
( a -- ud)
```

is to allow you to use it repeatedly in converting a string containing various non-numeric characters. For instance, you could parse the string

```
6/20/85
```

into three single-length numbers using three invocations of $\boxed{\text{CONVERT}}$ in a row. The address returned by the first $\boxed{\text{CONVERT}}$ will be the address passed to the second $\boxed{\text{CONVERT}}$, and so on.

Most systems include the word $\boxed{\text{NUMBER}}$ which is based on $\boxed{\text{CONVERT}}$ and is usually simpler to use. In the Forth-83 Standard (Uncontrolled Reference Words), $\boxed{\text{NUMBER}}$ works like this:

NUMBER	(a -- d)	Converts the text beginning at $a+1$, with regard to BASE, to a binary value. The string may contain a leading minus sign which will negate the value.

Thus, a better way to define PLUS would be:

```
: PLUS  \   n2   ( n1 -- sum )
     BL WORD  NUMBER DROP  + ;
```

$\boxed{\text{NUMBER}}$ is used by the Forth system itself; it's the "numbers runner" called by the text interpreter when a word is not found in the dictionary. $\boxed{\text{NUMBER}}$ then tries to convert the string, and if successful, leaves its value on the stack; otherwise it aborts.

Of course, every Forth system handles this process somewhat differently, since there are many different ways that numbers may need to be input. The box on page 248 shows a particular definition of $\boxed{\text{NUMBER}}$ that reads any of the characters

```
:  ,  -  .  /
```

as valid punctuation characters, causing the value to be treated as a double-length number. If such a character appears within the number, the variable $\boxed{\text{DPL}}$, which stands for "decimal place," will contain the number of digits to the right of the right-most character. For instance, if the string is "200.2", $\boxed{\text{DPL}}$ will contain one. If *no* punctuation appears, $\boxed{\text{DPL}}$ will be set to -1.

(The definition assumes that $\boxed{\text{CONVERT}}$ increments $\boxed{\text{DPL}}$ for each digit successfully converted unless $\boxed{\text{DPL}}$ is -1. Also, it uses $\boxed{\text{WITHIN}}$ as we defined it in the problems for Chapter 4. Finally, it uses the 83-Standard "true" flag as

---

A Definition of NUMBER

```
: NUMBER?   ( adr -- d t=successful)
```

`DUP 1+ C@`	Get the first digit.
`ASCII - =`	Is it a minus sign?
`DUP >R`	Save the flag on return stack.
`-`	And if so, add 1 to *adr*, setting it to point to the first digit (subtracting the −1 flag is the same as adding 1).
`-1 DPL !`	Indicate no punctuation yet.
`0 0 ROT`	Provide double-length zero as the accumulator.
`BEGIN CONVERT`	Convert until invalid digit.
`DUP C@ DUP ASCII : =`	Is the invalid digit a colon, or
`SWAP ASCII , ASCII / 1+` `    WITHIN OR`	a comma, hyphen, period, or slash?
`WHILE  0 DPL !   REPEAT`	If so, reset DPL and continue.
`-ROT R> IF DNEGATE THEN`	Bring *d* to top; negate if flag on return stack indicates.
`ROT C@ BL = ;`	Is last invalid character a blank as it should be?

```
: NUMBER   ( adr -- d)
    NUMBER?  NOT ABORT" ?" ;
```
Abort if conversion not successful.

---

an arithmetic −1. For earlier systems in which "true" is "1", change ⎢−⎢ to ⎢+⎢ on Line 4.)

In Forth, if you enter a number with no punctuation, only a single-length number is pushed onto the stack. Given this version of ⎢NUMBER⎢, the text interpreter would have to invoke:

```
... NUMBER  DPL @ -1 = IF DROP THEN ...
```

or something equivalent.

BUILDING A NUMBER-INPUT ROUTINE WITH KEY

In this section, we'll show how ⎢KEY⎢ can be used in the development of a special keystroke interpreter.

Suppose we want a word which, like ⎢EXPECT⎢, awaits the input of keystrokes, but which will accept only numeric characters. Other characters will have no effect, except for backspace, which will behave as usual, and the return key, which will signal the end of input. Unlike $\boxed{\text{EXPECT}}$, this word will not terminate when the given number of digits have been entered, because the user may wish to backspace and correct the last digit before pressing return.

We'll call the word EXPECT# and give it the stack effect

```
( a max-width -- actual-width)
```

where *a* is the place to receive the string and *max-width* is the maximum number of digits to receive. The *actual-width* may be handy if we need to test whether the user entered any digits at all.

We'll need to do some things, such as backspacing the cursor, that may require different code on different systems. It is good practice to factor these routines into Forth words, defined separately from the rest of the application. This makes our code more easily *transportable,* because to change the system will, if anything, only require changing the relevant words. This practice is called *localizing* or *hiding* information.

On most computers, we can define:

```
: BACKSPACE   8 EMIT ;
```

but some systems that use memory-mapped video may require different definitions.

Also, on different systems $\boxed{\text{KEY}}$ receives the carriage return and backspace keys as different characters. The following words will hide this information as well:

```
: BS?  ( c -- t=backspace-key)  8 = ;   \ some sys. use 12
: CR?  ( c -- t=return-key)    13 = ;   \ some sys. use 0
```

The main structure of EXPECT# is a $\boxed{\text{BEGIN}}$ $\boxed{\text{WHILE}}$ $\boxed{\text{REPEAT}}$ loop, with the $\boxed{\text{WHILE}}$ test depending on detecting the return key. The loop begins with $\boxed{\text{KEY}}$. If the key is a valid digit, we "ACCEPT" it (store it in the buffer and increment the pointer); if it's a backspace, we "REVERSE" (blank the last position entered and decrement the pointer). Using $\boxed{\text{KEY}}$ in a loop this way, you can define any sort of keyboard interpreter or editor you need.

The final definition, DIGITS, is an example of EXPECT# in use. There's nothing in the listing that we haven't covered already in this book. So you have no excuse not to study it a bit. (For advanced study, see reference [1].)

```
Block# 350
   0 \ Numeric input     1 of 2
   1
   2 : BACK  8 EMIT ;
   3 : BS? ( c -- t=backspace-key)  8 = ;  \ some sys use 12
   4 : CR? ( c -- t=return-key)    13 = ;  \ some sys use 0
   5 : #? ( c -- t=valid-digit)  ASCII 0  ASCII 9 1+ WITHIN ;
   6
   7
   8
   9
  10
  11
  12
  13
  14
  15


Block# 351
   0 \ Numeric input    2 of 2
   1 : ACCEPT  ( 1st-adr last-a+1 curr-adr c -- 1st-adr last curr')
   2   >R  2DUP > IF  R@ DUP EMIT  OVER C! 1+ THEN  R> DROP ;
   3 : REVERSE ( 1st-adr last-a+1 curr-adr c -- 1st-adr last curr')
   4   DROP SWAP >R  2DUP < IF  BACK SPACE BACK  1-  DUP 1 BLANK
   5   THEN  R> SWAP ;
   6 : EXPECT#  ( a max-width -- actual-width)
   7   OVER +  OVER  BEGIN  KEY  DUP CR?  NOT WHILE
   8     DUP #?  IF  ACCEPT        ELSE
   9     DUP BS? IF  REVERSE       ELSE  DROP
  10   THEN THEN   REPEAT  ROT 2DROP  SWAP - ;
  11
  12 : DIGITS  ( #digits -- d )
  13   PAD SWAP  2DUP 1+ BLANK  EXPECT# DROP  PAD 1- NUMBER ;
  14
  15
```

STRING COMPARISONS

Here are two words that you can use to compare character strings:

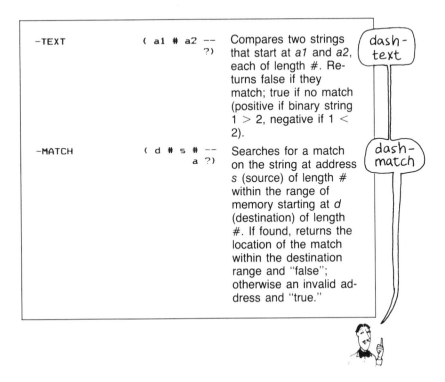

–TEXT	(a1 # a2 -- ?)	Compares two strings that start at *a1* and *a2*, each of length #. Returns false if they match; true if no match (positive if binary string 1 > 2, negative if 1 < 2).
–MATCH	(d # s # -- a ?)	Searches for a match on the string at address *s* (source) of length # within the range of memory starting at *d* (destination) of length #. If found, returns the location of the match within the destination range and "false"; otherwise an invalid address and "true."

| –TEXT | can be used to test either whether two character strings are equal or whether one is alphabetically greater or lesser than the other.† Chapter 12 includes an example of using | –TEXT | to determine whether strings match exactly.

Since for speed | –TEXT | compares cell-by-cell, you must take care on cell-address machines to give | –TEXT | even cell addresses only. For example, if you want to compare a string that is being entered as input with a string that is in an array, bring the input string to the pad (using | TEXT | rather than | WORD |) because | PAD | is an even address. Similarly, if you want to test a string that is in a block buffer, you must either guarantee that the string's address is even or, if you cannot know for sure, move the string to an even address (using | CMOVE |) before making the test.

By the way, the hyphen in | –TEXT | is as close as ASCII comes to "¬", the logical symbol meaning "not." This is why we conventionally use this prefix

† **For Users of Intel, DEC, and Zilog Processors:** To make the "alphabetical" test, you must first reverse the order of bytes.

for words which return a *negative true* flag. (Negative true means that a zero represents true and a nonzero represents false.)

If your system doesn't have $\boxed{-\text{TEXT}}$, you can load the high-level definition below. Of course, $\boxed{-\text{TEXT}}$ is usually written in assembler code, for speed.

```
: -TEXT  ( a1 # a2 -- f=match ¦ pos=1>2 ¦ neg=1<2 )
     2DUP + SWAP  DO  DROP 2+  DUP 2- @
        I @ -  DUP  IF DUP ABS / LEAVE  THEN
     2 +LOOP  SWAP DROP ;
```

$\boxed{-\text{MATCH}}$ finds an ideal application in editor commands such as $\boxed{\text{F}}$ and $\boxed{\text{S}}$ which must search for a given string in a larger region of memory. As with $\boxed{-\text{TEXT}}$, you'd want $\boxed{-\text{MATCH}}$ defined in machine code for speed. If you lack it entirely, however, here's a high-level definition that should suffice. (To play it safe and compatible, the following definition uses no tricks such as exits from loops that would otherwise accelerate it.)

```
VARIABLE 'SOURCE     ( address of source string)
VARIABLE SOURCE#     ( length of source string)
VARIABLE FLAG        ( t=no-match)
: -MATCH ( d # s # -- a t=no-match)
   SWAP 'SOURCE !  DUP SOURCE# !  - DUP O< NOT IF
      1+ O DO  O FLAG !
         'SOURCE @  SOURCE# @  O DO
            OVER I + C@  OVER I + C@ - IF -1 FLAG ! LEAVE THEN
         LOOP  DROP
      FLAG @ O= IF  LEAVE  THEN  1+  LOOP
   FLAG @  THEN ;
```

STRING LITERALS

A *string literal* is a text string that is compiled into the dictionary, with some means provided for us to get its address. The most general word for creating string literals is called $\boxed{\text{STRING}}$.† It works like this:

```
CREATE MESSAGE  BL STRING HELLO
MESSAGE COUNT TYPE_HELLO ok
```

$\boxed{\text{STRING}}$ takes as its argument the ASCII character that will serve as the string's delimiter, then scans forward for the string, compiling it as a counted string in the dictionary.

† **For non-polyFORTH Users:** On many (but not all) systems, you can define

```
: STRING ( c -- )  WORD C@ 1+ ALLOT ;
```

We assume that in this system $\boxed{\text{WORD}}$'s buffer happens to be at $\boxed{\text{HERE}}$, so we don't need to move the string and count into the dictionary. The address returned by $\boxed{\text{WORD}}$ is the address containing the count, so $\boxed{\text{C@}}$ places this count on the stack. $\boxed{\text{ALLOT}}$ then advances the dictonary pointer to the end of the string (plus one because of the count), leaving room for it in the dictionary.

We can use STRING to create string arrays. Remember how we defined LABEL in our egg-sizing application, using nested IF THEN statements? This time, let's make all the labels the same length (eight characters each) and "string them together" within a single string literal:

```
CREATE "LABEL"
ASCII " STRING Reject  Small   Medium  Large   Xtra LrgError  "
```

Invoking "LABEL" will give us the address of the string; we can type any particular label by offsetting into the array. For example, if we want label 2, we simply add 1 (to get past the count byte), then add 16 (2 × 8) and type the eight characters of the name:

```
"LABEL" 1+  16 +  8 TYPE
```

Now let's redefine LABEL so that it takes a category number from 0 through 5 and uses it to index into the string array, like this:

```
: LABEL  ( category# -- )
   8 * "LABEL" +  8 TYPE SPACE ;
```

This kind of string array is sometimes called a *superstring*. As a naming convention, the name of the superstring usually has quotes around it.

Our new version of LABEL will run a little faster because it does not have to perform a series of comparison tests before it hits upon the number that matches the argument. Instead it uses the argument to compute the address of the appropriate string to be typed.

Notice, though, that if the argument to LABEL exceeds the range zero through five, you'll be typing garbage. If LABEL is only going to be used within EGGSIZE in the application, there's no problem. But if an "end user," meaning a person, is going to use it, you'd better "clip" the index, like this:

```
: LABEL  0 MAX  5 MIN  LABEL ;
```

We'll see STRING again when we present a definition of ." in Chapter 11.

Another word for creating string literals exists in many Forth systems, although it has no standard name. We'll call it LIT". It may be used only within a definition. It can be compared to ." except that instead of typing the string, it leaves the address of the counted string. In fact, the expression

```
: 1TEST   LIT" What's happening?" COUNT TYPE ;
```

is equivalent to

```
: 2TEST   ." What's happening?" ;
```

LIT" is more powerful (and therefore less-generally useful) than STRING. (In fact, STRING may be used to define LIT".)

(The 83 model by Laxen and Perry uses the word ", which is similar to

LIT" except that it returns the address *and* count. In our opinion, that choice of factoring is not as flexible; therefore, our examples will use the version previously described as LIT" . Just be aware of the difference and you'll have no trouble.)

The following words were covered in this chapter.

UPDATE	(--)	Marks the most recently referenced block as modified. The block will later be automatically transferred to mass storage if its buffer is needed to store a different block or if FLUSH is executed.
SAVE-BUFFERS	(--)	Writes the contents of all updated buffers to their corresponding mass-storage blocks. All buffers are un-updated, but may still be assigned.
FLUSH	(--)	Performs SAVE-BUFFERS then unassigns all block buffers. Useful for mounting or changing mass storage media.
EMPTY-BUFFERS	(--)	Marks all block buffers as empty without necessarily affecting their actual contents. Updated blocks are not written to mass storage.
BLOCK	(u -- a)	Leaves the address of the first byte in block *u*. If the block is not already in memory, it is transferred from mass storage into whichever memory buffer has been least recently accessed. If the block occupying that buffer has been updated (i.e., modified), it is rewritten onto mass storage before block *u* is read into the buffer.
BUFFER	(u -- a)	Functions like BLOCK, except that the block is not necessarily read from mass storage.
TYPE	(a # --)	Transmits # characters, beginning at address, to the current output device.
-TRAILING	(a #1 -- a #2)	Eliminates trailing blanks from the string that starts at the address by reducing the count from *#1* (original byte count) to *#2* (shortened byte count).
>TYPE	(a # --)	Same as TYPE except that the output string is moved to the pad prior to output. Used in multiprogrammed systems to output strings from disk blocks.

MOVE	(a1 a2 # --)	Copies a region of memory # bytes long, cell-by-cell beginning at *a1*, to memory beginning at *a2*. The move begins with the contents of *a1* and proceeds toward high memory.
CMOVE	(a1 a2 # --)	Copies a region of memory # bytes long, byte-by-byte beginning at *a1* to memory beginning at *a2*. The move begins with the contents of *a1* and proceeds toward high memory.
CMOVE>	(a1 a2 # --)	Copies a region of memory # bytes long, beginning at *a1*, to memory beginning at *a2*, but starts at the *end* of the string and proceeds toward low memory.
BLANK	(a # --)	Fills # bytes of memory beginning at *a* with ASCII blank.
KEY	(-- c)	Returns the ASCII value of the next available character from the current input device.
EXPECT	(a # --)	Awaits # characters (or a carriage-return) from the keyboard and stores them starting at *a* and continuing toward high memory; responds to the backspace by backing up the cursor.
SPAN	(-- a)	Contains the number of characters received by EXPECT.
WORD	(c -- a)	Reads one word from the input stream, using the character as a delimiter. Moves the string to the address returned, with the count in the first byte.
COUNT	(a -- a+1 #)	Converts the address of a counted string (whose length is contained in the first byte) into the form appropriate for TYPE by leaving the address of the first character, and the length on the stack.
>IN	(-- a)	User variable containing the present character offset within the input stream.
BLK	(-- a)	User variable containing the number of the mass storage block being interpreted as the input stream. If the value of BLK is zero, the input stream is taken from the input message buffer.

CONVERT	(ud1 a1 -- ud2 a2)	Beginning at *a1* + 1 (the byte containing the count is ignored), CONVERT converts the string to a binary value with regard to BASE. The new value is accumulated into *d1*, being left as *d2*. It continues until it encounters a character that can't be converted in the current number base; this address is left on the stack as *a2*.
NUMBER	(a -- d)	Converts the text beginning at *a*+1, with regard to BASE, to a binary value. The string may contain a leading minus sign which will negate the value.
-TEXT	(a1 # a2 -- ?)	Compares two strings that start at *a1* and *a2*, each of length #. Returns false if they match; true if no match (positive if binary string 1 > 2, negative if 1 < 2).
-MATCH	(d # s # -- a ?)	Searches for a match on the string at address *s* (source) of length # within the range of memory starting at *d* (destination) of length #. If found, returns the location of the match within the destination range and "false"; otherwise an invalid address and "true."
STRING	(c --)	Compiles the string literal delimited by *c* into the dictionary as a counted string.
LIT" xxx "	run-time: (-- a)	Compiles the string literal *xxx*, delimited by double quote. At run-time, returns the address of the counted string. Used only within definitions.

REVIEW OF TERMS

Expecting — halting execution of a program while awaiting input from the keyboard, as opposed to "scanning for."

Information hiding — a good practice in the art of programming in which the programmer localizes information about how a particular thing works (especially something that might change in later versions or be reused) within a routine or group of collected routines.

Relative pointer — a variable which specifies a location in relation to the beginning of an array or string—not the absolute address.

Scanning for — looking ahead in the input stream for the remaining text or for a substring delimited by a given character.

Superstring   in Forth, a character array which contains a number of strings. Any one string may be accessed by offsetting into the array.

Virtual memory   the treatment of mass storage (such as the disk) as though it were resident memory; also the mechanisms of the operating system which make this treatment possible.

REFERENCE

1.   Ham, Michael, "Think Like a User, Write Like a Fox," *Forth Dimensions*, VI/3, p. 23.

PROBLEMS

10-1. Enter some famous quotations into an available block, say 228. Now define a word called CHANGE which takes two ASCII values and changes all occurrences within block 228 of the first character into the second character. For example,

`65 69 CHANGE`

will change all the A's into E's.

10-2. Define a word called FORTUNE which will display a prediction such as "You will receive good news in the mail." The prediction should be chosen at random from a list of sixteen or fewer predictions. Each prediction is sixty-four characters, or less, long.

10-3. (a) First, define a word called Y/N? to be used in an application that requires a yes/no response from the user. The definition will await a single keystroke, then return a flag that is true if the key was "Y", or false if any other key.

(b) Sometimes the user is in lowercase and types a lowercase "y" meaning yes. Rewrite Y/N? so that it accepts upper and lowercase "y" as yes.

(c) Sometimes the user means to press "Y" (as in "Yes, I want to save the file I've been working on for the last three hours!") but strikes another key by mistake. Rewrite Y/N? so that it ignores any key except upper/lowercase "Y" and "N", not quitting till it receives one of them, and returning "true" for "Y" and "false" for "N."

10-4. According to Oriental legend, Buddha endows all persons born in each year with special, helpful characteristics represented by one of twelve animals. A different animal reigns over each year, and every twelve years the cycle repeats itself. For instance, persons born in 1900 are said to be born in the "Year of the Rat." The art of fortune-telling based on these influences of the natal year is called "Juneeshee."

The order of the cycle is:

Rat Ox Tiger Rabbit Dragon Snake
Horse Ram Monkey Cock Dog Boar

Write a word called .ANIMAL that types the name of the animal corresponding to its position in the cycle as listed here; e.g.,

```
0 .ANIMAL_RAT_ok
```

Now write a word called (JUNEESHEE) which takes as an argument a year of birth and prints the name of the associated animal. (1900 is the year of the Rat, 1901 is the Ox, etc.)

Finally, write a word called JUNEESHEE which prompts the user for his/her year of birth. At the prompt, output four underline characters, leaving a field to type the year into, then output four "backspaces," resetting the cursor to the beginning of the field. Use the definition of EXPECT# given in this chapter ("Building a Number-Input Routine with $\boxed{\text{KEY}}$"). When the user presses "return," the routine displays the name of the person's Juneeshee animal.

10-5. In this chapter, we defined the word "add" to input buzzphrases into a database. That version entered strings one at a time. Redefine "add" so that it scans for three fields, separated by commas, representing the three columns on each line; for example,

> start
>
> add integrated,management,criteria

and increments by rows.

10-6. We mentioned that $\boxed{\text{CONVERT}}$ could be used to parse a sophisticated numeric string such as "6/20/86". Write a definition called >DATE that scans such a string at a given address, returning the date as two 16-bit numbers on the stack: the high-order cell containing the year (1986) and the low-order cell containing the month and day, with the month in the high-order byte. Then write a word called SCAN-DATE, which scans the input stream for such a string, leaving the same values on the stack as >DATE.

10-7. In Chapter 8, we showed how to create a cell array (array of 16-bit numbers) in the dictionary. In this exercise, we'll create a *virtual array*—not in main memory but on disk—consisting of 16-bit values.

First, find three available, contiguous blocks to hold the array. These blocks should not contain any text, since you'll be using them to save binary numbers. Define a variable that points to the first of these blocks.

Now write a word called ELEMENT with the stack effect:

```
( index -- address)
```

that is, it converts a cell index into an absolute address within a block buffer. Notice that the first block will hold only 512 cells; beyond that, the address returned will point into the second block of the set, and so on. This word should also call UPDATE .

Test your work so far by writing routines to initialize the first 600 cells to some values, and to display the contents.

Next, redefine ELEMENT to reserve the first cell of this array as a count of how many elements have already been stored. Also define USED to return the address of this count field.

Write a routine to intialize the array to "empty." Then define PUT to take a 16-bit value from the stack and add it to the array at the next available position.

Next, define ENTER to add two 16-bit values on the stack to the array, with the cell underneath added first. Finally, define TABLE to display the data, eight numbers per line. (Thanks to Kim Harris.)

11
EXTENDING THE COMPILER WITH DEFINING WORDS AND COMPILING WORDS

This chapter marks the beginning of a new plateau in your aquaintance with Forth. The previous ten chapters have explored capabilities that you might find in any language—arithmetic, control flow and logic, data structures, input/output, mass storage, and so on—even colon can be compared to the "procedure" operator in some languages.

In this chapter, however, we'll launch into another dimension of possibilities as we learn to extend the Forth compiler itself. The ability to create new defining and compiling words is vital to writing exquisitely readable, maintainable applications, and perhaps represents Forth's greatest strength.

WHAT IS A DEFINING WORD?

A defining word, simply, is any word that creates a new dictionary header. Some of the defining words we've seen so far are:

```
:
VARIABLE
CONSTANT
CREATE
```

What they all have in common is that they "define" words; they add new names to the dictionary.

Unlike other languages, Forth lets us create our own defining words. Why would we want to? In general, defining words promote good factoring. We've mentioned the concept of factoring here and there, particularly in Chapter 8. Well-factored applications are easier to read, easier to think about, and easier to maintain.

The use of defining words promotes good factoring because it allows us to create whole *classes*, or *families*, of words with similar characteristics. The characteristics that bind the members together are specified not in the definition of each member, but in the defining word.

Before we can show an example, we'll have to learn how to define a defining word. The root of all defining words is the simplest defining word of all, CREATE.† CREATE takes a name from the input stream and creates a dictionary heading for it.

CREATE EXAMPLE

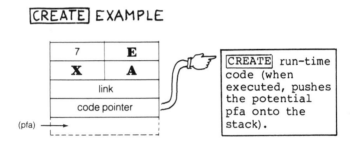

CREATE run-time code (when executed, pushes the potential pfa onto the stack).

CREATE is the *parent*, EXAMPLE is the *child*. What does the child do, when executed? It pushes its own pfa onto the stack. How does it know to do that? We didn't explicitly give it any code to execute. The answer is that EXAMPLE *doesn't* contain any run-time code; its code pointer simply points back to its parent, CREATE, which *does* have the run-time code.

CREATE is the basis for all other defining words. For instance, suppose Forth didn't have the word VARIABLE. We could define it as:

```
: VARIABLE    CREATE  O , ;
```

† **fig-Forth:** Remember to redefine CREATE as

```
: CREATE    <BUILDS DOES> ;
```

We've invoked CREATE within a colon definition! What does this do? Let's follow the action, in proper time sequence:

Time 1

`: VARIABLE   CREATE   0 , ;`

Define the defining-word VARIABLE .

Time 2

`VARIABLE ORANGES`

Execute VARIABLE , in turn performing two actions:
— CREATE a dictionary header with the name ORANGES and a code pointer that points to CREATE 's run-time code;
—"0 ," stores a 16-bit zero into the parameter field of the new variable, and allots the cell.

Time 3

`ORANGES`

Execute ORANGES. Since ORANGES points to the run-time code for CREATE , it pushes its pfa onto the stack.

Of course, we don't really need the word VARIABLE at all. We could always say:

`CREATE EXAMPLE   0 ,`

However, this syntax is not as elegant as when we factor the creating and allotting into a single definition.

Our definition of VARIABLE only shows half the power of defining words. All we've changed by using VARIABLE instead of CREATE is time 2, the point at which we define the word ORANGES. At time 3, on the other hand, ORANGES behaves exactly as it would have had we used CREATE .

But Forth also lets us create defining words that specify the *run-time* behavior of all their children. To illustrate, the following could be a valid definition for CONSTANT (although in fact, like VARIABLE , CONSTANT is usually defined in machine code):

`: CONSTANT   CREATE , DOES> @ ;`

The magic here is being performed by DOES> which marks the beginning of the run-time code for all children of this defining word. As you know, constants (i.e., children of the defining word CONSTANT) return their value, which is stored in their parameter field. Thus, the @ after DOES> fetches the value of the constant from its own pfa.

In any defining word, CREATE marks the beginning of the compile-time operations (time 2); DOES> marks the end of the compile-time operations and the beginning of the run-time operations (time 3).

Let's follow the action once again:

```
: CONSTANT   CREATE ,   DOES> @ ;
```

Time 1   Define the defining-word CONSTANT.

```
76 CONSTANT TROMBONES
```

Time 2   Execute CONSTANT in turn performing three actions:

DOES> @ ;

TROMBONES
link
code

TROMBONES
link
code
76

TROMBONES
link
code ———
76

CREATE a dictionary header with the name TROMBONES.

"Comma" the value (e.g., 76) from the stack into the constant's parameter field.

Reset TROMBONE's code pointer field to point to the code after DOES>.

TROMBONES

Execute TROMBONES. Since TROMBONES now points to the code following DOES>, it fetches the value (76), pushing it onto the stack.

Time 3   the stack.

Notice that at time 3, DOES> first pushes onto the stack the child's pfa. In other words, the definition

```
: VARIABLE   CREATE  0 , ;
```

is equivalent to

```
: VARIABLE   CREATE  0 , DOES> ;
```

which, at run-time, pushes the pfa, but otherwise does nothing.

Since a defining word specifies two behaviors (compile-time and run-time), special stack-effect conventions have been adopted. Here's how the definition of CONSTANT would be commented:

```
: CONSTANT  ( n -- )  CREATE ,
   DOES>  ( -- n) @ ;
```

The stack-effect comment on the top line depicts the compile-time behavior; the one on the bottom line, after DOES> , represents the stack behavior of the children.

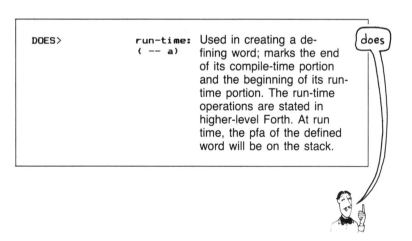

| DOES> | run-time: (-- a) | Used in creating a defining word; marks the end of its compile-time portion and the beginning of its run-time portion. The run-time operations are stated in higher-level Forth. At run time, the pfa of the defined word will be on the stack. | does |

DEFINING WORDS YOU CAN DEFINE YOURSELF

In this section, we'll discuss three useful classes of defining words. The first type allows us to factor similar code out of a series of colon definitions. In the last chapter we wrote:

```
: 1ADJECTIVE    10 CHOOSE  0 .BUZZWORD ;
: 2ADJECTIVE    10 CHOOSE  1 .BUZZWORD ;
: NOUN          10 CHOOSE  2 .BUZZWORD ;
```

If we had more than three of these parts of speech to define, we'd be smart to factor out the similarities into a separate word, named for "part of speech":

```
: PART  ( column# -- )  10 CHOOSE  SWAP .BUZZWORD ;
: 1ADJECTIVE    0 PART ;
: 2ADJECTIVE    1 PART ;
: NOUN          2 PART ;
```

However, this is still wasteful of memory. Since the only difference between the three words is a number, they don't need to be defined as colon definitions at all, but rather:

```
: PART  ( column# -- )  CREATE ,
   DOES> @  10 CHOOSE  SWAP .BUZZWORD ;
0 PART 1ADJECTIVE    1 PART 2ADJECTIVE    2 PART NOUN
```

This definition of PART is similar to that of $\boxed{\text{CONSTANT}}$† except that, at run time, it goes beyond pushing the column number onto the stack—it also selects a random row number and invokes .BUZZWORD.

The second broad category of defining words allows us to factor out repetitious code used at compile time. Suppose that we want to assign ranges of blocks on a disk to a group of students, 25 blocks per student starting at Block 360. We want a series of constants, indicating each student's starting block. We might define:

```
360 CONSTANT JILL
385 CONSTANT DICK
410 CONSTANT DON
435 CONSTANT CHRIS
460 CONSTANT THEA
485 CONSTANT LARRY
```

I don't know about you, but my addition is rusty and prone to errors. Besides, what if we change our minds and decide to give each student 30 blocks? It's more elegant to factor the compile-time calculations into a word:

```
: +STUDENT   ( n -- n+25 n )   DUP   25 +   SWAP ;
      360  \  beginning of student blocks
+STUDENT CONSTANT JILL      +STUDENT CONSTANT DICK
+STUDENT CONSTANT DON       +STUDENT CONSTANT CHRIS
+STUDENT CONSTANT THEA      +STUDENT CONSTANT LARRY
.   .( End of student blocks ) CR
```

The final "dot" gets rid of the left-over block number.

But the foregoing approach still is not as elegant as what we can do with defining words. Watch this:

```
: STUDENT   ( n -- n+25)   CREATE   DUP ,   25 +
    DOES>   ( -- n)   @ ;
360  \  beginning of student blocks
STUDENT JILL     STUDENT DICK    STUDENT DON
STUDENT CHRIS    STUDENT THEA    STUDENT LARRY
.   .( End of student blocks ) CR
```

The defining-word STUDENT is both creating "constants" and handling all our calculations at compile time.

A third use of defining words is to create advanced data structures such as dimensional arrays. You'll sometimes hear Forth criticized for lacking sophisticated data structures. However, it's rare that any set of data structures will serve all applications.

Forth goes one better, and offers us the *tools* to easily create customized data-structure defining words. Thus, we can create data *structures* that also

---

† **For Purists:** Sometimes it makes sense to incorporate existing defining words if they do most or all of what you want to do at compile time. Here we could substitute the word $\boxed{\text{CONSTANT}}$ for the phrase $\boxed{\text{CREATE}}$ $\boxed{,}$ with exactly the same effect. The Standard does not address this technique, however, and it may not work on all systems.

possess their own, unique run-time *operations*. Computer scientists call these structures *abstract data types*.

We'll show two examples. The simpler one is a defining word that creates a one-dimensional array. We can, of course, make such an array without using a defining word:

```
CREATE VALVES  30 ALLOT  \   array of 1-byte valve settings
: VALVE  ( i -- a)  \  convert valve# into absolute address
   VALVES + ;
```

Here the word VALVE lets us index into the array VALVES; for instance the expression

```
6 VALVE C@
```

would give us the current setting of hydraulic valve #6.

The above solution is preferable if the application requires only one or two such arrays. When more are needed, a defining word will simplify things:

```
: ARRAY  ( #bytes -- )  \  define 1-dimensional byte array
   CREATE  ALLOT
   DOES>  ( i -- a)  + ;

30 ARRAY VALVE
6 VALVE C@
```

Check this out. At time 1, we define ARRAY. At time 2 we execute ARRAY, in turn invoking $\boxed{\text{CREATE}}$ (to define VALVE) and $\boxed{\text{ALLOT}}$ (to reserve 30 bytes for the array). At time 3 we execute VALVE, in turn invoking the run-time code of ARRAY, which consists of adding the index (6) to the base address of the array.

By changing the definition of a defining word before recompiling, you can change the characteristics of all the member words of that family. This ability makes program development much easier. For instance, if our application requires the arrays to be initialized to zero, we might redefine ARRAY accordingly. First, we'll define a word similar to $\boxed{\text{ALLOT}}$ but which also erases (sets to 0) the allotted region:

```
: 0ALLOT  ( #bytes -- )  HERE OVER  ERASE  ALLOT ;
```

Then we'll substitute 0ALLOT for $\boxed{\text{ALLOT}}$ in our definition of ARRAY:

```
: ARRAY  ( #bytes -- )  \  define 1-dimensional byte array
   CREATE  0ALLOT
   DOES>  ( i -- a)  + ;
```

Or we can incorporate certain kinds of error checking while we are developing the program, then eliminate them after we're sure the program runs correctly. Here's a version of ARRAY that, at run-time, ensures that the index is valid (that it points within the array):

```
: ARRAY  ( #bytes)  CREATE DUP ,  ALLOT
    DOES> ( i -- a)  2DUP @ U< NOT  ABORT" Range Error " + 2+ ;
```

which breaks down as follows:

DUP , ALLOT	Compiles the count and allots the given number of bytes.
DOES> 2DUP @	At run time, given the index on the stack, produces: (i pfa i #)
U< NOT	Tests that the index is not less than the maximum, that is, the stored count. Since $\boxed{U<}$ is an unsigned compare, negative arguments will appear as very high numbers and thus will also fail the test.
ABORT" Range error"	Aborts if the comparison check fails.
+ 2+	Otherwise adds the index to the pfa, plus an additional two to skip over the cell that contains the count.

Here's another way that the use of defining words can help during development. Let's say you suddenly decide that all of the arrays you've defined with ARRAY are too large to be kept in computer memory and should be kept on disk instead. All you have to do is redefine the run-time portion of ARRAY. This new ARRAY will compute which block on the disk a given byte would be contained in, read the block into a buffer using $\boxed{\text{BLOCK}}$, and return the address of the desired byte within the buffer. An array defined in this way could span many consecutive blocks (using the same technique as in Problem 10-7).

Our second example is a defining word that creates two-dimensional byte arrays of given size:

```
: MATRIX  ( #rows #cols -- )   CREATE  OVER ,  * ALLOT
    DOES> ( row col -- a)  DUP @ ROT * + + 2+ ;†
```

---

† **For Optimizers:** This version will run even faster:

```
: MATRIX  ( #rows #cols -- )
    OVER CONSTANT HERE 2+ ,  * ALLOT
    DOES> ( row col -- a)  2@ ROT * + + ;
```

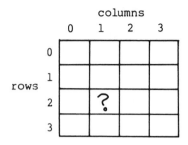

To create an array four bytes by four bytes, we would say

    4 4 MATRIX BOARD

To access, say, the byte in row 2, column 1, we could say

    2 1 BOARD C@

Here's how our MATRIX works in general terms. Since the computer only allows us to have one-dimensional arrays, we must simulate the second dimension. While our imaginary array looks like this: ⟶

column:	0	1	2	3
0		4	8	12
1		5	9	13
2		6	10	14
3		7	11	15

Our real array looks like this:

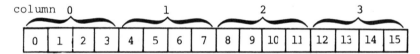

If we want the address of the byte in row 2, column 1, it can be computed by multiplying our column number (1) by the number of rows in each column (4) and then adding our row number (2), which indicates that we want the sixth byte in the real array.

This calculation is what children of MATRIX must do at run time. You'll notice that, to perform this calculation, each member word needs to know how many rows are in each column of its particular array. For this reason, MATRIX must store this value into the beginning of the array at compile time.

For the curious, here are the stack effects of the run-time portion of MATRIX:

OPERATION	CONTENTS OF STACK
	row col pfa
DUP @	row col pfa #rows
ROT	row pfa #rows col
*	row pfa col-index
+ +	address
2+	corrected-address

It is necessary to add two to the computed address because the first cell of the array contains the number of rows.

Here's a bonus example, not terribly useful but at least visually interesting:

```
\ Shapes, using a defining word
: STAR   42 EMIT ;
: .ROW  ( b -- )  \  display star for each bit in byte
   CR  8 0 DO  DUP 128 AND  IF STAR ELSE SPACE THEN
      2* LOOP  DROP ;
: SHAPE  ( b1 b2 b3 b4 b5 b6 b7 b8 -- )  \ define 8-row shape
   CREATE  8 0 DO C, LOOP
   DOES>  DUP 7 + DO  I C@ .ROW  -1 +LOOP  CR ;

\ Shapes:
HEX
18 18 3C 5A 99 24 24 24   SHAPE MAN
81 42 24 18 18 24 42 81   SHAPE EQUIS
AA AA FE FE 38 38 38 FE   SHAPE CASTLE
DECIMAL
```

.ROW prints a pattern of stars and spaces that correspond to the 8-bit number on the stack. For instance,

```
2 BASE ! ok
00111001 .ROW
  *** * ok
DECIMAL ok
```

Our defining word SHAPE takes eight arguments from the stack and defines a shape which, when executed, prints an 8-by-8 grid that corresponds to the eight arguments. For example,

```
MAN
    **
    **
   ****
  * ** *
 *  **  *
   *  *
   *  *
   *  *
ok
```

In summary, defining words can be extremely powerful tools. When you create a new defining word, you extend your compiler. Traditional languages do not provide this flexibility because traditional compilers are inflexible packages that say, "Use my instruction set or forget it!"

The real power of defining words is that they can simplify your problem. Using them well, you can shorten your programming time, reduce the size of your program, and improve readability. Forth's flexibility in this regard is so radical in comparison to traditional languages that many people don't even believe it. Well, now you've seen it.

The next section introduces still another way to extend the ability of Forth's compiler.

WHAT IS A COMPILING WORD?

When ordinary Forth words appear in colon definitions, they are compiled into the dictionary; the words are passive during compilation. A *compiling word*, on the other hand, is one that appears in a colon definition and actively does compiling work. Words such as [IF], [THEN], [BEGIN], [REPEAT], and [."] are all compiling words.

Just as Forth does not presume to offer every defining word you'd ever need, neither does it pretend to supply the gamut of compiling operators. The ability to control the compiler by creating your own compiling words allows a greater freedom of expression than you can get with other languages. It lets you localize intelligence within appropriate compiling operators—not scattered throughout the application—making programs easier to write, easier to read, easier to think about, and easier to maintain.

Perhaps your application would be expressed more elegantly if your language supported a case statement that matches text strings. Or perhaps you'd like to add extra error-checking to your control structure operators. Or—you never know—you may want a [DO] loop that uses a 32-bit index. If you need it, you can add it.

We'll give more examples of useful compiling words as we go along. Some of our examples may already exist in your system. Even if you don't intend to create any compiling words of your own right away, an understanding of how to create them is vital for understanding how Forth's own compiling words are created. Remember, Forth is written in Forth; so anything it can do, you can do!

Before we get to any useful examples, let's begin with the mechanics of creating compiling words. As we've mentioned, compiling words are executed, not compiled, when encountered by the colon compiler within a definition. This is the key to creating a compiling word. To understand how this works, let's look at the colon compiler.

The colon compiler is similar to the text interpreter. It scans the input stream looking for words, and tries to find them in the dictionary. Ordinarily, instead of executing them immediately—as [INTERPRET] does—it compiles their addresses into the dictionary. However, it recognizes certain words as compiling words, and executes only those, immediately, just as the text interpreter would.

How does the colon compiler know the difference? By checking the definition's *precedence bit* (Chapter 9, "The Structure of a Dictionary Entry"). If the bit is "off," the address of the word is compiled. If the bit is "on," the word is executed immediately; such words are described as *immediate*.

The word IMMEDIATE makes a word immediate. It is used in the form

```
: name    definition ; IMMEDIATE
```

that is, it is invoked right after the compilation of the definition.

Suppose we define this word:

```
: TEST    ; IMMEDIATE
```

This is an *immediate* word that does nothing. If we invoke it in the definition of another word, for example,

```
: 2CRS    CR  TEST  CR ;
```

here is what will get compiled:

2CRS
link
code
adr of CR
adr of CR
adr of EXIT

TEST does not get compiled in the definition. In fact, it *executes* during the compilation of 2CRS. Of course, TEST doesn't do anything as is, so it's not of much use. Here's another experiment. Suppose we have a word called TULIP. We define

```
: TEST    COMPILE TULIP ; IMMEDIATE
```

Now we redefine 2CRS just as before:

```
: 2CRS    CR  TEST  CR ;
```

Here's what has been compiled this time:

2CRS
link
code
adr of CR
adr of TULIP
adr of CR
adr of EXIT

This time, TEST did something during compilation of 2CRS—it compiled the address of TULIP. True, in this example we might as well have said:

```
: 2CRS   CR  TULIP   CR ;
```

but the point is that TEST has the power to compile, or not compile, anything it wants, because it is immediate.

Yes, we slipped a new word in on you, COMPILE . It's best that we introduced it this way, because it's easiest to understand in context.

```
: TEST   COMPILE TULIP ; IMMEDIATE
```

COMPILE computes the address of the next word in the definition and saves it as a number.

```
: 2CRS   CR   TEST   CR ;
```

When the immediate word in which COMPILE appears is invoked, it compiles the saved address into the definition being defined. Think of this process as *deferred compilation*.

Here's a simple example that can actually be useful: Suppose we've written a debugging tool called DEBUG, which we want to execute throughout our application. Because we want to turn the debugging on or off, we'll actually use the word TEST, which is defined like this:

```
: TEST   TESTING? IF DEBUG THEN ;
```

that is, it checks a flag at run-time to determine whether to invoke DEBUG. This is fine, except that our application is performance-critical; stopping to test a flag on every loop is throwing off our timings. When we are *not* debugging, we don't want any code testing whether or not we're debugging.

The solution is to redefine TEST as

```
: TEST   TESTING? IF  COMPILE DEBUG  THEN ;  IMMEDIATE
```

Now, of course, we have to recompile the application to switch testing modes, but that only takes a minute. In testing mode, TEST will compile DEBUG in the appropriate places in the application. Otherwise, it won't compile anything at all. The IF decision is being made at compilation time.

Now let's get down with a trickier, but more familiar, compiling word. The word ." does not really *display* a string, as we're inclined to think. In fact, it compiles the string into the dictionary, so that it can later be displayed. What word displays it, then? A primitive called (.") on some systems, or dot" on others. Let's play out this drama in time steps, as we did before with defining words. This definition for ." will work on most Forth systems, but it's the principle, not the details, that matters here.

Time 1

```
: dot"   R>  COUNT  2DUP + >R  TYPE ;
: ."   COMPILE dot"  ASCII " STRING ; IMMEDIATE
```

Define dot" and ." .

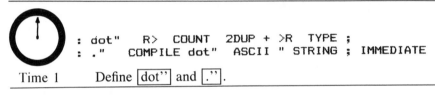

Time 2

```
: GREET   ." Hi, there " ;
```

Execute ." which is an immediate word (and therefore executes during the compilation of GREET) — in turn performing two actions:

—Compile the address of dot" into the definition of GREET.

GREET	link	code	dot"		. . .

—Compile the string delimited by double-quote as a counted string literal.

GREET	link	code	dot"	10	H	i	,		t	h	e	r	e		. . .

Time 3

GREET

Execute GREET, in turn invoking the run-time code, dot" , which displays the string.†

To review, the following two words are useful in creating new compiling words:

IMMEDIATE	(—)	Marks the most recently defined word as one which, when encountered during compilation, will be executed rather than be compiled.
COMPILE xxx	(—)	Used in the definition of a compiling word. When the compiling word, in turn, is used in a source definition, the code field address of *xxx* will be compiled into the dictionary entry so that when the new definition is executed, *xxx* will be executed.

† **For the Very Curious:** dot" begins by getting an address off the return stack. In this case, it is the address of the counted string. COUNT converts this address to address and count, suitable for TYPE . But there's one other thing we must do: we must adjust the return stack pointer so that, when we return, it points past the end of the string. This address we compute by adding 2DUP ed copies of the address and count together; we then restore this corrected address to the return stack. (If your system includes a source listing, check its definition of ." before experimenting.)

MORE COMPILER-CONTROLLING WORDS

As you may recall, a number that appears in a colon definition is called a *literal*. An example is the "4" in the definition

    : FOUR-MORE   4 + ;

The use of a literal in a colon definition requires two cells. The first contains the address of a routine which, when executed, will push the contents of the second cell (the number itself) onto the stack.†

The name of this routine may vary; let's call it the "run-time code for a literal," or simply (LITERAL) . When the colon compiler encounters a number, it first compiles the run-time code for a literal, then compiles the number itself.

9	**F**
0	**U**
link	
code pointer	
(LITERAL)	
4	
+	
EXIT	

The word you will use most often to compile a literal is LITERAL (no parentheses). LITERAL compiles both the run-time code and the value itself. To illustrate:

    4
    : FOUR-MORE (n -- n+4) LITERAL + ;‡

Here the word LITERAL will compile as a literal the "4" that we put on the stack before beginning compilation. We get a dictionary entry that is identical to the one shown above.

For a more useful application of LITERAL , recall that in Chapter 8 we created an array called LIMITS that consisted of five cells, each of which contained the temperature limit for a different burner. To simplify access to this array, we created a word called LIMIT. The two definitions looked like this:

    CREATE LIMITS 10 ALLOT \ 5-cell array of limits
    : LIMIT (burner# -- adr-of-limit) 2* LIMITS + ;

---

† **For Memory Conservationists:** While a literal requires two cells, a reference to a constant requires only one cell. Thus you can save memory by defining a number as a constant, if you use it often enough to compensate for the memory occupied by the constant's header. There is hardly any difference between the time required to execute a constant and a literal.

‡ **If Your System Prevents This:** In some Forth systems, semicolon takes the trouble to make sure the stack level hasn't changed since colon. The idea is to protect you from silly errors. Unfortunately, it also prevents you from passing an argument to LITERAL . If your system aborts when you try this, fool it with:

    : OUTSIDE (literal -- garbage) 0 SWAP ; IMMEDIATE
    4
    : FOUR-MORE   OUTSIDE LITERAL + ; DROP

Now let's assume that we will access the array only through the word LIMIT. We can eliminate the head of the array (name, link, and code fields) by using this construction instead:

```
HERE  10 ALLOT  \ 5-cell array of limits
: LIMIT  ( burner# -- adr-of-limit)  2* LITERAL + ;
```

In the first line, we put the address of the beginning of the array ([HERE]) on the stack. In the second line, we compile this address as a literal into the definition of LIMIT.

By eliminating the head for LIMITS, we save dictionary space.

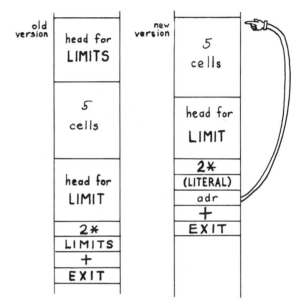

There are two other compiler control words that you should know. The words [[] and []] can be used inside a colon definition to stop compilation and start it again, respectively. Whatever words appear between them will be executed "immediately"—that is, at compile time. For example, imagine a colon definition in which we need to type line 3 of block 180. To get the address of line 3, we could use the phrase

```
180 BLOCK  3 64 *  +
```

but it's time-consuming to execute

```
3 64 *
```

every time we use this definition. Alternatively, we could write

```
180 BLOCK  192 +
```

but it's unclear to human readers exactly what the 192 means.

The best solution is to write

```
180 BLOCK  [ 3 64 * ] LITERAL  +
```

The arithmetic is performed only once, at compile time, and the result is compiled as a literal.

. . .
(LITERAL)
192
. . .

We said that $]$ restarts compilation. In fact, $]$ is invoked by $:$, and in many systems $]$ *is* the compiler.

Here's a trivial example that may give you some ideas for more practical applications. This definition must be loaded from a disk block:

```
: LIST-THIS   [ BLK @ ] LITERAL  LIST ;
```

When you execute LIST-THIS, you will list whichever block LIST-THIS is defined in. (At compile time, $\boxed{BLK}$ contains the number of the block being loaded. $\boxed{LITERAL}$ compiles this number into the definition as a literal, so that it will serve as the argument for $\boxed{LIST}$ at run time.)

By the way, here's the definition of $\boxed{LITERAL}$:†

```
: LITERAL  ( n -- )  COMPILE (LITERAL)  , ; IMMEDIATE
```

First it compiles the address of the run-time code, then it compiles the value itself (using comma).

Another compiler-controlling word is $\boxed{[COMPILE]}$. Suppose we want to rename $\boxed{IF}$. Obviously, we can't just write:

```
: implies  IF ; IMMEDIATE
```

because $\boxed{IF}$ is itself immediate; this code compiles a jump that is not resolved by a matching $\boxed{THEN}$. Somehow we must defeat $\boxed{IF}$'s defenses (its precedence bit) and get it compiled as though it were not immediate.

This is where $\boxed{[COMPILE]}$ comes in. If we define:

```
: implies   [COMPILE] IF ; IMMEDIATE
: otherwise [COMPILE] ELSE ; IMMEDIATE
: anyway    [COMPILE] THEN ; IMMEDIATE
```

we can use a new syntax for conditionals:

```
: fork   ( ?) implies  ." True "  otherwise  ." False "
    anyway  ." flag" ;
```

You may be wondering why we can't use $\boxed{COMPILE}$, as in:

```
: implies   COMPILE IF ; IMMEDIATE
```

---

† **For Memory Conservationists:** Clever systems on computers that tolerate odd addresses distinguish between cell and byte literals, using only three bytes for the latter.

Recall that COMPILE performs *deferred compilation*; that is, it would not compile IF into the word "implies," as we want, but rather into the word that *invokes* "implies" (e.g., fork).

[COMPILE], on the other hand, causes ordinary compilation, but of an immediate word that otherwise would have been executed.

Incidentally, the use of the square brackets in the name [COMPILE] is a Forth naming convention that indicates "execution at compile time." In fact, you could simulate the effect of [COMPILE] like this:

```
: implies   [ ' IF , ] ; IMMEDIATE
```

(or whatever's correct for your dialect). Here, we use the interpreter to find the address of IF, then "comma" this compilation address into the definition. The compiler is prevented from executing the immediate word IF.

Now here comes your trial by fire. If you can survive this next bit, you'll be an expert on compiling words!

Suppose we have the words BRIGHT and -BRIGHT, which change the video mode to bright and normal, respectively, for all succeeding text. Our mission is to define the word B." (for "bright dot-quote") to automatically change the mode to bright, display a string, and then reset the mode to normal.

There are two solutions, both of which are useful for study. First, let's recognize that the action of changing the video mode must occur when the string is *displayed*, not when it is *compiled*. Our first solution, then, is to create an equivalent to dot", which we'll call bdot", and let B." imitate ." except for compiling bdot" instead of dot":

```
: dot"    R> COUNT  2DUP + >R  TYPE ;
: ."      COMPILE dot"  ASCII " WORD  C@ 1+ ALLOT ; IMMEDIATE
: bdot"   BRIGHT R>  COUNT  2DUP + >R  TYPE  -BRIGHT ;
: B."     COMPILE bdot"  ASCII " WORD  C@ 1+ ALLOT ; IMMEDIATE
```

The foregoing solution is messy and probably not transportable. The alternate solution simply invokes ." and looks like this:

```
: B."   COMPILE BRIGHT  [COMPILE] ."
   COMPILE -BRIGHT ; IMMEDIATE
```

This is a compiling word, so let's see what it compiles. If we use it in the definition

```
: TEST   B." Wow!" ;
```

this is what gets compiled:

TEST	link	code	BRIGHT	dot"	4	W	O	W	!	-BRIGHT	EXIT

Our compiling word has done three things:

1. compiled into TEST the address of BRIGHT (so that BRIGHT will execute at TEST's run-time);
2. invoked $\boxed{.''}$ which in turn compiled $\boxed{\text{dot''}}$ and compiled the string in line; and
3. compiled the address of -BRIGHT.

The disadvantage of this solution over the previous one is that every invocation of B.'' compiles two extra addresses. The first solution is more efficient and therefore preferable if you have the system source listing and lots of invocations of B.''. The second solution is simpler to implement, and adequate for a small number of invocations.

If the foregoing ideas seem hard to grasp and the concept of time never seemed so confusing, rest assured that you will acquire a comfortable familiarity with all these words the more you use them. Other languages may be easier to learn; but what other languages let you extend the compiler like this?

As we've said before, an invaluable way to study Forth is to study Forth's source (written in Forth). See how these compiling words are used in other definitions, and how they themselves are defined.

To summarize, here are the additional compiler control words we introduced in this section:

LITERAL	compile-time: (n --) run-time: (-- n)	Used only inside a colon definition. At compile time, compiles a value from the stack into the definition as a literal. At run-time, the value will be pushed onto the stack.
[	(--)	Leaves compile mode.
]	(--)	Enters compile mode.
[COMPILE] xxx	(--)	Used in a colon definition, causes the immediate word *xxx* to be compiled as though it were *not* immediate; *xxx* will be executed when the definition is executed.

left-bracket

right-bracket

bracket-compile

A HANDY HINT
ENTERING MULTILINE DEFINITIONS FROM THE KEYBOARD

Some Forth systems won't let you type multiple-line definitions from the keyboard, because
pressing the return key takes you out of compilation mode. The solution, on such systems,
is to begin each subsequent line with a new invocation of the compiler:

```
: BOXTEST  ( length width height -- ) RETURN
]  6 >  ROT 22 >  ROT 19 >  AND AND RETURN
]  IF  ." Big enough " THEN ; RETURN _ok
```

THE STATE FLAG

Our final concept pertaining to the compiler is a thing called *state*. Most Forth
systems have a variable called $\boxed{\text{STATE}}$ which contains "true" when you are
compiling and "false" when interpreting. Here's a tool for illustrating this point;
it displays the value of the variable $\boxed{\text{STATE}}$:

```
: .STATE   STATE ? ; IMMEDIATE
```

Now type

```
.STATE_0_ok
```

Forth is interpreting at the time we invoke .STATE. (The fact that .STATE
is immediate has no effect; the interpreter doesn't check the precedence bit.)
Now invoke .STATE within a new definition:

```
: TEST   .STATE ;_-1_ok
```

This time $\boxed{\text{STATE}}$ is "true," because .STATE was invoked by the compiler.

Why would we ever need to know the state? Whenever we want to construct
a word that must *appear* to behave the same inside or outside a colon definition,
but in fact must behave differently. An example is the word $\boxed{\text{ASCII}}$.

In ordinary usage, $\boxed{\text{ASCII}}$ appears within colon definitions. For example:

```
: TEST  ( -- ascii-a)  ASCII A ;
```

When we *execute* TEST, the number 65 will appear on the stack.
$\boxed{\text{ASCII}}$ has performed the conversion at compilation time; ASCII must be a
compiling word. It will scan the input stream for the character, then compile it
as a literal so that it will be pushed onto the stack when TEST is executed. We
may define the compiling version of $\boxed{\text{ASCII}}$ as follows:

```
: ASCII  ( -- c)
\ Compile:   c   ( -- )
   BL WORD 1+ C@  [COMPILE] LITERAL ; IMMEDIATE
```

(A note on the comments: the stack comment on the first line represents the run-time behavior, the syntax for using the word. The comment on the second line shows what happens at compile time; namely that a character is read from the input stream and nothing is left on the stack.)

In the above definition, WORD scans the input stream for blank-delimited text, and returns the address where the counted string can be found. We assume this text is one-character only, so we skip the count with 1+, and C@ the value. Next we invoke LITERAL which compiles the run-time code for a literal followed by the value itself, which is what we want.

Now consider what happens if we want ASCII to work *outside* of definitions as well; for example, the phrase

```
ASCII A
```

will leave the number 65 on the stack (this can be useful for creating tables, etc.)

We are now asking ASCII to do something different than before; in this version we want to define it simply

```
: ASCII  ( -- c )  BL WORD 1+ C@ ;
```

So, in order to get the single word ASCII to handle both cases, we'll have to define it to be sensitive to the state:

```
: ASCII  ( -- c )
\ Compile:   c   ( -- )
\ Interpret:   c   ( -- c )
   BL WORD 1+ C@
   STATE @ IF  [COMPILE] LITERAL   THEN ;  IMMEDIATE
```

Such a word is called *state-smart*.

At first glance, state-smartness seems reasonable, even desirable, especially with a word such as ASCII that is only used in compilation.

A difficulty arises with state-smart words, however, when the programmer tries to reuse them in another definition and have them behave in the normal way. An example would be trying to use a state-smart compiling word in the definition of another compiling word. As the layers of state-smartness deepen, the programmer must go to greater lengths to keep track of what is supposed to do what where.

Dumb words are actually safer to use than smart words, because their behavior is predictable. Historically, in some earlier systems the word ." was state-smart. With the 83 Standard, however, the two functions were factored into two different words, ." (which handles the compiling usage within definitions), and .((which handles the run-time usage during interpretation of blocks as they load).

The word ' (tick) shares a similar history, and is now a dumb word. Its function when it appears within a definition is identical to that when it appears interpretively: it finds the definition whose name is in the input stream at run time. The version of tick that works as a compiling word is called ['].

Some Forth developers argue that *nothing* should be state-smart. Going back to ASCII, this would mean one of two choices: 1) allow ASCII to be used only within definitions, and if necessary create a different word such as ascii (lower case) for the interpretive version; or 2) make ASCII interpretive only. Its usage would therefore be

```
: TEST    [ ASCII A ] LITERAL ;
```

By convention, another word could then be defined for simplicity:

```
: [ASCII]    ASCII    [COMPILE] LITERAL ;    IMMEDIATE
```

which would be used:

```
: TEST    [ASCII] A ;
```

AN INTRODUCTION TO FORTH FLOWCHARTS

Flowcharts provide a way to visualize the logical structure of a definition, to see where the branches branch and where the loops loop. Old-fashioned flowcharting techniques haven't been adequate for describing Forth's structured organization. Instead, various Forth programmers have devised alternate schemes.

The question of which diagramming approach works best for Forth remains open; programmers use whatever methods work best for them. The subject of flowcharting could occupy a chapter of its own, but we're running out of chapters.

The diagrams that we will use are loosely based on a type of flowchart called the ''D-chart.'' Here's how our diagrams work:

Sequential statements are written one below the other, without lines or boxes:

```
        statement
        next statement
        next statement
```

Lines are used to show non-sequential control paths (conditional branches and loops). The Forth statement

```
condition IF true ELSE false THEN statement
```

would be diagrammed

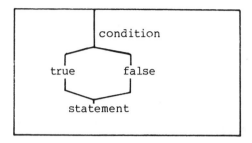

If either phrase is omitted, a vertical line is drawn in its place:

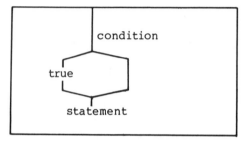

It is immaterial whether "true" is left or right.

A BEGIN UNTIL structure is diagrammed like this:

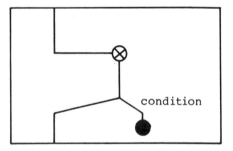

The entire loop structure is shifted to the right from the "normal" flow of execution, connected by a horizontal line at the top. If additional levels of nested loops were to be shown, they would be shifted still further to the right.

The black dot is the symbol for the end of the loop. It indicates that control is returned to the return point, symbolized by the circled X. The condition will cause the loop either to be repeated or to be exited. The diagonal line sloping down to the left indicates the return to the outer level of execution.

A [BEGIN] [WHILE] [REPEAT] loop is similar:

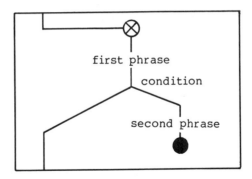

We've given this brief introduction to Forth flowcharts so that we can visualize the structure of two very important words.

CURTAIN CALLS

This section gives us a chance to say "Good-bye" to the text interpreter and the colon compiler and perhaps to see them in a new light.

All along we've referred to the word [INTERPRET] as the text interpreter. Its formal description is:

INTERPRET	(--)	Performs text interpretation of the input stream, indexed by >IN, until input is exhausted.

Although it's designed for use by the Forth system itself, it can be used in tools you define yourself. As a quick example, suppose you have written a loop which is acting funny. To help debug it, you'd like a word that stops each time around and lets you enter a line of interactive commands. When you press return, the loop continues. Such a tool is possible, using [INTERPRET].

To get a feel for the possibilities, define

```
: TEST    0 BEGIN  DUP .  1+  QUERY INTERPRET  0 UNTIL ;
```

Type TEST. It will display a zero, and wait. When you press return, it will loop again, displaying a one. Or you can type any command you like before pressing return; INTERPRET will see that it gets done before continuing with the loop. When you want out of the loop, type QUIT or make an error that causes an abort. Either action clears the return stack, taking you out of INTERPRET and out of TEST. (For a more useful version of this tool, see [1].)

Every Forth dialect has a different way of defining INTERPRET, but by describing the algorithm and drawing its D-chart, we can convey the sense of its operation. Here is what INTERPRET does, in plain English:

> *Begin a loop. Within the loop, scan the next word from the input stream and try to look up. If it's defined, execute it, then make sure the stack has not underflowed. (If it has, exit the loop and display an error message.) If it's* not *defined, try to convert it to a number, leaving it on the stack. Then repeat the loop until the input stream is exhausted.*

Let's apply our D-charting techniques to this algorithm:

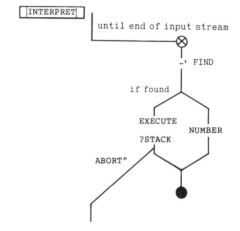

Now let's compare the interpreter's structure with that of the colon compiler:

> *Begin a loop. Within the loop, scan the next word from the input stream and try to look up. If it is defined, then treat it as a word. If the word is immediate, then execute it and make sure the stack has not underflowed. If it is* not *immediate, emplace its compilation address. If the word is* not *defined, try to convert it to a number, compiling it as a literal. Then repeat the loop until the input stream is exhausted, or the system state returns to interpreter mode.*

Picture it this way:

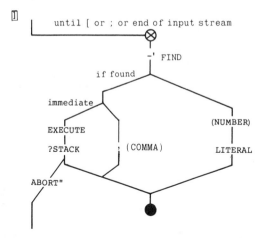

(If your system provides its own source code, we strongly encourage you to study the actual definitions of INTERPRET and of].)

Compare the two diagrams and you'll see that] could be called a text interpreter with the ability to decide whether to execute or to compile any given word. It is the simplicity of this design that lets you add new compiling words so easily.

In summary, we've shown two ways to extend the Forth compiler:

1. Add new, specialized compilers, by creating new defining words.
2. Extend the existing compiler by creating new compiling words.

While traditional compilers try to be universal tools, the Forth compiler is a collection of separate, simple tools . . . with room for more. Which approach seems more useful:

COMPLEXITY   OR SIMPLICITY?

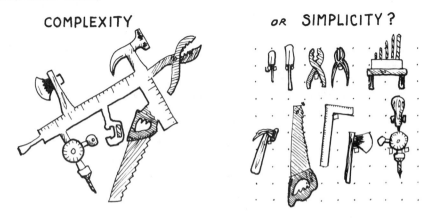

Here's a summary of the words we've covered in this chapter:

`DOES>`	`run-time:` `( -- a)`	Used in creating a defining word; marks the end of its compile-time portion and the beginning of its run-time portion. The run-time operations are stated in higher-level Forth. At run time, the pfa of the defined word will be on the stack.
`IMMEDIATE`	`( -- )`	Marks the most recently defined word as one which, when encountered during compilation, will be executed rather than be compiled.
`COMPILE xxx`	`( -- )`	Used in the definition of a compiling word. When the compiling word, in turn, is used in a source definition, the code field address of *xxx* will be compiled into the dictionary entry so that when the new definition is executed, *xxx* will be executed.
`LITERAL`	`compile-time:` `( n -- )` `run-time:` `( -- n)`	Used only inside a colon definition. At compile time, compiles a value from the stack into the definition as a literal. At run time, the value will be pushed onto the stack.
`[`	`( -- )`	Leaves compile mode.
`]`	`( -- )`	Enters compile mode.
`[COMPILE] xxx`	`( -- )`	Used in a colon definition, causes the immediate word *xxx* to be compiled as though it were *not* immediate; *xxx* will be executed when the definition is executed.
`STATE`	`( -- a)`	Variable containing system state flag; "true" if compiling, "false" if interpreting.
`INTERPRET`	`( -- )`	Performs text interpretation of the input stream, indexed by >IN, until exhausted.

REVIEW OF TERMS

Compile-time behavior
1. when referring to *defining* words: the sequence of instructions that will be carried out when the defining word is executed—these instructions perform the compilation of the member words;
2. when referring to *compiling* words: the behavior of a compiling word during compilation of the definition.

Compiling word
a word used inside a colon definition to take some action during the compilation process.

D-chart a graphic representation of the control structure of a routine or, in Forth, of a definition.

Defining word a word that, when executed, compiles a new dictionary entry. A defining word specifies the compile-time and run-time behavior of each member of the "family" of words that it defines.

Immediate word a dictionary entry for which the precedence bit is set, causing the word to be executed, not compiled, by the compiler.

Precedence bit in Forth dictionary entries, a bit that indicates whether a word should be executed rather than be compiled when it is encountered during compilation.

Run-time behavior **1.** when referring to *defining* words: the sequence of instructions that will be carried out when any member word is executed;
2. when referring to *compiling* words: a routine that will be executed when the compilee is executed. Not all compiling words have run-time behavior.

REFERENCE

1.   "Add a Break Point Tool," *Forth Dimensions*, Vol. V, No. 1, p. 19.

PROBLEMS

11-1. Define a defining word named LOADS that will define words which load a block when they are executed. For example,

    600 LOADS CORRESPONDENCE

would define the word CORRESPONDENCE. When CORRESPONDENCE is executed, block 600 would get loaded.

11-2. Define a defining word BASED. that will create number output words for specific bases. For example,

    16 BASED. H.

would define H. to be a word that prints the top of the stack in hex but does not permanently change BASE .

    DECIMAL
    17 DUP H. . RETURN _11_17_ok

11-3. Define a defining word called PLURAL, which will take the address of a word such as CR or STAR and create its plural form, such as CRS or

STARS. You'll provide PLURAL with the address of the singular word by using tick. For instance, the phrase

```
' CR   PLURAL CRS
```

will define CRS in the same way as though you had defined it

```
: CRS    ?DUP IF  0 DO CR  LOOP   THEN ;
```

11-4. The French words for DO and LOOP are TOURNE and RETOURNE. Using the words DO and LOOP, define TOURNE and RETOURNE as French "aliases." Now test them by writing yourself a French loop.

11-5. Write a word called LOOPS that will cause the remainder of the input stream, up to the carriage return, to be executed the number of times specified by the value on the stack. For example,

```
7 LOOPS   42 EMIT    SPACE RETURN _*_*_*_*_*_*_*_ok
```

11-6. In this chapter, we introduced the example of a defining word called SHAPE. To define the shape, we had to list eight numbers, each representing the bit pattern of a row. Design the syntax for a more elegant way to describe these 8 × 8-pixel shapes; for instance, using a picture rather than hex numbers.

Now implement your design (use the existing definition for .ROW). Test it according to your syntax.

12

$3\frac{1}{2}$ EXAMPLES

Programming in Forth is more of an "art" than programming in any other language. Like painters drawing brushstrokes, Forth programmers have complete control over where they are going and how they will get there. Charles Moore has written, "A good programmer can do a fantastic job with Forth; a bad programmer can do a disastrous job."

A good Forth programmer must be conscious of "style." Some elements of good Forth style include:

simplicity

the use of many short definitions rather than a few longer ones

a correspondence between words and easy-to-understand actions or data structures

well-chosen names

well laid-out blocks, clearly commented

One good way to learn style, aside from trial and error, is to study existing Forth applications, including Forth itself. In this book we've included the definitions of many Forth system words, and we encourage you to continue this study on your own.

This chapter introduces three applications which should serve as examples of good Forth style.

The first example shows the use of well-factored definitions and the creation of an application-specific "language."

The second example demonstrates the way to translate a mathematical equation into a Forth definition; you will see how speed and compactness can be increased by using fixed-point arithmetic.

The third example reveals the power of defining words, at the same time illustrating the construction of a Forth assembler.

A final, bonus example is presented with no explanation, as an exercise for you in learning to read Forth applications.

FILE AWAY!

Our first example consists of a simple filing system.† It is a powerful and useful application, and a good one to learn Forth style from. We have divided this section into three parts:

1. A "how to" for the end user. This will give you an idea of what the application can do.
2. Notes on the way the application is structured and the way certain definitions work.
3. A listing of the application, including documentation blocks.

USER NOTES: SIMPLE FILE SYSTEM

This computer filing system lets you store and retrieve information quickly and easily. At the moment, it is set up to handle people's names, occupations, and phone numbers.‡ Not only does it allow you to enter, change, and remove records, it also allows you to search the file for any piece of information. For example, if you have a phone number, you can find the person's name; or, given a name, you can find the person's job, etc.

For each person, there is a *record* that contains four *fields*. The names that specify each of these four fields are

```
surname   given   job   phone
```

("Given," of course, refers to the person's given name, or first name.)

FILE RETRIEVAL

You can search the file for the contents of any field by using the word "find" followed by the field-name and the contents, as in

```
find job newscaster RETURN  Dan Rather ok
```

---

† **For Serious File-Users:** Forth vendors that cater to professional programmers offer far more sophisticated data base packages.

‡ **For Programmers:** You can easily change these categories or extend the number of fields the system will handle.

If any "job" field contains the string "newscaster," then the system prints the person's full name. If no such file exists, it prints "Not in file."

Once you have found a field, the record in which it was found becomes "current." You can get the contents of any field in the current record by using the word "get." For instance, having entered the line above, you can now enter

```
get phone RETURN _555-9876_ok
```

The "find" command will only find the *first* instance of the field that you are looking for. To find out if there is another instance of the field that you last found, use the command "another." For example, to find another person whose "job" is "newscaster," enter

```
another RETURN _Connie_Chung_ok
```

and

```
another RETURN Frank_Reynolds_ok
```

When there are no more people whose job is "newscaster" in the file, the "another" command will print "No other."

To list all names whose field contains the string that was last found, use the command "all":

```
all
Dan Rather
Connie Chung
Frank Reynolds
_ok
```

Since the surname and given name are stored separately, you can use "find" to search the file on the basis of either one. But if you know the person's *full* name, you can often save time by locating both fields at once, by using the word "fullname." "fullname" expects the full name to be entered with the last name first and the two names separated by a comma, as in

```
fullname Wonder,Stevie RETURN _Stevie_Wonder_ok
```

(There must not be a space after the comma, because the comma marks the end of the first field and the beginning of the second field.) Like "find" and "another," "fullname" repeats the name to indicate that it has been found.

You can actually find *any pair* of fields by using the word "pair." You must specify both the field names and their contents, separated by a comma. For example, to find a newscaster whose given name is Dan, enter

```
pair job newscaster,given Dan RETURN _Dan_Rather_ok
```

FILE MAINTENANCE

To enter a new record, use the command "enter," followed by the surname, given name, job, and phone, each separated by a comma only. For example,

```
enter Nureyev,Rudolf,ballet dancer,555-1234 RETURN _ok
```

To change the contents of a single field within the *current* record, use the command "change" followed by the name of the field, then the new string. For example,

```
change job choreographer RETURN _ok
```

To remove the current record completely, use the command "remove":

```
remove RETURN _ok
```

After adding, changing, or removing records, and before turning off the computer or changing disks, be sure to use the word

```
FLUSH_ok
```

PROGRAMMER NOTES:
APPLICATION STRUCTURE

This section is meant as a guide, for the novice Forth programmer, to the listing that follows. We'll describe the structure of this application and cover some of the more complicated definitions.

Turn now to the listing. You'll first notice that this application has been written in a somewhat different style than the others in this book. In fact, it uses the conventions that FORTH, Inc. uses in its own applications.

The blocks on the left-hand pages are called *shadow blocks*; they document the code in the source blocks immediately to their right. For instance, the Forth definition of HELP appears on line 1 of block 240, while the explanation appears on the first line of block 561.

The use of shadow blocks has several advantages. First, the documentation is on-line. Most systems feature a word that toggles back and forth between the source block and its shadow block (the word is called Q in polyFORTH). The programmer can easily write and update the documentation as the program is being developed and maintained. And it's easy to find the documentation for any word in the application using a combination of LOCATE and Q.

And since related words appear in the same block, they can all be described jointly. This saves the useless repetition and wordiness commonly found in alphabetical glossaries.

HELP is defined in block 240 as a word that lists the "help block" (block 561) which contains all the commands for the end-user. The help block appears as soon as 240 is loaded (so that the user can read it while the application is compiling), or any time the user types HELP.

On line two of block 240 is the phrase "241 243 THRU" which loads the lower-level portion of the application. The remainder of 240 loads the highest-level words. Placing the user command set in the load block, rather than in the last block, allows the user commands to be documented in the load block's shadow block.

Now look at the nine end-user commands in block 240. Notice how simple these definitions are, compared to their power!

This is a characteristic of a well-designed Forth application. Notice that the word -FIND, the elemental file-search word, is factored in such a way that it can be used in the definitions of "find," "another," and "all," as well as in the internal word, (PAIR), which is used by "pair" and by "fullname."

We'll examine these definitions shortly, but first let's look at the overall structure of this application.

One of the basic characteristics of this application is that each of the four fields has a name which we can enter in order to specify the particular field. For example, the phrase

    surname PUT

will put the character string that follows in the input stream into the "surname" field of the current record. The phrase

    surname .FIELD

will print the contents of the "surname" field of the current record, and so on.

There are two pieces of information that are needed to identify each field: the field's starting address relative to the beginning of a record and the length of the field.

In this application, a record is laid out like this:

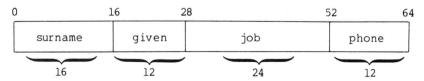

For instance, the "job" field starts twenty-eight bytes in from the beginning of every record and continues for twenty-four bytes.

We chose to make a record exactly sixty-four bytes long so that the fields will line up in columns when we LIST the file. This was for our convenience in programming, but this system could be modified to hold records of any length and any number of fields.†

We've taken the two pieces of information for each field and put them into a two-cell table associated with each field name. Our definition of "job," therefore, is

CREATE job 28 , 24 ,

3	**j**
o	**b**
link	
code pointer	
28	
24	

Thus, when we enter the name of a field, we are putting on the stack the address of the table that describes the "job" field. We can fetch either or both pieces of information relative to this address.

Let's call each of these entries a "field specifying table," or a "field table" for short.

Part of the design for this application is derived from the requirements of "find," "another," and "all"; that is, "find" not only has to find a given string within a given type of field, but also needs to "remember" the string and the type of field so that "another" and "all" can search for the same thing.

We can specify the kind of field with just one value, the address of the field table for that type of field. This means that we can "remember" the type of field by storing this address into a variable. KIND was created for this purpose, to indicate the "kind" of field.

To remember the *string*, we have defined a buffer called WHAT to which the string can be moved. (WHAT is defined relative to the pad, where memory can be reused, so as not to waste dictionary space.)

The word KEEP serves the dual purpose of storing the given field type into KIND and the given character string into WHAT. If you look at the definition of the end-user word "find" you will see that the first thing it does is KEEP

---

† **For Those Who Want to Modify This File System:** To change the parameters of the fields, just make sure that the beginning byte ("tab") for each field is consistent with the lengths of the fields that precede it. For example, if the first field is thirty bytes long, as in

CREATE 1FIELD   0 ,   30 ,

then make the tab for the second field thirty, as in

CREATE 2FIELD   30 ,   12 ,

and so on.

Finally, set the value of /RECORD to the length of the entire record (the last field's tab plus its length). Using /RECORD, the system automatically computes the number of records that can fit into a single block (1024 /RECORD /) and defines the constant REC/BLK accordingly. (Or see the problem at the end of this chapter.)

You may also change the location of the new file (e.g., to create several different files) by changing the value of the constant FILES. You may also change the maximum number of blocks that your file can contain by replacing the "2" in the next line. This value will be converted into a maximum number of records, by being multiplied by REC/BLK, and kept as the constant MAXRECS.

the information on what is being searched for. Then "find" executes the internal word − FIND, which uses the information in KIND and WHAT to find a matching string.

"another" and "all" also use − FIND, but they don't use KEEP. Instead they look for fields that match the one most recently "kept" by "find."

So that we can "get" any piece of information from the record which we have just "found," we need a pointer to the "current" record. This need is met with the variable RECORD#. The operations of the words TOP and DOWN in block 242 should be fairly obvious to you.

The word RECORD uses RECORD# to compute the absolute address (the computer-memory address, somewhere in a disk buffer) of the beginning of the current record. Since RECORD executes $\boxed{\text{BLOCK}}$, it also guarantees that the record really *is* in a buffer.

Notice that RECORD allows the file to continue over a *range* of blocks. $\boxed{\text{/MOD}}$ divides the value of RECORD# by the number of records per block (sixteen in this case, since each record is sixty-four bytes long). The quotient indicates which block the record will be in, relative to the first block; the remainder indicates how far into that block this record will be.

While a field table contains the *relative* address of the field and its length, we usually need to know the field's absolute address and length for words such as $\boxed{\text{TYPE}}$, $\boxed{\text{MOVE}}$, and $\boxed{\text{−TEXT}}$. Look at the definition of the word FIELD to see how it converts the − address of a field table into an absolute address and length. Then examine how FIELD is applied in the definition of .FIELD.

The word PUT also employs FIELD to compute the address and count of the destination field for READ. READ scans the input stream for a string delimited by comma and moves it to the destination field. Notice that READ invokes SAFE − CMOVE, which is defined here to clip the number-of-characters moved in case the source is wider than the destination.

There are two things worth noting about the definition of FREE in block 243. The first is the method used to determine whether a record is empty. We've made the assumption that if the first byte of a record is empty, then the whole record is empty, because of the way "enter" works. If the first byte contains a character whose ASCII value is less than thirty-three (thirty-two is blank), then it is not a printing character and the line is empty. (Sometimes an empty block will contain all nulls, other times all blanks; either way, such records will test as "empty.") As soon as an empty record is found, LEAVE ends the loop. RECORD# will contain the number of the free record.

Another thing worth noting about FREE is that it aborts if the file is full, that is, if it runs through all the records without finding one empty. We can use a $\boxed{\text{DO}}$ loop to run through all the records, but how can we tell that the loop has run out before it has found an empty record?

The best way is to leave a "true" flag on the stack before beginning the loop. If an empty record is found, we can change the flag to zero (with the word $\boxed{\text{NOT}}$) before we leave the loop. When we come out of the loop, we'll have a "true" if we never found an empty record, a "false" if we did. This flag will be the argument for ABORT".

We use a similar technique in the definition of −FIND. −FIND must return a flag to the word that executed it: "find," "another," "all," or (PAIR). The flag indicates whether a match was found before the end of the file was reached. Each of these outer words needs to make a different decision based on the state of this flag. This flag is a "true" if a match is not found (hence the name −FIND). The decision to use negative logic was based on the way −FIND is used.

The flag needs to be "true" if a match is not found; therefore the easiest way to design this word is to start with a "true" on the stack and change it to a "false" only if a match is found. But notice while the loop is running, there are two values on the stack: the flag we just mentioned and the field table address for the type of field to be searched. Since we need the address every time through the loop and the flag only once, if at all, we have decided to keep the address on top of the stack and the flag underneath. For this reason, we use the phrase

```
SWAP NOT SWAP
```

By the way, we could have avoided the problem of carrying both values on the stack by putting the phrase

```
KIND @ FIELD
```

inside the loop, instead of

```
KIND @
```

at the beginning and

```
DUP FIELD
```

inside. But we didn't, because we always try to keep the number of instructions inside a loop to a minimum. Naturally, it is the loops that take the most time running.

Now that you understand the basic design of this application, you should have no trouble understanding the rest of the listing, using the shadow blocks as a guide.†‡§ (Thanks to Jay Melvin for the shadow blocks.)

† **For fig-Forth Users:** To load the files application, make sure you have compiled these definitions *first*:

```
: VARIABLE   O VARIABLE ;
: CREATE   <BUILDS DOES> ;
: BLANK ( a # -- ) BLANKS ;
: WORD ( -- a)   WORD  HERE ;
: >IN ( -- a)   IN ;
```

Then, in block 243 change the phrase

```
ABORT" File Full"
```

to

```
IF ." File Full" QUIT  THEN
```

and, in block 240, change every occurrence of

```
' >BODY
```

to

```
[COMPILE] '
```

Finally, load the additional commands needed, as shown in the final footnote.

‡ **For polyFORTH Users:** To load the files application make sure you have first compiled this definition:

```
: >BODY   ;
```

then load any needed definitions from the final footnote.

§ **For Systems Lacking Other Words:** Load these definitions as needed (after loading definitions in preceding footnotes).

```
-1 CONSTANT TRUE
: ASCII ( -- c)  BL WORD 1+ C@ [COMPILE] LITERAL ; IMMEDIATE
: \   IN @ 64 / 1+  64 * IN ! ;
: -TEXT ( a1 # a2 -- ?)  2DUP + SWAP DO  DROP 2+
    DUP 2- @  I @ - DUP  IF DUP ABS / LEAVE THEN
    2 +LOOP  SWAP DROP ;
: TEXT ( c)  PAD 80 BLANK  WORD COUNT  PAD SWAP CMOVE ;
```

561 LIST

```
 0 HELP  displays these SIMPLE FILES instructions.
 1 enter  is used to create the data base by accepting text into
 2   the current record's four fields; heed commas and spacing.
 3   Usage:  enter Rather,Dan,newscaster,555-1212
 4 remove  blanks the current record and updates the disk buffer.
 5 change  moves the input text into the current record's
 6   specified  field.      Usage:  change job programmer
 7 find  matches the input text against memory and shows the data
 8   or indicates it is missing.   Usage:  find given Dan
 9 get  shows the data from the current record's specified field.
10   Usage:  get phone
11 another  will display next matching record beyond  RECORD# .
12 all  displays the entire data base's matching fields.
13 pair  finds the record having a match on two fields' contents.
14   Usage:  pair job newscaster,phone 555-9876
15 fullname  matches to both names.  Usage: fullname Rather,Dan
```

562 LIST

```
 0 ASCII text is saved on disk in records one line long pointed
 1   to by  RECORD#  and indexed (tabbed) by the four  field names.
 2   -TEXT  is used to compare buffered input against disk based
 3   data.  A match provokes loop exit with  RECORD#  set for
 4   typing the field selected by  KIND .
 5 Each field name contains its offset (tab) into the current
 6   record followed by its count (length) in bytes.  Their use
 7   allows  FIELD  to produce the virtual memory addresses used
 8   for accessing data.  Given a current record  (RECORD#) , that
 9   record's fields may be accessed by invoking the field name and
10   moving data to or from the resulting address.
11 RECORD#  is sequentially incremented for accessing records.
12 KIND  contains the address of the field of interest; used to
13   point into a record established by  RECORD# .
14 WHAT  is the buffer used to contain the input text for
15   comparison against the data base during searches.
```

563 LIST

```
 0 TOP  sets the record pointer to the beginning of the data base.
 1 DOWN  bumps the pointer to the next record.
 2
 3 SAFE-CMOVE  forces the count for the  CMOVE  to be not more than
 4   the field length.
 5 READ  blanks a buffer and moves a given count of bytes into it.
 6   Note that the field delimiter is an ASCII comma (,).
 7
 8 RECORD  is the virtual memory operator which produces an address
 9   within a disk block buffer.  The address is the beginning of
10   the current record.
11 FIELD  fetches a tab and length from one of four variable
12   addresses to prepare an address and count for typing.
13
14 PUT  moves keyboard input into an updated disk block buffer.
15
```

240 LIST

```
0 ( Simple files)   DECIMAL
1 : HELP    SCR @ 561 LIST  SCR ! ;  HELP
2 241 243 THRU
3 : enter   FREE  surname PUT  given PUT  job PUT  phone PUT ;
4 : remove   RECORD /RECORD BLANK  UPDATE ;
5
6 : change      '  >BODY PUT ;
7 : find ( field text)   '  >BODY KEEP  TOP -FIND  IF
8      MISSING  ELSE .NAME  THEN ;
9                              '
10 : get ( field)    '  >BODY .FIELD ;
11 : another   DOWN -FIND IF ." No other " ELSE  .NAME  THEN ;
12 : all   TOP BEGIN  CR  -FIND NOT  WHILE  .NAME  DOWN  REPEAT ;
13
14 : pair    '  >BODY KEEP  '  >BODY PAD 80 READ  (PAIR) ;
15 : fullname   surname KEEP  PAD 80 READ  given (PAIR) ;
```

241 LIST

```
0    ( Fields)
1 VARIABLE RECORD#   ( current record)
2 VARIABLE KIND    ( points to field table last used)
3 : WHAT ( - a)    PAD 100 + ;
4                  ( tab)     ( length)
5 CREATE surname    0 ,       16 ,
6 CREATE given     16 ,       12 ,
7 CREATE job       28 ,       24 ,
8 CREATE phone     52 ,       12 ,
9
10 64 CONSTANT /RECORD              ( bytes per record)
11 1024 CONSTANT /BLOCK             ( bytes per block)
12 /BLOCK /RECORD / CONSTANT REC/BLK  ( records per block)
13 244 CONSTANT FILES              ( file starts at this block)
14 2 ( blocks)  REC/BLK * CONSTANT MAXRECS   ( maximum #records)
15
```

242 LIST

```
0    ( Records)
1 : TOP   0 RECORD# ! ;
2 : DOWN   1 RECORD# +! ;
3 : SAFE-CMOVE ( a # a #)  >R SWAP R> MIN CMOVE ;
4 : READ ( a #)   2DUP BLANK  ASCII , WORD COUNT
5    2SWAP SAFE-CMOVE ;
6
7 : RECORD ( - a)   RECORD# @ REC/BLK /MOD FILES + BLOCK
8    SWAP /RECORD * + ;
9
10 : FIELD ( a - a' n)   2@ RECORD +  SWAP ;
11
12 : PUT ( a)   FIELD READ UPDATE ;
13
14
15
```

564 LIST

```
 0 .FIELD  types from the current record's specified field tab.
 1 .NAME  types  given  and  surname  from the specified record.
 2
 3 KEEP  is used to establish  WHAT  the text string is and the
 4   KIND  of field to be searched for comparison.
 5 FREE  sets the record pointer to the next available (empty)
 6   record; aborts if  MAXRECS is reached.  A record whose 1st
 7   byte contains 32 (space) or 0 (null) is empty.
 8 -FIND  compares byte by byte the text in  WHAT  to data in the
 9   selected field of each record.  Either a match is found or the
10   loop is exhausted, indicated by the "truth" flag.
11   This logic is used by  (PAIR) ,  find ,  all  and  another .
12 (PAIR)  uses two field addresses and takes two text strings
13   and compares these strings to data in the selected fields
14   of each record.
15
```

565 LIST

566 LIST

```
 0
 1
 2
 3
 4
 5
 6
 7
 8
 9
10
11
12
13
14
15
```

243 LIST

```
 0    ( Reports)
 1 : .FIELD ( a)    FIELD -TRAILING TYPE  SPACE ;
 2 : .NAME   given .FIELD  surname .FIELD ;
 3
 4 : KEEP  ( a)   DUP KIND ! 2+ @ ASCII , TEXT
 5    PAD WHAT ROT CMOVE ;
 6
 7 : FREE   TRUE  MAXRECS 0 DO  I RECORD# !  RECORD C@ 33 < IF
 8    NOT LEAVE  THEN  LOOP  ABORT" File full" ;
 9 : -FIND ( - t)   TRUE  KIND @  MAXRECS RECORD# @ DO
10    I RECORD# !  DUP FIELD WHAT -TEXT 0= IF
11        SWAP NOT SWAP  LEAVE  THEN  LOOP  DROP ;
12 : MISSING   ." Not in file " ;
13 : (PAIR) ( a)    MAXRECS 0 DO  I RECORD# !  -FIND IF
14    MISSING LEAVE  ELSE  DUP FIELD PAD -TEXT 0= IF
15       .NAME LEAVE  THEN  THEN  LOOP  DROP ;
```

244 LIST

```
 0 Fillmore      Millard      president               No phone
 1 Lincoln       Abraham      president               No phone
 2 Bronte        Emily        writer                  No phone
 3 Rather        Dan          newscaster              555-9876
 4 Fitzgerald    Ella         singer                  555-6789
 5 Chung         Connie       newscaster              555-9653
 6 Mc Cartney    Paul         songwriter              555-1212
 7 Washington    George       president               No phone
 8 Reynolds      Frank        newscaster              555-7865
 9 Sills         Beverly      opera star              555-9872
10 Ford          Henry        capitalist              No phone
11 Dewhurst      Colleen      actress                 555-1234
12 Wonder        Stevie       songwriter              555-0097
13 Fuller        Buckminster  world architect         555-3456
14 Rawles        John         philosopher             555-4567
15 Trudeau       Garry        humorist                555-4321
```

245 LIST

```
 0 Van Buren     Abigail      columnist               555-2233
 1 Abzug         Bella        politician              555-4433
 2 Thompson      Hunter S.    gonzo journalist        555-9452
 3 Marcuse       Herbert      philosopher             555-1849
 4 Jabbar        Kareem Abdul basketball player       555-4721
 5 Mc Gee        Travis       fictitious detective    555-8792
 6 Didion        Joan         writer                  555-0089
 7 Frazetta      Frank        artist                  555-9091
 8 Henson        Jim          puppeteer               555-0101
 9 Sagan         Carl         astronomer              555-7070
10
11
12
13
14
15
```

NO WEIGHTING

Our second example is a math problem that many people would assume could be solved only by using floating point. It will illustrate how to handle a fairly complicated equation with fixed-point arithmetic and demonstrate that for all the advantages of using fixed-point, range and precision need not suffer.

In this example, we will compute the weight of a cone-shaped pile of material, knowing the height of the pile, the angle of the slope of the pile, and the density of the material.

To make the example more "concrete," let's weigh several huge piles of sand, gravel, and cement. The slope of each pile, called the *angle of repose,* depends on the type of material. For example, sand piles itself more steeply than gravel.

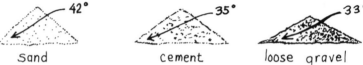

Sand   cement   loose gravel

(In reality, these values vary widely, depending on many factors; we have chosen approximate angles and densities for purposes of illustration.)

Here is the formula for computing the weight of a conical pile h feet tall with an angle of repose of θ degrees, where D is the density of the material in pounds per cubic foot:†

$$W = \frac{\pi h^3 D}{3 \tan^2 (\theta)}$$

This will be the formula that we must express in Forth.

† **For Skeptics:** The volume of a cone, V, is given by

$$V = \frac{1}{3}\pi b^2 h$$

where b is the radius of the base and h is the height. We can compute the base by knowing the angle or, more specifically, the tangent of the angle. The tangent of an angle is simply the ratio of the segment marked h to the segment marked b in this drawing:

If we call this angle "θ" (theta), then

$$\tan \theta = \frac{h}{b}$$

Thus, we can compute the radius of the base with

$$b = \frac{h}{\tan \theta}$$

When we substitute this into the expression for V, and then multiply the result by the density D in pounds per cubic foot, we get the foregoing formula.

Let's design our application so that we can enter the name of a material first, such as

DRY-SAND

then enter the height of a pile and get the result for dry sand.

Let's assume that for any one type of material the density and angle of repose never vary. We can store both of these values for each type of material into a table. Since we ultimately need each angle's tangent, rather than the number of degrees, we will store the tangent. For instance, the angle of repose for a pile of cement is 35°, for which the tangent is .700. We will store this as the integer 700.

CEMENT
131
700

Bear in mind that our goal is not just to get an answer; we are programming a computer or device to get the answer for us in the fastest, most efficient, and most accurate way possible. As we indicated in Chapter 5, to write equations using fixed-point arithmetic requires an extra amount of thought. But the effort pays off in two ways:

1. Vastly improved run-time speed, which can be very important when there are millions of steps involved in a single calculation, or when we must perform thousands of calculations every minute. Also,

2. Program size, which would be critical if, for instance, we wanted to put this application in a hand-held device specifically designed as a pile-measuring calculator. Forth is often used in this type of instrument.

Let's approach our problem by first considering scale. The height of our piles ranges from 5 to 50 feet. By working out our equation for a pile of cement 50 feet high, we find that the weight will be nearly 35,000,000 pounds.

However, because our piles will not be shaped as perfect cones and because our values are averages, we cannot expect better than four or five decimal places of accuracy.† If we scale our result to tons, we get about 17,500. This value will comfortably fit within the range of a single-length number. For this reason, let's write this application entirely with single-length arithmetic operators.

---

† **For Math Experts:** In fact, since our height will be expressed in three digits, we can't expect greater than three-digit precision. For purposes of our example, however, we'll keep better than four-digit precision.

Applications that require greater accuracy can be written using double-length arithmetic; to illustrate we've even written a second version of *this* application using 32-bit math, as you'll see later on. But we intend to show the accuracy that Forth can achieve even with 16-bit math.

By running another test with a pile 40 feet high, we find that a difference of one-tenth of a foot in height can make a difference of 25 tons in weight. So we decide to scale our input to tenths of a foot, not just whole feet.

We'd like the user to be able to enter

```
15 FOOT  2 INCH  PILE
```

where the words FOOT and INCH will convert the feet and inches into tenths of an inch, and PILE will do the calculation. Here's how we might define FOOT and INCH.

```
: FOOT  ( feet -- scaled-height)  10 * ;
: INCH  ( scaled-height -- scaled-height')
   100 12 */  5 +  10 /  + ;
```

(The use of INCH is optional.) Thus, "23 FOOT" will put the number 230 on the stack; "15 FOOT 4 INCH" will put 153 on the stack, and so on. (By the way, we could as easily have designed input to be in tenths of an inch with a decimal point, like this:

   15.2

In this case, NUMBER would convert the input as a double-length value. Since we are only doing single-length arithmetic, PILE could simply begin with DROP , to eliminate the high-order byte.)

In writing the definition of PILE, we must try to maintain the maximum number of places of precision without overflowing 15 bits. According to the formula, the first thing we must do is cube the argument. But let's remember that we will have an argument which may be as high as 50 feet, which will be 500 as a scaled integer. Even to *square* 500 produces 250,000, which exceeds the capacity of single-length arithmetic.

We might reason that, sooner or later in this calculation, we're going to have to divide by 2000 to yield an answer in tons. Thus the phrase

```
DUP DUP 2000 */
```

will square the argument and convert it to tons at the same time, taking advantage of */ 's double-length intermediate result. Using 500 as our test argument, the above phrase will yield 125.

However, our pile may be as small as 5 feet, which when squared is only 25. To divide by 2000 would produce a zero in integer arithmetic, which suggests that we are scaling down too much.

To retain maximum accuracy, we should scale down no more than necessary. 250,000 can be safely accommodated by dividing by 10. Thus we will begin our definition of PILE with the phrase

```
DUP DUP 10 */
```

The integer result at this stage will be scaled to one place to the right of the decimal point (25000 for 2500.0).

Now we must *cube* the argument. Once again, straight multiplication will produce a double-length result, so we must use $\boxed{*/}$ to scale down. We find that by using 1000 as our divisor, we can stay just within single-length range. Our result at this stage will be scaled to one place to the *left* of the decimal point (12500 for 125000.) and still accurate to 5 digits.

According to our formula, we must multiply our argument by *pi*. We know that we can do this in Forth with the phrase

```
355 113 */
```

We must also divide our argument by 3. We can do both at once with the phrase

```
355 339 */
```

which causes no problems with scaling.

Next, we must divide our argument by the tangent squared, which we can do by dividing the argument by the tangent *twice*. Because our tangent is scaled to 3 decimal places, to divide by the tangent we multiply by 1000 and divide by the table value. Thus we will use the phrase

```
1000 THETA @ */
```

Since we must perform this twice, let's make it a definition, called /TAN (for *divide-by-the-tangent*) and use the word /TAN twice in our definition of PILE. Our result at this point will still be scaled to one place to the left of the decimal (26711 for 267110, using our maximum test values).

All that remains is to multiply by the density of the material, of which the highest is 131 pounds per cubic foot. To avoid overflowing, let's try scaling down by two decimal places with the phrase

```
DENSITY @ 100 */
```

By testing, we find that the result at this point for a 50-foot pile of cement will be 34,991, which just exceeds the 15-bit limit. Now is a good time to take the 2000 into account. Instead of

```
DENSITY @ 100 */
```

we can say

```
DENSITY @ 200 */
```

and our answer will now be scaled to whole tons.

You will find this version in the listing of block 246 that follows. As mentioned, we have also written this application using double-length arithmetic, in block 248. In this version, you enter the height as a double-length number scaled to tenths of a foot, followed by the word FEET, as in 50.0 feet.

By using double-length integer arithmetic, we are able to compute the weight of the pile to the *nearest* whole pound. The range of double-length integer arithmetic compares with that of most floating-point arithmetic. The following is a comparison of the results obtained using a 10-decimal-digit calculator, single-length Forth and double-length Forth. The test assumes a 50-foot pile of cement, using the table values.

	IN POUNDS	IN TONS
calculator	34,995,634	17,497.817
Forth 16-bit	—	17,495
Forth 32-bit	34,995,634	17,497.817

Here's a sample of our application's output:

```
246 LOAD ok              ( compile single-length version)
CEMENT ok
10 FOOT PILE = 138 tons of cement ok
10 FOOT 3 INCH PILE = 151 tons of cement ok
DRY-SAND
10 FOOT PILE = 81 tons of dry sand ok

248 LOAD ok              ( compile double-length version)
CEMENT ok
10.0 FEET = 279939 pounds of cement or 139.969 tons ok
```

A NOTE ON OUR STRING-COMPILING TECHNIQUE

The defining word MATERIAL takes three arguments for each material, one of which is the address of a string. .SUBSTANCE uses this address to display the name of the material.

To put the string in the dictionary and to give an address to MATERIAL, we have defined a word called ," (comma-quote). First, it leaves [HERE] on the stack for MATERIAL, because it is here that the string will be compiled. Then it invokes [STRING] to compile the string literal delimited by double-quote. On some systems, you must define:

```
: STRING  ( c)  WORD C@ 1+ ALLOT ;
```

```
Block# 246
  0 \ Weight of conical piles  -- single-length
  1 VARIABLE DENSITY   VARIABLE THETA       VARIABLE I.D.
  2 : ," ( -- a) HERE ASCII " STRING ;
  3 : .SUBSTANCE   I.D. @  COUNT TYPE SPACE ;
  4 : MATERIAL   ( 'string density theta -- )   CREATE , , ,
  5   DOES> DUP @ THETA ! 2+ DUP @ DENSITY ! 2+ @ I.D. ! ;
  6
  7 : FOOT  ( feet -- scaled-height) 10 * ;
  8 : INCH ( scaled-height -- scaled-height')
  9   100 12 */  5 + 10 / + ;
 10
 11 : /TAN  ( n -- n') 1000 THETA @ */ ;
 12 : PILE ( scaled-height -- )
 13   DUP DUP 10 */  1000 */   355 339 */  /TAN /TAN
 14   DENSITY @  200 */  ." = " .  ." tons of "  .SUBSTANCE ;
 15 247 LOAD


Block# 247
  0 \ Table of materials
  1 \ string-address    density      theta
  2 ," cement"          131         700     MATERIAL CEMENT
  3 ," loose gravel"    93          649     MATERIAL LOOSE-GRAVEL
  4 ," packed gravel"   100         700     MATERIAL PACKED-GRAVEL
  5 ," dry sand"        90          754     MATERIAL DRY-SAND
  6 ," wet sand"        118         900     MATERIAL WET-SAND
  7 ," clay"            120         727     MATERIAL CLAY
  8
  9
 10
 11
 12 CEMENT
 13
 14
 15


Block# 248
  0 \ Weight of conical piles  -- double-length
  1 VARIABLE DENSITY   VARIABLE THETA       VARIABLE I.D.
  2 : ," ( -- a) HERE ASCII " STRING ;
  3 : .SUBSTANCE   I.D. @  COUNT TYPE SPACE ;
  4 : DU.3 ( du -- ) <# # # # ASCII . HOLD #S #> TYPE SPACE ;
  5 : MATERIAL   ( 'string density theta -- )   CREATE , , ,
  6   DOES> DUP @ THETA ! 2+ DUP @ DENSITY ! 2+ @ I.D. ! ;
  7 : CUBE ( d -- d') 2DUP OVER  10 M*/  DROP  10 M*/ ;
  8 : /TAN ( d -- d') 1000 THETA @ M*/ ;
  9 : FEET ( d -- ) CUBE 355 339 M*/ DENSITY @ 1 M*/
 10   /TAN /TAN 5 M+  1 10 M*/
 11   2DUP ." = " D. ." pounds of " .SUBSTANCE
 12   1 2 M*/ ." or " DU.3 ." tons " ;
 13 247 LOAD
 14
 15
```

A FORTH ASSEMBLER

Forth is often used in applications that require great processing speed. For example, in signal processing, data is arriving in "real time" and the computer must keep up with it. Usually, Forth is fast enough as is, but as with other high-level languages, Forth is not as fast as straight assembly language. (The new Forth engines, such as the Novix NC4000, directly execute high-level Forth instructions in hardware *faster* than traditional processors execute their own machine language. The assembler described in this section is required only for Forth systems running on non-Forth engines.)

In typical applications, nearly all computing time is spent performing very little code. The routines that are executed the most are sometimes called the *inner loops*. When an application written in high-level code runs too slowly, you can improve its performance dramatically just by translating one or two *inner loops* into assembly language.

In most high-level languages, it is a difficult process to generate a subroutine separately with an assembler and then link it into the body of the application. In Forth, however, this process is trivial; assembly-language definitions look a lot like regular high-level definitions. Whereas the body of a colon definition contains high-level code:

```
: NEWNAME   ( high-level code ...) ;
```

the body of an assembler definition contains assembly-language instructions:

```
CODE NEWNAME   ( assembly code ...)   END-CODE
```

(The terminating word varies from system to system; END-CODE is 83 Standard.)

A word that is defined by CODE exists in the dictionary along with everything else, and can be executed or invoked just like anything else. It also can be defined to manipulate values on the stack, so you can pass it arguments just as you would a colon definition. In fact, when you execute a word, there's no way you can tell whether it was defined in high level or in code (except perhaps by timing it).

The nice part is that you can write your entire application in high level. After it works, you can measure where most of the computing time is being spent. Then, redefine only those routines in machine code that require speeding up. Recompile the application and—bingo!—better performance. The alternative—trying to predict the bottlenecks ahead of time—doesn't prove as effective.

In this section, we'll show the development of a particular assembler—one for the 8080. Obviously, each processor needs to have its own kind of assembler, and this one assembles code for the 8080 only. If you enter the example shown here, you can actually generate 8080 assembler code in your machine, which is the point of the exercise. If you try to *execute* your code definitions, however, you will no doubt crash.

The example will show how easy Forth assemblers are to use, explain the elementary principles involved in constructing them, and provide an excellent demonstration of the power of Forth defining words.

Let's begin with the defining word CODE. The purpose of CODE is to create a dictionary header which, when executed, will jump to an address containing our machine code. This turns out to be easier than it sounds. Remember (from Chapter 9) that all definitions have a code pointer field that points to machine code? In a CODE definition, this pointer should point to the definition's own parameter field!

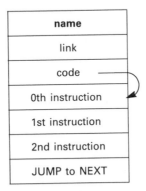

Thus, a simple definition of CODE would be:

```
: CODE   CREATE  HERE  HERE 2- ! ;
```

Now we need a set of words that will allow us to assemble machine instructions into the dictionary. Let's pick an easy one to start with. The 8080 instruction CMA performs a complement on register A. Its opcode, in binary, is

```
00101111
```

To assemble this instruction, we might simply define:

```
HEX
: CMA    2F C, ;
```

Another simple instruction is XCHG, which exchanges the D&E register pair with the H&L registers. Its opcode is

```
11101011
```

Hence, we can define:

```
: XCHG   EB C, ;
```

Let's look at what we've already done. We've given ourselves a syntax for defining machine-code definitions. We can now write:

```
CODE TEST   CMA   XCHG  ...
```

and know that we have defined the word TEST to execute the machine instructions

CMA and XCHG. You can even try this, and do a $\boxed{\text{DUMP}}$ to verify that it worked. (But don't invoke $\boxed{\text{TEST}}$!)

We'll defer the problem of ending a $\boxed{\text{CODE}}$ definition till a bit later. Let's return now to defining our assembler instructions. We've aleady defined two commands, both of which are simple 8-bit opcodes. There actually are quite a few 8080 instructions of this same type. For this reason, let's use a defining word to define all the instructions of this type. We'll call the defining word 1MI, for "1st type of machine instruction":

```
: 1MI   ( opcode -- )   CREATE C,   DOES> C@ C, ;
```

and use it in the following definitions (the first two are rewrites of the commands we already built):

```
HEX
2F 1MI CMA      EB 1MI XCHG      OO 1MI NOP      76 1MI HLT
F3 1MI DI       FB 1MI EI        07 1MI RLC      OF 1MI RRC
17 1MI RAL      1F 1MI RAR       E9 1MI PCHL     F9 1MI SPHL
E3 1MI XTHL     27 1MI DAA       37 1MI STC      3F 1MI CMC
CO 1MI RNZ      C8 1MI RZ        DO 1MI RNC      D8 1MI RC
EO 1MI RPO      E8 1MI RPE       FO 1MI RP       F8 1MI RM
C9 1M1 RET
```

(The defining word 1MI creates a family of commands, each of which contains a unique opcode, but all of which share a common behavior: to compile their individual opcode into the dictionary. The new definition of CMA is functionally no different from the earlier one using colon. The only difference is that the $\boxed{\text{C,}}$ that assembles the opcode into the dictionary appears in the $\boxed{\text{DOES>}}$ part of 1MI, and the opcode itself (2F) resides in CMA's parameter field.)

We've already defined a good portion of the entire 8080 instruction set. But the rest of the opcodes are not quite so simple. For example, the 8080 instruction ADD adds the contents of a specified register into register A (the accumulator). For example, in typical assembler notation one would write:

```
ADD B
```

to add the contents of register B into A.

The opcode for the ADD instruction, in binary, is

```
10000SSS
```

"SSS" represents three bits that are used to indicate the specified register. ("S" stands for "source.") The B register is indicated by "000"; hence, "ADD B" would be assembled as

```
10000000
```

Similarly, the L register is represented by "101" (5); hence, "ADD L" would be assembled as

```
10000101
```

In other words, the desired opcode can be produced by OR ing binary

```
10000000
```

(hex 80) with the number that indicates the register. Let's define ADD as:

```
: ADD  ( register# -- )  80  OR  C, ;
```

The simplest way to get the register# on the stack is to define all the registers as constants:

```
0 CONSTANT B
1 CONSTANT C
2 CONSTANT D
3 CONSTANT E
4 CONSTANT H
5 CONSTANT L
7 CONSTANT A
```

(These are all the registers applicable to the ADD instruction.)

Now, for instance, we can use the syntax

```
B ADD
```

to assemble the opcode for adding register B into the accumulator. Using the postfix syntax takes a little getting used to, but it makes the assembler a lot simpler and retains Forth's extensibility (by letting you easily define macros).

There happen to be several opcodes like ADD that contain a specified register number in the low-order three bits. Therefore, it makes sense to make another defining word for this class:

```
: 2MI   CREATE C,  DOES> ( register# -- ) C@ OR C, ;
```

With this new defining word, we can define

```
80 2MI ADD    88 2MI ADC    90 2MI SUB    98 2MI SBB
A0 2MI ANA    A8 2MI XRA    B0 2MI ORA    B8 2MI CMP
```

(2MI behaves the same as 1MI; that is it saves the unique opcode for each instruction in the parameter field of the commands it defines [the children]. The difference is that when we execute one of the *children*, 2MI specifies that we OR the saved opcode with the register number that has been placed on the stack.)

Another class of machine instructions also embed register numbers within the opcode, but in a different place. For example, the INR (increment) instruction's opcode is

```
00DDD100
```

(hex 04) where "DDD" specifies the register to be incremented. ("D" stands for "destination.") We can still use the register constants we defined earlier, but we have to shift the bits three places to the left before we OR them into the opcode (this is the same as multiplying them by eight):

```
: INR   ( register# -- ) 8 * 04 OR C, ;
```

Using the same logic, we can create a defining word instead:

```
: 3MI    CREATE C,
    DOES> ( register# -- ) C@ SWAP 8 * OR C, ;
```

```
04 3MI INR
```

In our syntax, then, the instruction "C INR" will assemble this opcode:

```
00001100
```

We can now use 3MI to define a new set of instructions, as you can see by turning to the listing at the end of this section.

Only two more defining words are needed to create the rest of the instruction set. 4MI is used for those opcodes that require an additional 8-bit literal, such as ADI (add immediate to A). 5MI defines those opcodes that require an additional 16-bit literal, such as CALL and JMP. The MOV, MVI, and LXI instructions are unique; therefore, each is defined without a defining word, using colon.

One thing you will notice in studying the listing is the inclusion of control-structure operators such as [IF], [ELSE], [THEN], [BEGIN], [UNTIL], [WHILE], and [REPEAT]. They are *not* the same words we have studied in this book (which compile jumps into high-level Forth definitions), but special versions created just for the assembler that assemble jumps and resolve addresses—just as traditional assemblers do—but letting you use the syntax of a structured language!

How is it possible to compile different versions of [IF], [THEN], and so on into the dictionary and not have them confused with the high-level versions? Because the assembler commands are in the [ASSEMBLER] vocabulary, not in the [FORTH] vocabulary. The definition of [CODE] in our listing invokes the word [ASSEMBLER] to make this vocabulary current every time we begin a code definition.

Another delightful feature of Forth assemblers like this one is that they are extensible. If you find yourself repeating a particular sequence of instructions in several places, you may want to use a *macro* instead. Here is a macro that assembles instructions to "rotate register A left" then "add the contents of B":

```
: SHIFT+   RLC B ADD ;
```

Think about this for a moment. When the word SHIFT+ appears in the middle of an assembler definition, it assembles these two instructions into the dictionary:

```
RLC B ADD
```

just as if we had typed them instead. It does not compile the address of SHIFT+;

nor is SHIFT+ invoked as a subroutine call when we *execute* our code. There is no performance penalty for using a macro because the assembled code is exactly the same as it would be without the macro.

One macro that you will see defined in the assembler itself is the word [NEXT]. It is defined here as

```
: NEXT    (NEXT) JMP ;
```

In other words, it assembles an instruction to jump to the address given by [(NEXT)]. The code for the address interpreter (which we introduced in Chapter 9) resides at this address. The address interpreter is the heart of Forth, the routine that executes each address in a compiled Forth definition in turn. Each [CODE] definition must conclude by invoking the address interpreter. Thus, each assembler definition must end with the word "NEXT." In this particular assembler, definitions must also end with [END-CODE], which does additional tidying up.

Here are two examples using the assembler defined here:

```
HEX
CODE FLIP   ( n -- n' )   \ Swap hi & lo bytes of n
    H POP    L A MOV    H L MOV    A H MOV    H PUSH
    NEXT    END-CODE
```

(We pop "n" from the stack into the HL register pair; move the L (lo) part into register A; move the H (hi) part into L; move A into H; push the HL pair back onto the stack; jump to [NEXT].)

```
CODE CLFOLD   ( a # -- )   \ Convert lower-case to upper
    D POP    H POP
    BEGIN    D A MOV    E ORA   0= NOT WHILE
      M A MOV   60 CPI   CS NOT IF
        20 SUI    A M MOV    THEN
    D DCX    H INX    REPEAT    NEXT    END-CODE
```

(Pop the count into the DE register pair; pop the address into the HL register pair; begin the loop; see if the count is zero by [OR]ing the D and E registers in the accumulator; while the count is nonzero move the character from referenced memory into the accumulator; if it is greater than hex 60 [lowercase "a" or above], then subtract decimal 32 to make it uppercase and restore it to memory; then decrement the count and increment the address; repeat; jump to next.)

To summarize, the advantage of this type of assembler is that you remain "in Forth" while assembling. If you wish to refer to a device address by name, rather than by number, you may define it as an ordinary constant, and name the constant within your assembler definition. You can use colon definitions as macros, or even refer to a variable, since a variable returns its address and can therefore be assembled in a "load immediate" instruction. The full power of Forth is available as you assemble machine-code routines.

The assembler given here is based on John Cassady's 8080 assembler for fig-Forth, which he placed in the public domain. We have changed it somewhat in accordance with the 83 Standard, and, to simplify this tutorial we have eliminated certain system-dependent aspects. For the original, see [1]. Assemblers for other processors have also been published ([2], [3], [4]).

```
\ 8080 Assembler
\ tutorial version based on figForth 8080 assem. by John Cassady
HEX
VOCABULARY ASSEMBLER
: CODE    CREATE  HERE  HERE 2- !    ASSEMBLER ;
ASSEMBLER DEFINITIONS
: ENDCODE    CURRENT @ CONTEXT ! ;
0 CONSTANT B    1 CONSTANT C    2 CONSTANT D    3 CONSTANT E
4 CONSTANT H    5 CONSTANT L    6 CONSTANT PSW  6 CONSTANT M
6 CONSTANT SP   7 CONSTANT A
: 1MI    CREATE C,  DOES> C@ C, ;
: 2MI    CREATE C,  DOES> C@ OR C, ;
: 3MI    CREATE C,  DOES> C@  SWAP 8 * OR  C, ;
: 4MI    CREATE C,  DOES> C@ C, C, ;
: 5MI    CREATE C,  DOES> C@ C, , ;

\ 8080 Assembler
HEX
00 1MI NOP       76 1MI HLT       F3 1MI DI        FB 1MI ED
07 1MI RLC       0F 1MI RRC       17 1MI RAL       1F 1MI RAR
E9 1MI PCHL      F9 1MI SPHL      E3 1MI XTHL      EB 1MI XCHG
27 1MI DAA       2F 1MI CMA       37 1MI STC       3F 1MI CMC
80 2MI ADD       88 2MI ADC       90 2MI SUB       98 2MI SBB
A0 2MI ANA       A8 2MI XRA       B0 2MI ORA       B8 2MI CMP
09 3MI DAD       C1 3MI POP       C5 3MI PUSH      02 3MI STAX
0A 3MI LDAX      04 3MI INR       05 3MI DCR       03 3MI INX
0B 3MI DCX       C7 3MI RST       D3 4MI OUT       DB 4MI SBI
E6 4MI ANI       EE 4MI XRI       F6 4MI ORI       FE 4MI CPI
22 5MI SHLD      2A 5MI LHLD      32 5MI STA       3A 5MI LDA
CD 5MI CALL

\ 8080 Assembler
HEX
C9 1MI RET       C3 5MI JMP       C2 CONSTANT 0=   D2 CONSTANT CS
E2 CONSTANT PE   F2 CONSTANT 0<
: NOT    8 OR ;
: MOV    8 *   40 + + C, ;
: MVI    8 *    6 + C, C, ;
: LXI    8 *    1+ C, , ;
: THEN    HERE SWAP ! ;
: IF    C,  HERE 0 , ;
: ELSE    C3 IF SWAP THEN ;
: BEGIN    HERE ;
: UNTIL    C, , ;
: WHILE    IF ;
: REPEAT    SWAP JMP  THEN ;
: NEXT    (NEXT) JMP ;
```

A BETTER BUZZ

The solution to the buzz-phrase generator problem in Chapter 10 has a limitation: we have to force carriage returns in the definition of PARAGRAPH. This is a hassle, and it leads to ragged output.

When we try to extend the application so that it generates several paragraphs, we find it necessary to let the application make its own decisions about when to do carriage returns. The following listing is presented without further comment. Practice your ability to read Forth code. See if you can rewrite the application more clearly.

Here is a sample of the application's output:

```
In this paper we will demonstrate that by applying available
resources towards functional digital capability coordinated
with compatible organizational utilities it is possible for
even the most responsive digital outflow to avoid transient
unilateral mobility.

On the one hand, studies have shown that with structured
deployment of total fail-safe mobility balanced by
systematized unilateral through-put it becomes not unfeasable
for all but the least random organizational projections to
avoid responsive logistical concepts.

On the other hand, however, practical experience indicates
that with structured deployment of qualified transitional
mobility balanced by representative logistical through-put it
is necessary for all representative unilateral engineering to
function as optional digital superstructures.

In summary, then, we propose that with structured deployment
of random management flexibility balanced by stand-alone
digital criteria it is necessary for all qualified fail-safe
outflow to avoid partial undocumented engineering.
```

```
Block# 156
   0 ( Buzzphrase generator, self-formatting version      11/28/84 )
   1 VARIABLE REMAINING   \ #characters remaining to be scanned
   2 VARIABLE ACROSS      \ current horizontal output cursor position
   3 70 CONSTANT RMARGIN \ right margin
   4
   5 : SCANWORD  ( a search-length -- adr-of-blank!end-of-field)
   6   2DUP +  ROT ROT  OVER + SWAP DO  I C@ BL =
   7      IF  DROP I LEAVE THEN  LOOP ;
   8 : GETWORD   ( a -- a word-count)  \ get next word to format
   9    DUP  REMAINING @  DUP  0> IF SCANWORD ELSE DROP  THEN  OVER -
  10    DUP  1+  NEGATE  REMAINING +! ;
  11 : FITS  ( count -- t=fits on this line)
  12    ACROSS @ +  RMARGIN < ;
  13 : SPACE'    ACROSS @  IF SPACE  1 ACROSS +!  THEN ;
  14 : CR'   CR  0 ACROSS ! ;
  15 157 LOAD   158 LOAD
```

```
Block# 157
   0 ( Buzzphrase generator, self-formatting version      11/28/84 )
   1 : .WORD  ( a # -- )   \ type word, doing CR if necessary
   2    DUP  FITS IF  SPACE'  ELSE CR'   THEN
   3    DUP  ACROSS +!  TYPE ;
   4 : NEXTWORD  ( a # -- next-adr )
   5    +  1+ ;
   6 : DISPLAY  ( a #chars -- )  \ output formatted text
   7    REMAINING !
   8    BEGIN   GETWORD  DUP WHILE  2DUP .WORD  NEXTWORD  REPEAT
   9    2DROP ;
  10 : BUZZWORDS  ( -- a)  161 BLOCK ;    \ random words
  11 : FILLERS  ( -- a)  160 BLOCK ;      \ glue phrases
  12 : INTROS  ( -- a)  159 BLOCK ;       \ sentence openers
  13 : BUZZWORD  ( row# column# -- a )    \ get address of word
  14    20 * SWAP  64 * +  BUZZWORDS + ;
  15
```

```
Block# 158
   0 ( Buzzphrase generator, self-formatting version      11/28/84 )
   1 : .BUZZWORD  ( row# col# -- )  BUZZWORD  20 DISPLAY ;
   2 : PART  ( column# -- )  CREATE ,        \ define parts of speech
   3    DOES> @  10 CHOOSE  SWAP .BUZZWORD ;
   4 0 PART 1ADJECTIVE
   5 1 PART 2ADJECTIVE
   6 2 PART NOUN
   7 : PHRASE    1ADJECTIVE  2ADJECTIVE  NOUN ;
   8 : FILLER  ( group# -- )  [ 4 64 * ] LITERAL   *
   9    3 CHOOSE  64 * +  FILLERS +  64 DISPLAY ;
  10 : SENTENCE   4 0 DO  I FILLER  PHRASE  LOOP  ." ." CR' ;
  11 : INTRO  ( paragraph# -- )
  12    CR'  64 *  INTROS +  64 DISPLAY ;
  13 : PAPER   CR' CR'  4 0 DO  I INTRO  SENTENCE  LOOP ;
  14
  15
```

Block# 159
```
 0 In this paper we will demonstrate that
 1 On the one hand, studies have shown that
 2 On the other hand, however, practical experience indicates that
 3 In summary, then, we propose that
 4
 5
 6
 7
 8
 9
10
11
12
13
14
15
```

Block# 160
```
 0 by using
 1 by applying available resources towards
 2 with structured deployment of
 3
 4 coordinated with
 5 to offset
 6 balanced by
 7
 8 it is possible for even the most
 9 it becomes not unfeasable for all but the least
10 it is necessary for all
11
12 to function as
13 to generate a high level of
14 to avoid
15
```

Block# 161
```
 0 integrated        management        criteria
 1 total             organization      flexibility
 2 systematized      monitored         capability
 3 parallel          reciprocal        mobility
 4 functional        digital           programming
 5 responsive        logistical        concepts
 6 optimal           transitional      time phasing
 7 synchronized      incremental       projections
 8 compatible        third generation  hardware
 9 qualified         policy            through-put
10 partial           decision          engineering
11 stand-alone       undocumented      outflow
12 random            context-sensitive superstructures
13 representative    fail-safe         interaction
14 optional          omnirange         congruence
15 transient         unilateral        utilities
```

REFERENCES

1. Cassady, John J., "8080 Assembler," *Forth Dimensions*, III/6, p. 180.

2. Duncan, Ray, "Forth 8086 Assembler," *Dr. Dobb's Journal*, 09/05, pp. 28–35, May 1984.

3. Perry, Michael A., "A 68000 FORTH Assembler," *Dr. Dobb's Journal*, 08/09, pp. 28–43, September 1983.

4. Ragsdale, William F., "A FORTH Assembler for the 6502," *Dr. Dobb's Journal*, 06/09, pp. 12–24, September 1981; reprinted in *Forth Dimensions*, III/5, pp. 143–50, January/February 1982.

PROBLEMS

12-1. In the Simple Files application, we used the following definitions for the four fields:

```
                  (tab)        ( length)
CREATE surname      0 ,          16 ,
CREATE given       16 ,          12 ,
CREATE job         28 ,          24 ,
CREATE phone       52 ,          12 ,
```

and then added the definition

```
64 CONSTANT /RECORD
```

to define the length of the entire record.

The problem is that, to change the length of the surname field, one would have to also edit the starting position (tab) of the other three fields, along with the value of /RECORD. There must be a way to automate this. Define the syntax and write the code.

12-2. Using the data base "language" implemented in the Simple Files example, define the new word "call" to search for a first name and return the full name and phone number. For example:

```
Call Connie
Connie Chung 555-9653 ok
```

ANSWERS TO PROBLEMS

CHAPTER 1

```
1.  : GIFT   ." bookends" ;
    : GIVER  ." Stephanie" ;
    : THANKS   CR  ." Dear "  GIVER  ." ,"  CR
       5 SPACES   ." Thanks for the "  GIFT  ." . "  ;

2.  : TEN-LESS  ( n -- n-10)  -10 + ;  or
    : TEN-LESS  ( n -- n-10)  10 - ;
```

3. When you defined THANKS, the compiler referred to the
    definition of GIVER that existed at the time. If you now
    add another GIVER, THANKS is not affected. (But if you
    also redefine THANKS, the new THANKS will use the new
    GIVER.)

CHAPTER 2

```
1.  DUP DUP:   ( 1 2 -- 1 2 2 2)
    2DUP:      ( 1 2 -- 1 2 1 2)

2.  : NIP  ( a b -- b)  SWAP DROP ;      .

3.  : TUCK  ( a b -- b a b)  SWAP OVER ;

4.  : -ROT  ( a b c -- c a b)  ROT ROT ;

5.  SWAP 2SWAP SWAP
```

6.   : 3DUP   (n1 n2 n3 -- n1 n2 n3 n1 n2 n3)   DUP 2OVER ROT ;

7.   : 2-7   (c a b -- n)   OVER + * + ;

8.   : 2-8   (a b -- n)   2DUP - ROT ROT + / ;

9.   : CONVICTED-OF   (-- empty-accumulator)   0 ;
      : WILL-SERVE   (sentence --)   .   ." YEARS " ;
      : HOMICIDE   (sentence -- sentence+20)   20 + ;
      : ARSON   (sentence -- sentence+10)   10 + ;
      : BOOKMAKING   (sentence -- sentence+2)   2 + ;
      : TAX-EVASION   (sentence -- sentence+5)   5 + ;

10.   : EGG.CARTONS   (#eggs --)
          12 /MOD   .   ." carton(s) and "   .   ." leftover(s) " ;

CHAPTER 4

1.   -1 0= NOT . _-1 ok
      0 0= NOT . _0 ok
      200 0= NOT . _-1 ok

2.   Don't ask.

3.   (assuming the legal age is 18 or over:)
      : CARD   (age --)
          17 > IF   ." Alcoholic beverages permitted "
          ELSE   ." Under age " THEN ;

4.   : ?SIGN   (n)   DUP 0= IF   ." Zero " ELSE
                       DUP 0< IF   ." Negative " ELSE
                                   ." Positive " THEN THEN DROP ;
      (or anything else that works)

5.   : <>   (n1 n2 -- ?)   = NOT ;

6.   : XOR   (x y -- ?)
          2DUP NOT AND   SWAP ROT NOT AND   OR ;

7.   : STARS   (n --)   ?DUP IF   STARS   THEN ;

8.   : NEGATE   (n -- -n)   0 SWAP - ;
      : ABS   (n -- |n|)   DUP 0< IF NEGATE THEN ;

9.   : /UP   (divd divr -- quot)   /MOD SWAP IF 1+ THEN ;

10.   : -ROT   (a b c -- c a b)   ROT ROT ;
      : WITHIN   (n l h+1 -- ?)   -ROT OVER > NOT   -ROT > AND ;
      Or here's a more efficient version, using tricks
      introduced in later chapters:
      : WITHIN   (n l h+1 -- ?)   OVER -   >R   -   R> U< ;

11.   : GUESS   (answer guess -- answer | --)
          2DUP =   IF ." Correct! " 2DROP   ELSE
          2DUP <   IF ." Too high " ELSE
                      ." Too low "   THEN DROP THEN ;

```
12.  : .NEGATIVE  ( n -- |n|)   0< IF ." Negative "  ABS THEN ;
     : SPELLER  ( n -- )  DUP ABS 4 > IF ." Out of range " ELSE
        DUP .NEGATIVE   DUP 0= IF  ." Zero "    ELSE
                        DUP 1 = IF  ." One "     ELSE
                        DUP 2 = IF  ." Two "     ELSE
                        DUP 3 = IF  ." Three "   ELSE
                                    ." Four "
     THEN THEN THEN THEN THEN  DROP ;

13.  assuming -ROT and WITHIN are still loaded:
     : 3DUP   ( a b c -- a b c a b c)  DUP 2OVER ROT ;
     : TRAP   ( answer lo-try hi-try -- answer | -- )
        3DUP  OVER =  -ROT = AND
           IF  ." You got it! "  2DROP DROP  ELSE
        3DUP SWAP  1 +  SWAP  WITHIN IF ." Between "
           ELSE  ." Not between " THEN  2DROP  THEN ;
```

CHAPTER 5

1. -1 is interpreted as the number "negative-one"; 1- is a
    Forth word that subtracts one from a value on the stack.

2. */ NEGATE

3. MAX MAX MAX .

4. a) : 2ORDER (n1 n2 -- n? n?) \ get larger value on top
           2DUP > IF SWAP THEN ;

    b) : 3ORDER (n1 n2 n3 -- n? n? n?) \ get largest on top
           2ORDER >R 2ORDER R> 2ORDER ;
       (Incidentally, you can keep going on like this...)
       : 4ORDER \ arrange four stack items, largest on top
           3ORDER >R 3ORDER R> 2ORDER ;
       ...the last command need always be only 2ORDER.)

    c) : BOXTEST (length width height --) \ in any order
           3ORDER 22 > ROT 6 > ROT 19 >
           AND AND IF ." Big enough " THEN ;
                                  (Thanks to Michael Ham.)

5. : PLOT (n --) CR 80 100 */ STARS ;

6. a) 0 32 - 10 18 */ . _-17_ok
    b) 212 32 - 10 18 */ . _100_OK
    c) -32 32 - 10 18 */ . _-35_ok
    d) 16 18 10 */ 32 + . _60_ok
    e) 233 273 - . _-40_ok

7. : F>C (fahr -- cent) 32 - 10 18 */ ;
    : C>F (cent -- fahr) 18 10 */ 32 + ;
    : K>C (kel -- cent) 273 - ;
    : C>K (cent -- kel) 273 + ;
    : F>K (fahr -- kel) F>C C>K ;
    : K>F (kel -- fahr) K>C C>F ;

```
Block# 270
   0 \ Answers; Chapter 6
   1 \ Problems 1 - 6
   2 : STARS  ( n)  0 ?DO  42 EMIT  LOOP ;
   3 : BOX  ( width height -- )  0 DO  CR  DUP STARS  LOOP  DROP ;
   4 : \STARS  ( #lines -- )  0 DO  CR  I SPACES  10 STARS  LOOP ;
   5 : /STARS  ( #lines -- )
   6    1- 0 SWAP  DO  CR  I SPACES  10 STARS  -1 +LOOP ;
   7 \ using BEGIN & UNTIL for /STARS:
   8 : A/STARS  ( #lines)
   9    BEGIN  1-  CR  DUP SPACES  10 STARS  DUP  0= UNTIL  DROP ;
  10
  11 \ DIAMONDS defined in two stages:
  12 : TRIANGLE  ( increment limit index -- )
  13    DO CR  9 I - SPACES  I 2* 1+ STARS  DUP +LOOP  DROP ;
  14 : DIAMONDS  ( #diamonds -- )
  15    0 DO  1 10 0 TRIANGLE  -1 0 9 TRIANGLE  LOOP  CR ;


Block# 271
   0 \ Answers; Chapter 6 cont'd
   1 \ Problem 7:
   2 : THRU  ( lo hi -- )  1+ SWAP DO  I DUP .  LOAD  LOOP ;
   3 \ Problem 8:
   4 : R%  ( n1 % -- n2)  10 */  5 +  10 / ;
   5 : DOUBLED  ( amount interest -- )
   6    OVER 2*  SWAP ROT  21 1 DO
   7      CR  ." Year "  I 2 .R  3 SPACES
   8        2DUP  R% +  DUP  ." Bal "  .
   9      DUP  2OVER DROP > IF
  10      CR CR  ." More than doubled in "  I .  ." years "  LEAVE
  11    THEN LOOP  2DROP  DROP ;
  12 \ Problem 9:
  13 : **  ( n1 n2 -- n1-to-the-n2-power)
  14    1 SWAP  ?DUP IF  0 DO  OVER * LOOP THEN  SWAP DROP ;
  15                        \ thanks to J.I. Anderson, Edinburgh, Scotland


Block# 272
   0 \ Answers; Chapter 7
   1 \ Problem 1:
   2 : N-MAX   0 BEGIN  1+  DUP 0< UNTIL  1- . ;
   3 ( Keeps incrementing the number on the stack by one until
   4   it looks negative, which means the limit has been passed.
   5   The final 1- sets it back to what it was just before it
   6   surpassed the limit.)
   7
   8 \ Problem 2 (a-f):
   9 : BINARY   2 BASE ! ;
  10 : BIT  ( bit# -- bit-position) 1 SWAP  0 ?DO  2*  LOOP ;
  11 : SET-BIT  ( bits1 bit# -- bits2 )  BIT OR ;
  12 : CLEAR-BIT  ( bits1 bit# -- bits2 )  BIT  -1 XOR  AND ;
  13 : GET-BIT  ( bits bit# -- bit )  BIT AND ;
  14 : TOGGLE-BIT  ( bits1 bit# -- bits2 )  BIT  XOR ;
  15 : CHANGED  ( bits1 bits2 -- bits3 )  XOR ;
```

```
Block# 273
  0 \ Answers; Chapter 7, cont'd
  1 \ Problem 3:
  2 : BEEP    ." Beep "  7 EMIT ;
  3 : DELAY    20000 0 DO LOOP ;
  4 : 3BELLS    BEEP DELAY BEEP DELAY BEEP ;
  5
  6 \ Problem 4a:
  7 : F>C    -320 M+  10 18 M*/ ;
  8 : C>F    18 10 M*/  320 M+ ;
  9 : K>C    -2732 M+ ;
 10 : C>K    2732 M+ ;
 11 : F>K    F>C  C>K ;
 12 : K>F    K>C  C>F ;
 13 \ Problem 4b:
 14 : .DEG    ( d -- )  DUP >R  DABS
 15     <#  # 46 HOLD  #S  R> SIGN  #>  TYPE SPACE ;
```

```
Block# 274
  0 \ Answers; Chapter 7, cont'd
  1 \ Problem 5:  ( returns 17513; this takes a while.)
  2 : DPOLY  ( x -- dv)
  3    DUP 7 M*  20 M+  ROT 1 M*/  5 M+ ;
  4 : ?DMAX   0 BEGIN  1+ DUP  DPOLY  0 0 D< UNTIL  1- . ;
  5
  6 \ Problem 6:
  7 In hex, DEC is a valid number.
  8
  9 \ Problem 7:
 10 : BINARY    2 BASE ! ;
 11 : 3-BASES
 12    17 0 DO   CR  ." Decimal"  DECIMAL  I 4 .R  8 SPACES
 13                 ." Hex "      HEX      I 3 .R  8 SPACES
 14                 ." Binary"    BINARY   I 8 .R  8 SPACES
 15     LOOP DECIMAL ;
```

```
Block# 275
  0 \ Answers; Chapter 7, cont'd
  1 \ Problem 8:
  2 ( Because of the decimal point, 3.7 is interpreted as a double-
  3   length number.  Therefore it occupies two stack positions.
  4   Since 37 is such a small number, the high-order part is all
  5   zeroes.  "Dot" is a single-length operator; two dots in a row
  6   will display both halves of a double-length number.  The high-
  7   order part of a double-length number is on top; this is what
  8   the first dot displays.  The second dot displays the
  9   low-order part: the 37.)
 10 ( The number 65536 is exactly one more than will fit in 16 bits.
 11   So the 17th bit becomes "1" and all other bits become "0".
 12   The 17th bit of a double-lenth number is the right-most bit
 13   of the high-order part.  It displays as a "1".  The low-order
 14   part displays as all zeros. )
 15 ( 65538 is two higher, so the low-order part looks like "2".)
```

```
Block# 276
   0 \ Answers; Chapter 7, cont'd
   1 \ Problem 9:
   2 ( Since this is not a word, Forth interprets it as a number.
   3   Since NUMBER interprets periods as decimal points indicating
   4   a double length number, it will push a double-length zero
   5   onto the stack.)
   6
   7 \ Problem 10:
   8 : .PH#   ( d -- )   <#  # # # #  ASCII - HOLD  # # #
   9    OVER IF  ASCII / HOLD  #S THEN  #> TYPE SPACE ;
  10
  11
  12
  13
  14
  15


Block# 277
   0 \ Answers; Chapter 8
   1 \ Problem 1-a:
   2 VARIABLE PIES  O PIES !
   3 : BAKE-PIE   1 PIES +! ;
   4 : EAT-PIE    PIES @  IF -1 PIES +!  ." Thank you "
   5    ELSE  ." What pie? "  THEN ;
   6 \ Problem 1-b:
   7 VARIABLE FROZEN-PIES   O FROZEN-PIES !
   8 : FREEZE-PIES   PIES @  FROZEN-PIES +!  O PIES ! ;
   9 \ Problem 2:
  10 : .BASE   BASE @  DUP DECIMAL .  BASE ! ;
  11 \ Problem 3  (extra-credit version):
  12 : S>D  ( n -- d)  DUP  O< ;  \ single-to-double
  13 : M.  ( d -- )  TUCK  DABS
  14    <#  DPL @  DUP  -1 <> IF  O ?DO  # LOOP  ASCII . HOLD  ELSE
  15    DROP  S>D  THEN  #S  ROT SIGN  #>  TYPE SPACE ;


Block# 278
   0 \ Answers; Chapter 8, Problem 4
   1
   2 CREATE #PENCILS  8 ALLOT  \ four colors of pencil
   3 O CONSTANT RED            2 CONSTANT BLUE
   4 4 CONSTANT GREEN          6 CONSTANT ORANGE
   5
   6 : PENCILS  ( offset -- a)  #PENCILS + ;
   7
   8 23 RED PENCILS !
   9 15 BLUE PENCILS !
  10 12 GREEN PENCILS !
  11  O ORANGE PENCILS !
  12
  13 \ To test, we can enter
  14 \    BLUE PENCILS ? 15 ok
  15
```

```
Block# 279
   0 \ Answers; Chapter 8, Problem 5
   1
   2 CREATE 'SAMPLES  20 ALLOT  ( 10 cells)
   3 : SAMPLES  ( i -- a ) 2* 'SAMPLES + ;
   4 : STARS  ?DUP IF  0 DO  42 EMIT  LOOP THEN ;
   5 : INIT-SAMPLES   10 0 DO  I 6 MOD  I SAMPLES !  LOOP ;
   6
   7 : PLOT  ( -- )
   8    10 0 DO  CR  I 2 .R  SPACE  I SAMPLES @  STARS  LOOP CR ;
   9
  10 INIT-SAMPLES
  11
  12
  13
  14
  15


Block# 280
   0 \ Answers; Chapter 8, Problem 6
   1 1 CONSTANT FEMALE         0 CONSTANT MALE
   2 2 CONSTANT MARRIED        0 CONSTANT SINGLE
   3 4 CONSTANT EMPLOYED       0 CONSTANT UNEMPLOYED
   4 8 CONSTANT CITIZEN        0 CONSTANT NON-CITIZEN
   5 VARIABLE JOHN
   6 VARIABLE  MARY
   7 : DESCRIBES  ( status status status status person -- )
   8    >R  OR  OR  OR  R> ! ;
   9 MALE MARRIED UNEMPLOYED NON-CITIZEN  JOHN DESCRIBES
  10 FEMALE SINGLE EMPLOYED CITIZEN  MARY DESCRIBES
  11
  12
  13
  14
  15


Block# 281
   0 \ Answers; Chapter 8, Problem 6, cont'd
   1 : .SEX  ( bits -- ) FEMALE AND  IF ." fe"  THEN  ." male " ;
   2 : .MARITAL  ( bits -- )
   3    MARRIED AND  IF ." married " ELSE ." single " THEN ;
   4 : .JOB-STATUS  ( bits -- )
   5    EMPLOYED AND  0= IF ." un" THEN  ." employed " ;
   6 : .CITIZENSHIP  ( bits -- )
   7    CITIZEN AND  0= IF ." non-" THEN ." citizen " ;
   8 : REPORT  ( person -- )
   9    @ DUP .SEX  DUP .MARITAL  DUP .JOB-STATUS  .CITIZENSHIP ;
  10
  11
  12
  13
  14
  15
```

```
Block# 282
  0 \ Answers; Chapter 8, Problem 7
  1 CREATE BOARD  9 ALLOT
  2 : SQUARE    ( square# -- a)  BOARD + ;
  3 : CLEAR    BOARD    9 0 FILL ;  CLEAR
  4 : BAR   ." ¦ " ;
  5 : DASHES   CR  9 0 DO  ASCII - EMIT  LOOP CR ;
  6 : .BOX  ( square# -- )   SQUARE C@  DUP 0= IF  2 SPACES  ELSE
  7    DUP 1 = IF  ." X "   ELSE  ." O "  THEN THEN  DROP ;
  8 : DISPLAY   CR  9 0 DO  I IF  I 3 MOD  0=  IF
  9    DASHES  ELSE  BAR  THEN  THEN  I .BOX  LOOP  CR QUIT ;
 10 : PLAY  ( player square# -- )
 11    1-  0 MAX  8 MIN  SQUARE C! ;
 12 : X!  ( square# -- )   1 SWAP  PLAY  DISPLAY ;
 13 : O!  ( square# -- )  -1 SWAP  PLAY  DISPLAY ;
 14
 15


Block# 283
  0 \ Answers; Chapter 9
  1
  2 \ Problem 1:
  3 VARIABLE   'EQUALS
  4 : EQUALS   ( n n -- )   'EQUALS @ EXECUTE  . ;
  5 : ADDING   ['] +  'EQUALS ! ;
  6 : MULTIPLYING   ['] *  'EQUALS ! ;
  7
  8 \ Problem 2:
  9 \ You can find out by entering
 10 \    HERE U.
 11 \ just after coming up, or after invoking a system-dependent
 12 \ command that empties the dictionary, such as COLD or EMPTY.
 13
 14
 15


Block# 284
  0 \ Answers; Chapter 9, cont'd
  1
  2 \ Problem 3:
  3 \ You can find out by entering
  4 \    PAD HERE - U.
  5
  6 \ Problem 4:
  7 \ a) No difference.  A variable returns its own pfa.
  8 \ b) A user variable returns the address of a cell in the
  9    user table.  The dictionary entry, which ' finds,
 10    is elsewhere.
 11
 12
 13
 14
 15
```

```
Block# 285
   0 \ Answers; Chapter 9, cont'd
   1 \ Problem 5, Solution 1:
   2 CREATE 'TO-DO  12 ALLOT   \ 6 cells
   3 : TO-DO  ( i -- a)  0 MAX  5 MIN  2* 'TO-DO + ;
   4
   5 : GREET    ." Hello, I speak Forth. " ;
   6 : SEQUENCE   11 1 DO  I .  LOOP ;
   7 : TILE   10 5 BOX ;   \ see answers, Chapter 6
   8 : NOTHING ;
   9
  10 ' GREET    0 TO-DO !         ' SEQUENCE  1 TO-DO !
  11 ' TILE     2 TO-DO !         ' NOTHING   3 TO-DO !
  12 ' NOTHING  4 TO-DO !         ' NOTHING   5 TO-DO !
  13
  14 : DO-SOMETHING  ( index -- )  TO-DO  @EXECUTE ;
  15
```

```
Block# 286
   0 \ Answers; Chapter 9, cont'd
   1 \ Problem 5, Solution 2:
   2 CREATE 'TO-DO  12 ALLOT   \ 6 cells
   3 : TO-DO  ( i -- a)  0 MAX  5 MIN  2* 'TO-DO + ;
   4
   5 : GREET    ." Hello, I speak Forth. " ;
   6 : SEQUENCE   11 1 DO  I .  LOOP ;
   7 : TILE   10 5 BOX ;   \ see answers, Chapter 6
   8 : NOTHING ;
   9
  10 : INITIALIZE    ( -- )
  11    6 0 DO ['] NOTHING  I  TO-DO !  LOOP
  12    ['] GREET  0 TO-DO !   ['] SEQUENCE  1 TO-DO !
  13    ['] TILE   2 TO-DO ! ;
  14 INITIALIZE
  15 : DO-SOMETHING  ( index -- )  TO-DO  @EXECUTE ;
```

```
Block# 287
   0 \ Answers; Chapter 10
   1 \ Problem 1:
   2 : CHARACTER   ( i -- a)
   3    228 BLOCK + ;
   4 : CHANGE  ( c1 c2 -- )  \ change c1 to c2
   5    1024 0 DO  OVER  I CHARACTER C@  = IF  DUP  I CHARACTER C!
   6    UPDATE  THEN  LOOP 2DROP ;
   7
   8 \ Problem 2:
   9 181 LOAD  \  Random numbers
  10 \ ??? CONSTANT FORTUNES  \  block number for messages
  11 : FORTUNE   CR  16 CHOOSE  64 *  FORTUNES BLOCK +
  12    64 -TRAILING TYPE  SPACE ;
  13 \ You'll have to invent your own "fortunes."  Edit them into
  14 \ an available block, one per line.  Then edit the block number
  15 \ into the definition of the constant FORTUNES above.
```

```
Block# 288
   0 \ Answers; Chapter 10, Problem 3
   1 \ part a:
   2 : Y/N?   ( -- t=yes ! f=other)  KEY   DUP EMIT   ASCII Y = ;
   3 \ part b:
   4 : Y/N?   ( -- t=yes ! f=other)
   5    KEY  95 AND  DUP EMIT   ASCII Y = ;
   6 \ part c; two possible solutions:
   7 : Y/N?   ( -- t=yes ! f=no )
   8    BEGIN  KEY  95 AND   DUP   ASCII Y = IF  DROP TRUE EXIT    ELSE
   9                         DUP   ASCII N = IF  0= EXIT   THEN THEN
  10    DROP   FALSE UNTIL ;
  11
  12 : Y/N?   ( -- t=yes ! f=no )
  13    BEGIN  KEY  95 AND   DUP ASCII Y =   OVER ASCII N =   OR NOT
  14       WHILE DROP REPEAT   ASCII Y = ;
  15
```

```
Block# 289
   0 \ Answers; Chapter 10, Problem 4
   1 : ANIMALS  LIT" RAT    OX      TIGER RABBITDRAGONSNAKE HORSE RAM
   2 MONKEYCOCK   DOG    BOAR   " ;
   3 : .ANIMAL   ( u -- )   \  u from 0 to 11
   4    6 *   ANIMALS 1+  +   6 -TRAILING TYPE ;
   5 : (JUNEESHEE)   ( year -- )
   6    1900 -   12 MOD
   7    ." You were born in the year of the "   .ANIMAL
   8    ASCII . EMIT  CR ;
   9 350 351 THRU   \ load definition of EXPECT#
  10 : DIGITS   ( #digits  -- d )
  11    DUP 0 DO  ASCII _ EMIT  LOOP  DUP 0 DO  BACKSPACE  LOOP
  12    PAD  SWAP  2DUP 1+ BLANK  EXPECT# DROP  PAD 1-  NUMBER ;
  13 : JUNEESHEE
  14    CR  ." In what year were you born? "  4 DIGITS
  15    CR  DROP (JUNEESHEE) ;
```

```
Block# 290
   0 \ Answers; Chapter 10, Problem 5
   1 VARIABLE ROW
   2 : start    0 ROW ! ;
   3 : add    \   1adjective,2adjective,noun    ( -- )
   4    ROW @ 0 BUZZWORD  60 BLANK UPDATE
   5    3 0 DO
   6       ASCII , WORD COUNT  ROW @ I BUZZWORD SWAP CMOVE  UPDATE
   7    LOOP  1 ROW +! ;
   8
   9 \ Or, using TEXT:
  10 : add    \   1adjective,2adjective,noun    ( -- )
  11    3 0 DO
  12       ASCII , TEXT  PAD  ROW @ I BUZZWORD  20 CMOVE  UPDATE
  13    LOOP  1 ROW +! ;
  14
  15
```

```
Block# 291
   0 \ Answers; Chapter 10
   1 \ Problem 6
   2 : >DATE    ( a - n n)
   3    0 0 ROT CONVERT   ROT >R   0 SWAP CONVERT   ROT >R
   4    0 SWAP   CONVERT   2DROP   1900 +    R> R> 256 * +   SWAP ;
   5 : SCAN-DATE    BL WORD >DATE ;
   6
   7 \ Problem 7
   8 VARIABLE STUFF    \   first block of file
   9 300 STUFF !       \   is block 300
  10 : ELEMENT  ( i -- a)
  11    2* 1024 /MOD  STUFF @  + BLOCK  +  UPDATE ;
  12 \ Test virtual array:
  13 : INIT-ARRAY   600 0 DO  I  I ELEMENT ! LOOP ;
  14 : .ARRAY   600 0 DO  I . SPACE  I ELEMENT ? LOOP ;
  15
```

```
Block# 292
   0 \ Answers; Chapter 10, Problem 7, cont'd
   1
   2 \ Now make the virtual array into a file:
   3 : USED   ( -- a)   STUFF @  BLOCK  UPDATE ;
   4 \ Redefine ELEMENT to skip over USED:
   5 : ELEMENT   ( i -- a)
   6    1+  2* 1024 /MOD  STUFF @  + BLOCK  +  UPDATE ;
   7
   8 : NO-STUFF    0 USED ! ;
   9 NO-STUFF
  10 : PUT  ( n -- )  USED @  ELEMENT !  1 USED +! ;
  11 : ENTER  ( n1 n2 -- )  SWAP  PUT PUT ;
  12
  13 : TABLE    CR  USED @  0 ?DO  I 8 MOD  0= IF  CR  THEN
  14    I ELEMENT @  8 .R  LOOP  CR ;
  15
```

```
Block# 293
   0 \ Answers; Chapter 11
   1 \ Problem 1:
   2 : LOADS  ( n -- )  CREATE ,  DOES> ( -- )  @ LOAD ;
   3
   4 \ Problem 2:
   5 : BASED. ( n -- )  CREATE ,
   6    DOES> ( n -- )  @ BASE @  SWAP  BASE !  SWAP .  BASE ! ;
   7
   8 \ Problem 3:
   9 : PLURAL    ( a -- )  CREATE ,
  10    DOES> ( -- )  @  SWAP  0 ?DO  DUP EXECUTE  LOOP  DROP ;
  11 ' CR PLURAL CRS
  12 4 CRS
  13
  14
  15
```

```
Block# 294
   0 \ Answers; Chapter 11, cont'd
   1 \ Problem 4:
   2 : TURNE    [COMPILE] DO ; IMMEDIATE
   3 : RETURNE  [COMPILE] LOOP ; IMMEDIATE
   4 : TRY   10 0 TURNE  I . RETURNE ;
   5
   6 \ Problem 5:
   7 : LOOPS ( #times -- )
   8    >IN @  SWAP 0 DO  DUP >IN !  INTERPRET  LOOP DROP ;
   9
  10
  11
  12
  13
  14
  15
```

```
Block# 295
   0 \ Answers; Chapter 11, Problem 6:
   1 : STAR    42 EMIT ;
   2 : .ROW  ( b -- )  \ display star for each bit in byte
   3    CR  8 0 DO  DUP 128 AND  IF STAR ELSE SPACE THEN
   4      2* LOOP  DROP ;
   5 VARIABLE PATTERN
   6 : BIT  ( t=non-blank -- )
   7    1 AND   PATTERN @ 2*  +  PATTERN ! ;
   8 : STARS>BITS  ( a -- b)
   9    0 PATTERN !  8 OVER + SWAP DO  I C@  BL <> BIT  LOOP
  10     PATTERN @ ;
  11 : READ-ROW  ( -- b)
  12    ASCII | WORD  COUNT +  8 -  STARS>BITS ;
  13 : SHAPE   CREATE   8 0 DO READ-ROW C,  LOOP
  14    DOES>  8 OVER + SWAP DO I C@ .ROW  LOOP  CR ;
  15
```

```
Block# 296
   0 SHAPE .L   XXX      |
   1             X        |
   2             X        |
   3             X        |
   4             X        |
   5             X        |
   6             X     X|
   7           XXXXXXXX|
   8 SHAPE .B   XXXXXX  |
   9             X     X|
  10             X     X|
  11           XXXXX  |
  12             X     X|
  13             X     X|
  14             X     X|
  15           XXXXXX  |
```

```
Block# 297
   0 \ Answers; Chapter 12, Problem 1:
   1 : wide   ( tab length -- newtab )
   2    CREATE  OVER , DUP , + ;
   3 0  \ starting position within record
   4 16 wide surname
   5 12 wide given
   6 24 wide job
   7 12 wide phone
   8 CONSTANT /RECORD   / bytes per record
   9 EXIT
  10 The above syntax compiles the exact same structures.  "wide"
  11 is a defining word, which keeps on the stack the current
  12 position within the field.  For each field, "wide" compiles the
  13 tab and the length, then adds them together to compute the next
  14 tab.  After "phone" is defined, the number left over is the
  15 width of the total record, and is made into the constant /RECORD
```

```
Block# 298
   0 \ Answers; Chapter 12, Problem 2:
   1 : call  (   given-name   ( -- )
   2    given KEEP  TOP -FIND IF  MISSING
   3       ELSE  CR .NAME  phone .FIELD  THEN ;
   4
   5
   6
   7
   8
   9
  10
  11
  12
  13
  14
  15
```

```
Block# 299
   0
   1
   2
   3
   4
   5
   6
   7
   8
   9
  10
  11
  12
  13
  14
  15
```

B

ALPHABETICAL INDEX OF FORTH WORDS

This list of Forth words is alphabetized in ASCII order. Boldface page numbers indicate the formal description of the word. Parenthesized numbers refer to footnotes.

! 169–69, **174**
" 253–54
152–53, **154**
#> 151–53, **154,** 155–56
#S 151–53, **154**
' 196–99, **199,** 280
'S **216**
(24, **26**
(LITERAL) 274
* **29,** 30
*. 110–12
*/ **103,** 104–8
*/MOD **107**
+ 20–21, **26**
+! 173, **174**
+LOOP 123–25, **131**
, 188, **190,** 213
- **29,** 87
-MATCH **251**

-ROT 50 (Probs)
-TEXT **251**
-TRAILING **232**
. 20–21, **26**
." 17, **26,** 272–73, 280
.(60, **62,** 242
.R 123, **131**
.S 46–47
/ **29,** 31–32, 39
/. 110–12
/LOOP (125)
/MOD **39**
0 175, **191**
0. **191**
0< 84, **92**
0= 84, **92**
0> 84, **92**
1 175, **191**
1+ **96**

FORTH WORDS
BY CATEGORY

Boldface page numbers indicate the formal description of the word. Parenthesized numbers refer to footnotes.

ARITHMETIC

SINGLE-LENGTH

* **29**, 30
*/MOD **107**
+ 20–21, **26**
− **29**, 87
/ 29, 31–32, 39
/MOD **39**
1+ **96**
1− **96**
2* **96**
2+ **96**
2− **96**
2/ **96**
ABS 94 (Probs), **97**
MOD **39**
NEGATE 94 (Probs), **97**

DOUBLE LENGTH

D+ **157**
D− **157**
DABS **157**
DNEGATE **157**

MIXED LENGTH

*. 110–12
*/ **103**, 104–8
/. 110–12
M* **158**
M*/ **158**, 159
M+ **158**
M/ **158**
UM* **158**
UM/MOD **158**

CHARACTER INPUT

?TERMINAL 238
COUNT 241, **243**
EXPECT 238–39, **240**
KEY 237–38, **240,** 248–50

KEY? 238
PARSE 242–43
TEXT 243
WORD 240–46, **243**

CHARACTER OUTPUT

-TRAILING **232**
." 17, **26,** 272–73, 280
>TYPE **232**
CR 11, **26**
EMIT 10, **26,** 143

PAGE 130, **131**
SPACE **26**
SPACES 10, **26**
TYPE 151–53, **231**

COMPARISONS

SINGLE-LENGTH

-
0< 84, **92**
0= 84, **92**
0> 84, **92**
< 84, **92**
<> **92,** 94 (Probs)
= **92**
> 84, **92**
MAX **97**
MIN **97,** 98
U< **148**

WITHIN 95 (Probs)
double-link 6
DO= **157**
D< **157**
D= **157**
DMAX **157**
DMIN **157**
DU< **157**

STRING

-MATCH **251**
-TEXT **251**

COMPILATION

(LITERAL) 274
, 188, **190,** 213
C, 189, **190**
CODE 308
COMPILE 272, **273,** 276–77
DOES> 262–63, **264**
IMMEDIATE 271, **273**
LIT" 253, **256**
LITERAL 274, 276, **278**

RECURSE 211
STATE 279–80, **286**
STRING 252, **256**
[275, **278**
['] 199
[COMPILE] 276–77, **278**
] 275, **278,** 284–85
END-CODE 308

CONSTANTS

0 175, **191**
0. **191**
1 175, **191**

BL 237
FALSE 127, **176**
TRUE **176**

DEFINING WORDS

2CONSTANT 176, **177**
: 8, 10, 15–16, **26,** 219, 260
; 8, 10, **26**
CONSTANT 174, **176,** 260, 262–63

CREATE 178–79, **181,** 188–89, 260, 261
VARIABLE 168, **174,** 260–62
2VARIABLE 176, **177**

DICTIONARY CONTROL

ALLOT 178–79, **181,** 213
EMPTY (60)
FORGET 52–3, **57,** 58

H 213, **216**
HERE 213, **216**

EDITOR COMMANDS

B 74, **78**
BRING 75, **77**
COPY 74, **78**
D 67, **78**
E 66–67, **78**
F 65, 69–70, **78**
G 75, **77**
I (editor) 66, 70–1, **78**
K 75, **78**
L 63, **78**

M 75
N 74, **78**
P 64, 71–72, **77**
R 67–68, **78**
S 74, **78**
T 64, **77**
TILL 68, **78**
U 72–73, **77**
WIPE 64, **78**
X 73, **77**

INTERNALS

>BODY 203, **210**
@EXECUTE 197, **199**
ASSEMBLER 219–20, **221,** 312
CONTEXT 220, **221**
CURRENT 220, **221**
DECIMAL **148,** 169
DEFINITIONS 220, **221**
dot" 272–73, 277
EDITOR 219–20, **221**

EXECUTE 14, 196–97, **199,** 207
EXIT 57, (99), 204, 206, 209, **210**
FORTH 219–20, **221,** 312
HEX **148,** 149, 169
NEXT 313
OCTAL **148,** 149, 169
PAD 214, **216**
QUIT 127, 130, **131,** 207–8, **210**

INTERPRETATION

` 196–99, **199,** 280
(24, **26**
.(60, **62,** 242
>IN 244–45, **246**
ASCII **144,** 279–81
BLK 245, **246**

INTERPRET 13, 195, 207, **283,** 284
QUERY 207, 239
SPAN **240**
TIB 215, **216**
\ 57, **58**
\S 57, **58**

STRUCTURE CONTROL

+LOOP 123–25, **131**
/LOOP (125)
?DO 120
ABORT 208, **210**
ABORT" 91, **92**, 126
AGAIN 127
BEGIN 126–28, **131**
DO 117–26, **131**, 207
ELSE 84, **92**

I (loops) 119–20, 207
IF 81–83, 86–87, **92**
J 123
LEAVE 121, 128–30, **131**
LOOP 117–26, **131**, 207
REPEAT 128, **131**
THEN 81–83, **92**
UNTIL 126–27, **131**
WHILE 128, **131**

TOOLS

.S 46–47
DUMP 186, **190**
INDEX 61, **62**
LIST 55, **57**
LOCATE 76, **77**

Q 292
SHOW 61, **62**
THRU 60, **62**
TRIAD 60, **62**
VLIST 13

VIRTUAL MEMORY

BLOCK 228, **230**
BUFFER **230**
EMPTY-BUFFERS 229, **230**
FLUSH 56, **57**, 228–29, **230**

LOAD 55, **57**
SAVE-BUFFERS 228–29, **230**
UPDATE 228, **230**

INDEX

Boldface page numbers indicate the formal description of the word. Parenthesized numbers refer to footnotes.

A

Abort, 91, **93**
Abstract data type, 266
Address, as loop index, 186–87
Address, finding, 196–97
Address, hardware, 175
Address interpreter, 203–4, **222**
And logic, 89–90, **93**, 144–46
Applications, Forth, 4–6
  arts, 4
  business, 4
  data acquisition, 4
  expert systems, 5
  graphics, 5
  medical, 5
  personal computer, 4
  portable devices, 5
  process control, 5
  robotics, 5
  silicon, 6
Arithmetic, 29–41
  addition and subtraction, 30
  division, 32, 39
  division with remainder, 39–41
  floating point, (*See* Floating point)
  fractional, (*See* Fractional arithmetic)
  left and right shift, 139–40, **164**
  multiplication, 33
  scaled integer, 101–7, **114,** 303
Array, 177–84, **191**
Array, byte, 187–88
Array, initializing, 188–89
ASCII, 141–44, 142 (table), **164**
Assembler, 219, 308–14